ROUTLEDGE LIBRARY EDITIONS:
THE MEDIEVAL WORLD

Volume 35

THE ENGLISH MEDIEVAL FEAST

THE ENGLISH MEDIEVAL FEAST

WILLIAM EDWARD MEAD

LONDON AND NEW YORK

First published in 1931 by George Allen & Unwin Ltd

This edition first published in 2020
by Routledge
2 Park Square, Milton Park, Abingdon, Oxon OX14 4RN

and by Routledge
52 Vanderbilt Avenue, New York, NY 10017

Routledge is an imprint of the Taylor & Francis Group, an informa business

© 1931 William Edward Mead

All rights reserved. No part of this book may be reprinted or reproduced or utilised in any form or by any electronic, mechanical, or other means, now known or hereafter invented, including photocopying and recording, or in any information storage or retrieval system, without permission in writing from the publishers.

Trademark notice: Product or corporate names may be trademarks or registered trademarks, and are used only for identification and explanation without intent to infringe.

British Library Cataloguing in Publication Data
A catalogue record for this book is available from the British Library

ISBN: 978-0-367-22090-7 (Set)
ISBN: 978-0-429-27322-3 (Set) (ebk)
ISBN: 978-0-367-19379-9 (Volume 35) (hbk)
ISBN: 978-0-367-19386-7 (Volume 35) (pbk)
ISBN: 978-0-429-20214-8 (Volume 35) (ebk)

Publisher's Note
The publisher has gone to great lengths to ensure the quality of this reprint but points out that some imperfections in the original copies may be apparent.

Disclaimer
The publisher has made every effort to trace copyright holders and would welcome correspondence from those they have been unable to trace.

THE ENGLISH MEDIEVAL FEAST

BY
WILLIAM EDWARD MEAD

LONDON
GEORGE ALLEN & UNWIN LTD
MUSEUM STREET

FIRST PUBLISHED IN 1931
SECOND IMPRESSION 1967

This book is copyright under the Berne Convention. Apart from any fair dealing for the purpose of private study, research, criticism or review, as permitted under the Copyright Act, 1956, no portion may be reproduced by any process without written permission. Enquiries should be addressed to the Publishers.

PRINTED IN GREAT BRITAIN
BY PHOTOLITHOGRAPHY
UNWIN BROTHERS LTD., WOKING

PREFACE

It is somewhat singular that the English Medieval[1] Feast, perhaps the most characteristic feature of the social life of four or five hundred years ago, has received in this generation comparatively little attention in books addressed to the general public. The older works, such as the excellent little book, published anonymously, under the title *Our English Home* (1860), Thomas Wright's *History of Domestic Manners and Sentiments during the Middle Ages* (1861), and his *Homes of Other Days* (1871), have long been out of print. The primary authorities on medieval food, published by Pegge (1782), Warner (1790), Morris (1862), Furnivall (1868), Mrs. Napier (1882), and Austin (1888), were printed in limited editions, and are for the most part out of reach of the average reader. Fortunately, the excellent English version of the *Ménagier of Paris* has recently appeared (1928).

Of the solid worth of these books there is no question, but notwithstanding the invaluable service of the editors of the old cookery books in presenting unchanged the primary material that has escaped destruction, they have, except for an occasional comment, given no comparative account of the old receipts and, except through glossaries, little or no help in making the material intelligible to readers unfamiliar with English of the fifteenth century.

As for the scope and purpose of the present volume, a few words will suffice. Obviously, it is not a practical book of instruction in medieval cookery, It aims rather to point out certain distinctive features of medieval cuisine which in most parts of the world have long since passed out of fashion but which form an important though much neglected chapter in the history of the English people. Few things are more extraordinary than the type of food that our ancestors commonly ate; and if we can imagine ourselves as attempting to join them in eating the astonishing dishes described in the following pages, we shall not only get a more vivid and accurate understanding of the life of our forefathers, but also more clearly realize the gulf that separates us from the fifteenth century.

But fascinating as the topic in itself is, I shall have to confess that the task which I approached light-heartedly after some years of general acquaintance developed a variety of unexpected difficulties and called for extensive investigation in more than one out-of-the-way field. There still remain questions easier to ask than to answer, but I trust that I have not unduly neglected those that are most important. One main difficulty has been to decide what to omit. At best, the multiplicity of receipts that are differentiated from other receipts in only trifling particulars has involved a certain amount of repetition. But since this very similarity is one of the most striking features of medieval cookery, I have felt obliged to present the material in reasonable measure even at some sacrifice of artistic finish. A book on this subject might be padded to an indefinite extent, but wherever illustrative material could be excluded without obvious loss I have not hesitated to omit it. If, however, the reader is satisfied with less than is here offered, he has only to turn the page.

It is hardly necessary to observe that much of this book is based upon contemporary material, and that if it were intended solely for students of early English literature all the passages taken from ancient cookery books and chronicles might be presented in the old orthography. But since in a book addressed to the general public no really useful purpose would be served by retaining the old and flagrantly inconsistent spellings, these have been for the most part brought into conformity with modern usage. An occasional passage presenting no difficulty to the average reader has been allowed to remain unchanged. In any case, I have as far as possible retained the old phrasing; and the reader who insists upon the old orthography has only to look up the original texts indicated in the references.

In passing, it should be noted that this book takes little account of the diet of the lower classes, but deals chiefly with the food prepared for royalty and the aristocracy on great occasions. The life of the peasantry and the lower middle classes during the Middle Ages is a fascinating topic, but it calls for more detailed treatment than can be given here. From necessity the food of the poor was simple and monotonous, and almost wholly limited to native products. The poor ate to live, while in too many cases the rich lived to eat.

Secondary authorities, especially Le Grand d'Aussy and Alfred Franklin, I have used sparingly and with caution, and only incidentally have I relied upon the work of modern writers.

The illustrations are taken from illuminations in medieval manuscripts, and, although those containing representations of feasts are almost wholly French, the essential features of a great feast were common to all the countries of Western Europe. Moreover, the illuminations for the most part are somewhat conventional and rarely reproduce in a photographic way the actual realities of any particular occasion.

In the preparation of the book I have had no direct assistance except from the ever-ready attendants in the North Library and in the Manuscript Department of the British Museum, and to them I am deeply indebted for innumerable favours. I must not, however, overlook the generous encouragement offered by the eminent Shakespearean scholar, the late Horace Howard Furness, and, particularly, by the late Sir Israel Gollancz, whose enthusiastic approval overcame the discouragement which attends the progress of any work requiring extended research.

W. E. M.

CONTENTS

CHAPTER		PAGE
	PREFACE	7
I.	SOME FEATURES OF ENGLISH MEDIEVAL LIFE	15
II.	THE FOOD FOR THE FEAST AND THE COST	32
III.	PREPARATION OF FOOD	42
IV.	MEDIEVAL DRINKS	123
V.	THE SCENE OF THE FEAST	129
VI.	SERVING THE FEAST	137
VII.	NOTABLE FEASTS	180
VIII.	FOOD AND HEALTH	214
	NOTES	225
	BIBLIOGRAPHICAL NOTE	261
	INDEX AND GLOSSARY	267

ILLUSTRATIONS

KING AT TABLE WITH FOUR BISHOPS *Frontispiece*
Richly decorated room. King at table with four bishops wearing their mitres, and two men with hats on. Knives and trenchers on the table. Serving-table with six metal plates and brass jar before a hutch, inside of which stands a cook apparently holding a ladle. Servants are bringing food to the table. Musicians blowing pipes in the gallery. Note the bench without a back on which two bishops are seated. (B.M. Royal MS. 14 E. IV.)

FACING PAGE

1. CARVER AT TABLE 48
Five persons at table, one holding a large cup to his lips. In front of the table a carver, kneeling, knife in hand, and holding the joint with the other hand.

    MERLIN LED BY A SPANIEL INTO THE BANQUETING HALL 48
Merlin led by a spaniel into the banqueting hall. At least fourteen guests. Knives, trenchers, and drinking-vessels on the table.

2. THE ABBOT'S KITCHEN, GLASTONBURY, 1435–40 49
From H. W. C. Davis's *Medieval England*. By permission of Methuen & Co., Ltd.

3. POULTRY SERVED WHOLE 64
Five men at a round table, on which are five trenchers, three knives, and three spoons, one drinking-cup, and a small wine-jug. One servant at the left is bringing a large covered dish, and another servant at the right has a tall glass cup containing a reddish-yellow drink. Behind him is a man with a large wine-jug. On the table are a roast goose and another fowl in a large dish.

4. A FISH DINNER 65
A very good representation of a feast—a fish dinner. On the table are trenchers, knives, a wine-jug, and a fish. Six persons, all sitting on one side of the table, are served with fish by two attendants. One guest is offering the king a "royal" cup, covered.

5. THE GREAT HALL, HAMPTON COURT PALACE 129
Photo. by J. Beagles & Co., Ltd.

6. THE GOLD CUP OF THE KINGS OF FRANCE AND ENGLAND 144

7. CEREMONIAL BRINGING OF DISHES TO THE TABLE IN A PROCESSION BY SERVANTS HEADED BY THE STEWARD BEARING HIS OFFICIAL STAFF 145

    SERVANTS BRINGING IN DISHES, PRECEDED BY MUSIC 145
Fiddler preceding two servants bearing dishes to the royal table, where a crowned king sits with two ladies. Before the table a servant on one knee offers a dish.

14   THE ENGLISH MEDIEVAL FEAST

                FACING PAGE
  SERVANT OFFERING A ROYAL CUP   145
  KING HEROD AND HIS DAUGHTER HERODIAS.

8. MEDIEVAL TABLES   160

  King crowned and four guests at table. Serving-table at left, on which are wine-jugs, and drinking-cups along with four plates set on edge. Steward with staff behind. On the chief table, three meat platters with poultry, two knives, and two drinking-cups. On the floor a kneeling attendant offers a royal drinking-cup to the king.

9. FOUR MEN AT TABLE   161

  SIX AT TABLE

  Royal cup in centre of (lower) table. One large fish, entire, on top of a hollow dish.

10. FEAST GIVEN BY RICHARD II IN WESTMINSTER PALACE 176

  Feast given by Richard II in his palace at Westminster, at which were present the greater part of the chivalry of England. On the serving-table are two wine-jugs, with cups, etc. Musicians at the left are blowing trumpets. In the foreground one attendant holds a covered "royal" cup. Another attendant, wearing a sword, carries a golden *nef*, etc.

  This is one of the most exquisite of the medieval illustrations of feasts. The banquet was served "le jour de Noel prochain après le partement du roy de France".

11. PEACOCK IN HIS PLUMAGE PRESENTED TO BE SERVED
   AT THE TABLE   177

  Peacock in plumage presented at table by a lady, kneeling, along with three other ladies, also kneeling. Squire ready to receive it. Crowned king sitting at table. Lady beside him in fifteenth-century headdress. No food or dishes on the table.

12. NEF OR SALT-CELLAR   192

  KING, QUEEN, AND FOUR GUESTS AT TABLE

  THE CARVER AT WORK

  Servant carving (in front), another at one end of the table bringing a platter with meat, a third servant at the other end bearing a jug in his left hand. Ornamental tapestry behind the table.

13. FEAST WITH KING AND QUEEN AT TABLE   193

  King and queen at table, and a musician at each end, one playing a sort of fiddle and the other blowing a pipe. The king (standing) holds a gold cup. Before him are three fish in a silver dish. A carver at the left has a knife in his hand. On the table beside the queen is another gold cup, and also bread and a silver wine-jug. Another attendant faces the carver. Note the rich background, the tapestry, the table-cloth, the musicians, the carver, the drinking-cups.

THE ENGLISH MEDIEVAL FEAST

CHAPTER I

SOME FEATURES OF ENGLISH MEDIEVAL LIFE

THE Middle Ages have often been idealized by writers who have fixed their attention upon features that were attractive and have ignored the rest. We may freely admit that much in medieval life was poetic and fascinating. But daily life in the Middle Ages, except when viewed through the eyes of the romancers, was doubtless at times dull enough, though not necessarily because of lack of occupation. In the upper ranks of society the care of one's estate, perhaps scattered through half a dozen counties, required vigilant oversight, even though the actual labour was commonly entrusted to competent overseers. The outbreak of war might impose upon the head of a great house the obligation to go overseas, or at least to make a heavy contribution toward the expense of an expedition. Part of the routine of every day was attendance at one or two religious services. But the day was not wholly given to labour or to devotion. When the season permitted the active members of the household were more likely to be found coursing over the hills and through the forests on the chase than spending their time in quiet contemplation or study. Various sports, such as bear-baiting or cock fighting, helped to while away the time for those who cared little for higher forms of entertainment.

But a great feast, particularly when accompanied, as it often was, by a brilliant tournament, to say nothing of other diversions, was incomparably the greatest attraction of medieval life. At a widely proclaimed feast one was certain to meet the most notable representatives of one's social circle; and there a young knight might have the inestimable privilege of sharing the same dish and drinking from the same cup with his lady-love, as also of paying courtly compliments and of showing his prowess in the tournament.

The Middle Ages eagerly seized upon any event that afforded a reasonable excuse for a banquet. But some occasions made a feast inevitable. A coronation, a great victory, a marriage in high life, the arrival of an ambassador, the enthronization of an archbishop, a birthday, especially the day on which the heir to an estate attained his majority, besides the Church festivals like Easter, Whitsunday, Christmas, and Twelfth Night,[1] all afforded an opportunity and an excuse for a great entertainment and at the same time a welcome relief from the monotony of the daily round. The intimate connection between the Church and the social life of the Middle Ages is obvious at every turn; and although the religious element is in many cases far from obtrusive in the actual feasts, the mere fact that a day was set apart as a Church holiday often determined its selection as a fitting time for a banquet.

Owing to the fact that a feast on a grand scale involved expenditure far beyond the means of the ordinary citizen, it was mainly an affair of the court, the nobility, a great ecclesiastic, or an occasional favoured son of fortune. As social life grew more complex and luxury increased, the feast became more and more a favourite means of manifesting the wealth and social importance of the donor. Closer contact with other countries through commerce and travel, to say nothing of wars, naturally brought about modifications of various features. But, despite all change, many characteristics remained common to the feasts of the period closely following the Battle of Hastings and those of the fifteenth century.

The five centuries from 1050 to 1550 include a series of transitions in English history from a period of highly organized feudalism to something like a modern state, though even in the sixteenth century many medieval features still survived. When we pause to enumerate merely a few of the most characteristic features of those centuries, feudalism, chivalry, the Crusades, the extension of monasticism, the building of cathedrals and the evolution of architectural styles, the flourishing of romance, the founding of universities, the development of town life, the spread of commerce, the revolution in military science, the Hundred Years' struggle with France, the Wars of the Roses, the progress of discovery, the Revival of Learning, the Reformation, we realize that, notwithstanding the persistent survival of many features of earlier times, we cannot regard the medieval period as a unit. It follows, then, that in so far as our immediate topic is concerned we must give our attention in the main to a comparatively brief period during which social conditions, at least in the higher circles, with which alone we have here to do, had in a sense been standardized. This period, for our purpose, we may regard mainly as the whole of the fifteenth and the first half of the sixteenth century. The year 1500 brought no revolution in the food supplied at feasts or in the social usages to which feasters were supposed to conform, though increasing wealth naturally led to more and more lavish display.

But, obviously, we cannot ignore the earlier centuries in which the social ideals of the English people were slowly taking shape and when the English and the Normans were gradually fusing together to form one people. The English have been notably conservative in making progress and, while cautiously introducing new features into their mode of living, they have retained to this day a multitude of quaint medieval usages and customs that in other countries have been long abandoned and forgotten.

So was it also in the fifteenth and sixteenth centuries. Notwithstanding the notable changes that we have enumerated, the general aspect of the country, the means of transportation, and in large measure the mode of living throughout the land up to the end of the fifteenth century, and even later, must have been strikingly similar to that in the two or three centuries that preceded. Differences in detail there were, of course, in plenty,[2] but, speaking broadly, we may say that even in the fifteenth and

SOME FEATURES OF ENGLISH MEDIEVAL LIFE

part of the sixteenth century the habits of thought of the mass of the population and the round of their daily life were essentially medieval.

The Medieval Feast may well be regarded as the most characteristic expression of social life during the period we are studying, and hence we cannot do better than to glance at some of the more notable features of the life of that time, particularly those that are in marked contrast with the life of our own day.

Certain aspects of the Middle Ages have been carefully studied and brilliantly depicted—the tournaments, the pilgrimages, the Crusades, and many other features of religious and secular life in times of war and of peace. But to know the life of some five hundred years ago as the people of that time saw it and lived it is a matter of the utmost difficulty, and it may be doubted whether any modern investigator has succeeded to the full in penetrating and divining the innermost soul of the Middle Ages. They are full of co-existing features strangely contradictory. In times when the lowest vice in high places went almost unrebuked we find examples of almost boundless self-denial and devotion to ascetic ideals. We meet also endless examples of what we should call childish wilfulness alongside of the prevailing medieval deference to conventionality. People in general were hedged about by traditional usages that almost had the force of laws and were violated at one's peril. Every man knew his place, and as a rule kept it. Class lines were rigidly drawn and, except in the Church, only a man of very exceptional type could hope to rise above his original station.

From all this and much more that might be adduced, the only safe conclusion appears to be that, although we may tabulate a variety of characteristic features, we cannot compress the long period vaguely known as the Middle Ages into a neat formula, and still less describe it in a single phrase. We must be content to consider it as a time when conventionality is the rule and also as a time when, as the French say, it is the unexpected that happens.

Many of the most notable men of the Middle Ages often act like impulsive children. The fantastic exploits depicted in the medieval romances are hardly more unreasonable than, for example, the First Crusade, undertaken with no conception of the dangers involved and with no adequate preparation. Enthusiasm without weighing consequences is a marked characteristic of medieval life, and is abundantly illustrated in the life of St. Francis of Assisi and of multitudes of others less known to fame. What they believe they hold with an intensity that admits of no denial. Bigotry and intolerance are only one aspect of the lack of restraint common to all classes. If they give themselves to a life of devotion they know no limit. If they sit down to a feast they eat to excess. The dancing epidemic in Germany and Italy in the Middle Ages illustrates how a sudden mania can sweep through whole populations and cause them to act like unreasonable beings. The intolerance that rooted out the heresy of the Albigenses is simply

SOME FEATURES OF ENGLISH MEDIEVAL LIFE

another illustration of the lack of balance and restraint that characterized the age. There was no lack of formal logic in those days, but the average man and woman was guided, not by reason, but by impulse.

Our conception of medieval life as a whole is often distorted and thrown out of proportion by the dazzling accounts in chronicles and romances of the festivities in which the nobility and royalty participate. The glitter and splendour of the feast and the tournament tend to obscure the fact that everyday living in the Middle Ages might be quite as humdrum and monotonous as any in our own time. The entire period might with no exaggeration be termed an inconvenient age, the shortcomings of which appear at every turn.

Broadly speaking, one of the most notable characteristics of medieval as compared with modern life is the extent to which men were isolated and thrown upon their own resources. In our own day we not only actually talk with men in the uttermost parts of the earth, but we pass from one country to another with a speed that three or four generations ago would have appeared miraculous. As a result of the difficulty of travel five hundred years ago multitudes of men lived all their lives in the same community without ever visiting any other. Their conceptions of foreign lands, and in general of other communities than their own, were often fantastic in the extreme.

The adventurous spirits who went upon crusades, or, like Chaucer's Knight, sought military service in foreign lands, belonged in a class quite apart from the vast majority of their fellow-countrymen. Those who remained at home in small towns or hamlets, in so far as they were not craftsmen or ordinary agricultural labourers, lived a life which at best must have been uniform in the extreme. The care of their estates naturally kept them occupied with a variety of humble tasks, and these, along with the ever-recurring religious festivals, to say nothing of rural sports, hunting, hawking, fishing, took up some of their too abundant leisure. But the occasions when the owner of a remote country estate could participate in a typical medieval feast on a grand scale must have been comparatively rare.

Doubtless the people of the pre-Reformation period, like people of our own day, regarded themselves as ultra-modern, and assuredly they had no conception of the defects of their civilization. But when we attempt to enumerate what the Middle Ages lacked we hardly know where to begin or to end. Brief comment upon a few of the discomforts and inconveniences of medieval life will show how great these were, and at the same time dissipate some of the glamour thrown about daily life in the time when knights wore armour and were supposed to spend their days in making love or in riding about in search of adventures.

In the romantic period of the early nineteenth century the popular impression was that during the Middle Ages the life depicted in the medieval romances substantially represented the normal state of society, quite ignoring the fact that, as a rule, the romances practically disregard the existence of all except the privileged classes and ignore a large part even of their daily life. We do, indeed, find the descriptions of medieval feasts in the romances strikingly corroborated by the accounts in the old chronicles, and up to a certain point we may therefore accept their evidence as a valuable supplement to what we learn from other sources. But caution in generalizing is necessary.

If we confine our study of medieval life to the old romances and chronicles, and especially if we dwell mainly upon the descriptions of feasts and other scenes of rejoicing, we may easily be led to suppose that in the Middle Ages luxury was carried to its highest pitch, and that modern life is sober and drab in comparison. From some points of view this is the case. Medieval life was picturesque and full of colour to an extent that we hardly realize. And even to-day, when we enter a great medieval hall or the nave of a vast Gothic cathedral, we feel the enchantments of the Middle Ages and almost envy the men and women who lived amid scenes so full of beauty and picturesqueness.

Two occasions call forth to the utmost the descriptive powers of the romancers—the tournament and the feast. And especially the feast, for the splendour of the hall, with its tapestries, its many coloured windows, its richly clad guests, the glittering gold and silver vessels, the red and golden wines, the lights, the music, the pantomimes, the dancing, made a picture which to this day remains in popular thought as the most typical feature of medieval life.

Through contact with other countries, especially in the time of the Crusades, Western nations gradually became familiar with the amenities of life in the East. Some of the earlier Crusades, especially the march of the ill-equipped and undisciplined horde that swarmed eastward on the first expedition, seem almost like movements of madmen. A single battery of modern machine-guns could easily have routed the entire host. The later Crusades were more carefully organized and in some measure achieved their purpose. In particular, the taking of Constantinople in 1204 revealed splendours hitherto unrealized even in the palaces of kings in Western Europe. The successive Crusades brought the West into direct contact with the East—with the rich fabrics woven in the looms of Damascus and Bagdad, with the curiously inlaid vessels of gold and silver, with goblets of oriental glass, with weapons adorned with exquisitely carved ivory. Not unnaturally, after the long stay of the Crusaders in the East, where in the cool, covered bazaars they had revelled in the sherberts, the spices, the dates, the figs, the almonds, and, above all, in the sweetmeats, they sought upon their return to their homes in the West to continue to enjoy in some measure the pleasures of oriental life. These in turn gradually became a necessity even for those who had never crossed the English Channel.

The importance of these modifications in English life we can hardly overestimate, but we must guard against conclusions that are too sweeping. We must not forget that the Middle Ages made up in splendour what they lacked in comfort. Magnificence in dress and in the adornment of the table at feasts was reserved in most households for special occasions, and was the more impressive owing to its comparative rarity. Houses that displayed almost boundless luxury at a great feast were strangely lacking in what are now regarded as the ordinary conveniences of life. And the guests who had been covered with jewels and silks and velvets at the feast commonly withdrew to bedrooms of the most cheerless type, furnished in a fashion that would now seem beggarly in a common artisan's dwelling.[3]

The ancient streets that now appear so picturesque when seen in brilliant sunlight were far from clean. The fronts of the houses were quaintly carved and decorated, but the rooms were usually low-studded and narrow, ill-ventilated, and shockingly lacking in sanitary conveniences. Nameless vessels were emptied from the upper windows into the street, and the resulting exhalations were not those of Araby the blest. The nostrils of fine ladies in the Middle Ages must very early have grown accustomed to odours that would now be intolerable, for what with open drains and filth in public places,[4] rotting straw and other refuse on the floor of the hall, and meats on the table long overkept, there must have been so constant a stench that one might have felt the lack of it as a real deprivation.

Obviously, then, if we with our standards of

living could be suddenly taken back into the Middle Ages we should realize at once in the most striking way the lack of modern comfort. When we enumerate the dozen or twenty things that contribute most to the amenities of modern life we find, with scarcely an exception, that these things were lacking in the Middle Ages. First and foremost, we note the almost entire lack of labour-saving machinery. Practically everything was accomplished by hand labour. This means, obviously, that much muscular energy was wasted that might have been more usefully employed. There were, indeed, certain simple devices, such as hand-looms, pulleys, water-wheels, and the blacksmith's bellows. But the use of steam was unknown, and, of course, the use of electricity. Hence manufacturing was literally manu-facturing, that is, hand work. Mass production, which in our time has brought hundreds of useful articles within the means of persons of modest incomes, was therefore unknown. But when we consider that hand labour, skilled by long experience, fashioned the dishes of the table, the furniture of the hall, the carved doors, the misereres, the choir stalls, and the exquisite porches of the vast medieval cathedrals, we are less inclined to regret that the Middle Ages lacked some of the mechanical devices that make life at present less strenuous than that of our ancestors.

One of the most serious problems in the housekeeping of five hundred years ago was that of lighting and heating. With us, the matter of lighting is very simple whether by day or by night. Except in large cities, where we must adapt ourselves to conditions imposed by adjoining buildings, we place our windows where we please and regulate their shape and size according to our needs and the length of our purse. In the Middle Ages, it must be noted, window glass was too rare and costly for ordinary use. At best, it was made in small pieces and carefully fitted together in such windows as have for centuries been the glory of the cathedrals of Chartres and Bourges and the shattered Rheims. Windows of this type were found in some of the finest of the medieval halls, but in so far as the ordinary private house had window glass, it was mostly of the coarse, greenish, translucent type, in thick, small pieces, where the blowpipe had left its mark. In general, during the fifteenth century glass was much too costly for large windows in private dwellings. The openings for air and light were closed, if ever, with heavy shutters that indeed kept out some of the cold and the snow, but also the light. To fill the chinks at the edges of the shutters or elsewhere, rags or straw were freely used. Where windows were diminutive a partial substitute for glass or for shutters appeared in the form of thin plates of horn, mica, or of bladders or oiled canvas.[5]

As for artificial lighting, most of the world fared badly. Indeed, the primitive conditions of the Middle Ages in illumination have disappeared only in our own time. Only a generation or more ago travellers throughout Europe were provided for the night with candles, duly charged in the bill. And, of course, the Middle Ages had nothing better.

Like so much of the other equipment of old English houses, most of the lights were of home manufacture. Wax candles were dear, and in most houses could be afforded only on great occasions. For ordinary use, tallow dips made from kitchen fat, with rushes for wicks, or torches made of rope, "steeped in pitch, tallow, oil, and rosin",[6] were deemed quite sufficient.[7] Doubtless wax candles burned with a clear and beautiful flame, but the ordinary tallow dip must have been ineffective for illumination and a source of filthy and noisome smoke. At best, the lighting could never have been brilliant, as compared with the electric lighting of our own time, but it was at all events picturesque.

Incidentally, we note that the inadequate lighting was still more painfully felt in the streets. Throughout Europe the streets of the largest cities were entirely unlighted at night during the greater part of the year, though in some English towns householders were required to have a light before their doors from Christmas to the feast of Epiphany on January 6th. Anyone compelled to traverse the streets at night commonly carried a torch dipped in pitch. Old houses in London still retain the iron extinguishers where the eighteenth-century linkboys used to quench their flambeaux.

Not less serious than the problem of lighting was that of heating. In this particular the old Romans were far ahead of the English. The Romans heated their villas in cold weather by means of terra-cotta pipes or narrow passages under the floors and in the side walls that carried heat all over the house. But nothing of the sort was used in England during the Middle Ages.

In the medieval kitchen warmth was purely incidental. The main purpose was to get sufficient heat for boiling, baking, and roasting. Deprived of the convenient coal fires and gas or electric ranges so common in our time, the cooks of centuries ago had mainly to rely upon open fires of wood and charcoal or, in favoured localities, upon sea-coal.[8] But the fire itself was a constant problem. To anyone in our day nothing seems simpler than making a fire. Six hundred years ago it was more or less an achievement. In the hands of an expert, flint and steel, along with abundant tinder and light kindlings, rapidly brought the desired result. But in families ill-provided with the ordinary necessities of life the extinguishing of the hearth fire may have been a serious calamity. In any case, continuous, uniform heating in winter must have been almost impossible. If, as at Penshurst, the hall was heated by billets of wood piled on firedogs or a brazier in the middle of the floor, the smoke had to find its way out through the louvre in the roof. In the later medieval period fireplaces with chimneys were often found, and in the kitchen were employed for roasting the vast haunches that were turned on the spits before the fire. But for supplying warmth the fireplaces in the hall were not too satisfactory, since the greater part of the heat went up the throat of the chimney.

It is difficult, therefore, to see how guests wearing

light clothing at a feast in the colder months could have been very comfortable. Draughts circulated everywhere in the great hall. To some extent the chilly currents might be guarded against by the use of high-backed settles, especially when placed near the fire. But another form of protection was common. Ordinarily in severe weather when a passing stranger of obvious social rank arrived at a castle he was hospitably received, and after he had bathed and made himself as presentable as possible he was provided with a fur-lined robe[9] in which to envelop himself. A robe of this sort covered the entire person, and when provided with a hood made one more or less indifferent to the temperature of a chilly room. But at the close of the day, when the spiced wine had been served and the gorgeous mantles were laid aside, the costume adopted for the night was simplicity itself. In these times of pyjamas and union suits it is something of a shock to learn that the only article of clothing for the night was the nightcap, and that night rail became general only late in the sixteenth century.

In view of the conditions just described we may perhaps better understand the outbursts of joy in medieval poetry at the approach of spring. Such raptures may seem natural enough in any country where the fields, bare and desolate throughout the winter, begin again to deck themselves in green, where the trees once more stand luxuriant in their foliage, and the birds, long absent, return to their nests and make love amid the branches. But in the Middle Ages the reason for the poet's joy is possibly not so sentimental. He is no longer confined to the house by severe weather. The bright sun has dried the roads and made them passable, and he can enjoy the mild air of spring without having to muffle himself in heavy clothing. And, lastly, he sees an end of the monotonous diet of salted meat and salted fish. At all events, whether such considerations moved the poets, the physical joys attending the approach of spring without doubt were uppermost in the mind of the average occupants of a medieval castle.

But comfort is a relative term, and we shall do well not to exaggerate the sufferings of those who ate food that we should find repulsive, and in general lived under conditions that to us would be hardly tolerable. Men and women adapt themselves to their environment, and somehow the people of the Middle Ages appear to have enjoyed life very well. Indeed, they seem to have been quite as well satisfied with their lot and their achievements as we are with our own. And when we pause to consider what they accomplished in art, in architecture, in philosophy, in government, in literature, and in social life, we must admit their originality and in some respects their superiority. We must remember that we have built upon their foundations. And it is by no means certain that they would have admitted the advantages of many of our so-called modern improvements. Certainly, from a spectacular point of view, the men who organized the medieval banquets, the fame of which still endures, had little to learn from us in such matters.

CHAPTER II

THE FOOD FOR THE FEAST AND THE COST

CATERING for a great house was a complicated matter; and in more than one of the old household books detailed instructions are given as to what is to be provided at different seasons of the year. Thus, in the *Northumberland Household Book*[1] we find directions for the purchase of capons, with the price to be paid, and likewise for the purchase of pigs, rabbits, geese, hens, chickens, pigeons, plovers, swans,[2] cranes, herons, mallards, teals, woodcocks, seagulls, quails, partridges, pheasants, curlews, peacocks, bustards, larks, etc.

Even in our own day the preparation of an elaborate dinner for hundreds or perhaps thousands of guests is no trifling affair. But as a rule it involves little more than accurate calculation of what is needed and the dispatch of orders that will, as a rule, be filled without delay. Far different was it in the medieval period, when transportation was difficult and letters or messengers travelled slowly. But, notwithstanding the difficulty, the constantly recurring feasts show that somehow the food was found, and in quantities that to modern notions seem incredible.

Enormous as these supplies may appear, we may well believe that the purveyors knew the type of guests for whom they had to prepare. Except in extreme winter weather or in the spring, when heavy rains made roads practically impassable, the

THE FOOD FOR THE FEAST AND THE COST

men and women of the upper classes lived a very active life in the open air, busied in the chase or in various sports, to say nothing of directing the work upon their estates. Their appetites corresponded to their activity, and they were not appalled when confronted with the mountainous heaps of food prepared for their consumption. Yet even the most inveterate glutton would have been unable in less than several hours to eat his way through to the end of a typical medieval banquet conceived on a fairly liberal scale.[3]

What would modern diners think of a feast like that provided at the installation of Archbishop Neville at York in 1467? A partial list of the food includes 300 quarters of wheat, 300 tuns of ale, 100 tuns of wine, 1 pipe of hippocras, 104 oxen, 6 wild bulls, 1,000 sheep, 304 calves, 304 "porkes", 400 swans, 2,000 geese, 1,000 capons, 2,000 pigs, 104 peacocks, besides over 13,500 birds, large and small, of various kinds. In addition there were stags, bucks, and roes, five hundred and more, 1,500 hot pasties of venison, 608 pikes and breams, 12 porpoises and seals, besides 13,000 dishes of jelly, cold baked tarts, hot and cold custards, and "spices, sugered delicates, and wafers plentie".[4] It is true that there were said to have been some six thousand guests at this famous feast, but a slight calculation shows that the allowance for each was enormous.

On a grand scale, but not of so gargantuan dimensions as the preceding, was the feast at the enthronization of Archbishop Warham at Canterbury on March 9, 1504, the cost of which is recorded as £513 3s.[5] Enormous quantities of wheat, of red wine, of white wine, of malmsey, of Rhenish wine, of beer, of wax, of linen, of meat and fish in many varieties, olive oil, honey, mustard, were provided, besides innumerable dishes, pieces of furniture, and servants.[6]

These two feasts were given to celebrate the enthronization of two great prelates of the English Church. Hardly less lavish in proportion to the number of guests was the supply of food for the feast at Ipswich on April 20, 1467, when Sir John Howard and Master Thomas Brewse were chosen Knights of the shire.[7] Of no insignificant proportions was the wedding feast of Gervys Clifton and Mary Neville on January 17, 1530,[8] as our notes abundantly show.

The feasts attended by royalty, no less than those provided for the clergy and the nobility, were more notable for profusion than for delicacy. In 1531, the very year in which Catherine of Aragon was ordered to leave Windsor, she and King Henry were present at a great feast lasting for five days at Ely House, in London, where also were the serjeants-at-law and the foreign ambassadors. Stow enumerates in detail the enormous quantity of food provided for the obviously select company of guests.[9]

A large part of the food for all these banquets consisted of native products, particularly beef, pork, and mutton, venison, poultry, fish, eggs, bread, milk, cheese, besides herbs and vegetables, to say nothing of ale, cider, and mead. Practically every great estate provided sufficient for ordinary everyday needs, though an ambitious entertainment naturally required eatables more or less out of the common run.

A typical illustration of the extent to which one's own estates might provide for daily needs is found in the Earl of Derby's *Household Books* for the year 1561.[10] The Earl had a retinue of not less than one hundred and forty servants in his various establishments, all but two of whom were men; and the extent of his domain supplied him with most of the necessaries of life. "His flocks and herds were the produce of his own lands, his park furnished his family with venison, and his warrens and fishponds readily supplied game and fish for the table. The malt was made in his own kilns, and the hops apparently grown on his own lands, whilst the ale, in no stinted quantity, was brewed by experienced hands. The ordinary weekly consumption of the household was about one ox, a dozen calves, a score of sheep, fifteen hogsheads of ale, and plenty of bread, fish, and poultry." The proportion of supplies from native sources in the fifteenth century was doubtless as great as it was in the sixteenth, and probably far greater.

To-day much of our food comes literally from the ends of the earth. Cold storage and rapid transport by land and by sea have made possible the transfer of all but the most perishable fruits and meats in practically perfect condition from the most distant lands. Strangely different were the facilities of transport some four or five hundred years ago.

Vessels were small and relatively unseaworthy. A voyage to Greece or to Egypt through the Mediterranean or to Russia through the Baltic was a hazardous adventure, and the cargo that the vessels carried consisted mainly of products unattainable except from distant lands, spices from Ceylon and India, wines from Greece and the islands of the Ægean Sea, caviare from Russia, dates from Africa, dried figs from Italy, raisins from Greece, oranges from Sicily and Spain, sugar from various Mediterranean ports.

In the course of time a thriving trade with the East,[11] partly through the Mediterranean by means of Genoese or Venetian vessels, early developed and prospered. The vessels of the Hanseatic League, with its great exchange port at Visby in the island of Gotland, sixty miles east of Sweden, brought hides and salt fish, along with caviare and other delicacies, through the Baltic from Russia and the Far East, and delivered them at the Steelyard in London. This foreign domination of sea trade continued throughout the fourteenth century, and foreign hucksters and foreign buyers of English wool were seen at every great fair throughout England. In the course of the fifteenth century Englishmen more and more engaged in foreign trade until the greater part had passed into English hands.[12] English vessels went forth laden with English cloth and other English products and returned with all sorts of foreign wares, and in particular with the luxuries that had become indispensable features of a great banquet.

THE FOOD FOR THE FEAST AND THE COST

When the foreign supplies arrived in England they commonly had, unless they were to be consumed in the port of entry, to be transported over the wretched medieval roads to the local market or direct to the castle, where alone, as a rule, they could find a purchaser. The roads throughout England so carefully constructed by the Romans had, in the course of centuries, degenerated to such an extent that weeks were required for a distance now covered in a few hours.

Upon the various periodic fairs[13] scattered about England the purveyors for feasts held in regions far from large centres like London or York or Bristol were mainly dependent for supplies other than those to be obtained from the estate of the lord of the manor or from the neighbouring country.

Our interest in the present study is not primarily economic, but rather in the type of food eaten by our ancestors; but assuredly the cost of food has some bearing on the subject, for notwithstanding the apparent cheapness of medieval food—owing to the difference in the relative value of money—the cost of a great feast or of maintaining a sumptuous table was sufficient to compel severe retrenchment or even to cripple one's estate.[14] Incidentally, we have noted the cost of some of the food and other materials provided for a great banquet, and we may add a few more items of the same sort, but with no attempt at completeness.[15]

In 1378, 2 Richard II, we find a characteristic list of the cost of various sorts of cooked meat and poultry. "The ordinance of the Cooks, ordered by the Mayor and Aldermen, as to divers fleshmeat and poultry, as well roasted as baked in pasties,—The best roast pig for 8d. Best roast goose, 7d. Best roast capon, 6d. Best roast hen, 4d. Best roast pullet, 2½d. Best roast rabbit, 4d. Best roast river mallard, 4½d. Best roast dunghill mallard, 3½d. Best roast teal, 2½d. Best roast snyte, 1½d. Five roast larks, 1½d. Best roast wodecok, 2½d. Best roast partridge, 3½d. Best roast plover, 2½d. Best roast pheasant, 13d. Best roast curlew, 6½d. Three roast thrushes, 2d. Ten roast finches, 1d. Best roast heron, 18d. Best roast bittern, 20d. Three roast pigeons, 2½d. Ten eggs, 1d. For the paste, fire, and trouble upon a capon, 1½d. For the paste, fire, and trouble upon a goose, 2d. The best capon baked in a pasty, 8d. The best hen baked in a pasty, 5d. The best lamb, roasted, 7d."[16]

With the foregoing prices for cooked meats we may compare the prices for uncooked poultry, in the seventh year of Richard II's reign:

"The best cygnet shall be sold for four pence; the best purcel [?] for sixpence; the best goose for sixpence; the best capon for sixpence; the best hen for sixpence; the best pullet for two pence; the best rabbit, with the skin, for four pence; and without the skin, for three pence;—and no foreigner shall sell any rabbit without the skin: the best river mallard [wild duck], for three pence; the best dunghill mallard [tame duck], for two pence; the best snipe, for one penny; the best woodcock, for three pence; the best partridge, for four pence; the best plover, for three pence; the best pheasant, for twelve pence; the best curlew, for sixpence; a dozen thrushes, for sixpence; a dozen finches, for one penny; the best heron, for sixteen pence; the best bittern, for eighteen pence; the best brewe [snipe?], for eighteen pence; the best egret, for eighteen pence; twelve pigeons for eight pence."[17]

Not only do meats appear amazingly cheap, but the remuneration of a cook seems very moderate, even allowing for the difference in the value of money:

"Item, that no Cook shall take more than one penny for putting a capon in a crust. F. 182."[18]

"Item, that a Cook shall not take more than one penny for putting a capon or a rabbit in a crust. G. 108."[19]

In 1418, 6 Henry V, "it was ordered, that oysters and mussels should be sold at 4d. the bushel, 2d. the half bushel, 1 penny the peck, and the half peck at one half penny".

In the *Northumberland Household Book* of the beginning of the sixteenth century, to cite only a few examples, we find the following, pp. 182 ff.:

Geese, 3 to 4d.	Snipes, 3 for 1d.
Plovers, 1 to 1½d.	Quails, 2d.
Mallards, 11d.	"Grate birdes", 4 for 1d.
Teals, 1d.	Small birds, 12 for 1d.
Woodcocks, 1 to 1½d.	Larks, 12 for 2d.
Seagulls, 1 to 1½d.	

The price for large birds is considerably higher:

Young herons, 12d. each.	Curlews, 12d. each.
Cranes, 16d. each.	Peacocks,[20] 12d. each.
Pheasants, 12d. each.	

In the public markets the cost of food was strictly regulated and stringent laws were enacted to ensure its quality. Bakers in particular were under close supervision and liable to corporal punishment for failure to conform to the laws concerning the making of bread.[21] In 1316 two London bakers charged with making bread of "false, putrid, and rotten materials" were sent to the pillory.[22] Ralph atte Sele was "put upon the pillory, with a whetstone hung from his neck, for slandering the mayor and aldermen, and falsely saying that his bread that had been found to be under weight, had been weighed when cold".[23] In 1417 it was "ordered that in time of Lent simnel[24] loaves should not be made nor yet any other white loaves, that are called 'painman', 'maincherin',[25] etc., but only three kinds of loaves, namely, 'tourte',[26] 'bis',[27] and white".[28]

The various City companies were proud of their reputation for fair dealing. An ordinance of the "Pepperers" of Soper Lane, as early as 1316, provided "that no one shall moisten any manner of merchandise, such as saffron, alum, ginger, cloves, and such manner of things as may admit of being moistened; that is to say, by steeping the ginger, or by turning the saffron out of the sack, and then anointing it, or bathing it in water; by reason whereof any manner of weight may be increased, or any deterioration arise to the merchandise".[29]

Attempts by dealers to take advantage of opportunities to purchase food before its arrival at the market were sharply punished. In 1379 it was decreed that "no poulterer, cook, piebaker, or other regrator whatsoever of victuals in flesh or in fish shall go to meet victuals coming towards the City, within or without, or shall buy any manner of victuals to resell in the markets, or elsewhere in the City, before ten of the clock shall have struck".[30]

CHAPTER III

PREPARATION OF FOOD

I

WE have already taken account of some of the inconveniences of medieval life and found many of the conditions of living far more simple and primitive than those in our own time. But at the threshold of the medieval kitchen simplicity vanished, though of course the convenient devices for saving time and labour so common in our day were quite unknown.

The kitchen of a great medieval house was commonly an elaborate establishment. In particular, the more important abbeys spared no expense in building and equipping kitchens sufficiently large to supply not only the needs of the monastery itself but also of the numerous guests who were entertained in the course of a year. Of enormous size were the kitchens at Gloucester Abbey (36 feet by 17 feet 6 inches), at Durham (36 feet $8\frac{1}{2}$ inches in diameter), Canterbury (45 feet in diameter). Besides these may be placed the great kitchen of Jervaulx Abbey in Yorkshire, with its three vast fireplaces, the whole supplemented by a smaller kitchen; and the famous Abbot's kitchen at Glastonbury, built in octagonal form and terminating in a picturesque lantern. This kitchen is paralleled by the kitchen of the abbey of Fontevrault in France, which is very similar.[1] An example of appointments on a grand scale is also afforded by the vast six-

PREPARATION OF FOOD

teenth-century kitchen of Christ Church College, at Oxford, Wolsey's princely foundation.

But most kitchens were built on a far smaller plan than those in the great monastic establishments. Whereas in the kitchens of Glastonbury or of Christ Church College there was ample room for roasting oxen entire and for a mighty turnspit full of small birds, at the average castle the roasting of oxen or the boiling of whole carcasses of swine had to be carried on in the courtyard or in the fields outside.

The floor of the kitchen was commonly of stone or brick. A great table or two with a top of massive oak planks hewn with the axe was conveniently placed for holding dishes of food in course of preparation. Huge copper pots and pans, ladles and strainers and graters, were hung upon the walls, along with spoons and skimmers and knives, and flesh-hooks for drawing the quarters of pork or beef out of the pots over the open fire. Labour-saving devices were practically unknown. In place of a simple mechanical contrivance for turning the spit regularly and without fatigue, a turnspit, miserably paid, would wearily perform his monotonous task. A chopping-block and a large wooden bowl for hacking meat and vegetables into small pieces must have been in constant use, if we may trust the old receipt books. One specimen will suffice: "Take eels and flay them, and chop them in fair slices. Hew fair butts of calf or pork, not too fat, all small. Take butts of pork and smite them in pieces. Take the paunch of a sheep and let it boil till it be tender, then lay it on a fair board and cut it in small pieces of the breadth of a penny "[2]; and so on without end.

But probably the most important aids to the medieval cook after the great cauldrons that hung over the open fire were his mortar and pestle. Into the mortar went the most heterogeneous ingredients: meats, vegetables, fruits, spices, sugar, nuts, particularly almonds. Out of the mortar came the impalpable messes so characteristic of the medieval table. Nearly every dish, whatever its name, was soft and mushy, with its principal ingredients disguised by the addition of wine or spices or vegetables. The skill of the cook was attested by the fact that his strange compounds were actually eaten. It was apparently not worth the pains of a cook of any reputation to prepare food simply, and hence practically everything had to be mashed or cut into small pieces and mixed with something else, preferably of so strong a flavour as to disguise the taste of most of the other ingredients. Nearly every dish was a riddle.

Of the grinding and braying in a mortar we find endless examples. On one page of a cookery book there are six receipts that prescribe grinding. Of these we may select portions of three.[3] "Take mulberries and wring them through a cloth. Take veal, hew it, seeth it, grind it small, and cast thereto", etc. So too, "take the flesh of good crabs and good salmon and bray it small", etc. For making "Rapeye", "Take figs and raisins and grind them in a mortar; . . . take pears, seethe them, and pare them, and bray them in a mortar." "Noteye" is made as follows: "Take a great portion of hazel leaves and grind in a mortar as small as thou may, while that they be young . . . take flesh of pork or of capon, and grind it small", etc.[4]

At first sight this constant maceration of food might seem to suggest a people who were toothless and had to be spared the trouble of mastication by having their food made easy to slip down their throats. But a simple explanation is to be found in the lack of forks. There was no easy way of cutting meat upon one's plate, and hence the cutting was done by the carver, who served the meat in small pieces to be taken up in one's fingers, or the contents of an entire dish were soft and mushy and had to be eaten with a spoon or dipped up with the fingers.

As is well known, the ordinary table fork did not come into use in England before the reign of James I, after the eccentric traveller Thomas Coryat had brought up a fork from Italy. And this simple implement contributed to bring about a revolution in cookery, for when with a fork a guest could hold his meat firmly upon his plate while cutting it and could pass food from his plate to his mouth without scooping it up in his fingers, the soft messes in fashion for so many generations were no more required, and dining gradually ceased to be a sticky and messy performance.

As a rule, even in our own day, those who wish to retain a good appetite do well not to frequent the kitchen. Doubly true must this have been at a time when sanitation was little understood, and the wretched scullions slept upon the bare floor of the kitchen in the palace of Henry VIII, and went about half clad during the day. Choice examples of what a professional cook or a hireling might be expected to do may be gleaned here and there in the cookery books. The following are fair specimens: "Gelye de chare [meat jelly] . . . seethe it again over the fire and skim it clean. Let a man evermore keep [watch] it, and *blow off the gravy*. And in case the liquor waste away, cast more of the same wine thereto, and *put thy hand therein*. And *if thy hand wax clammy*, it is a sign of goodness", etc.[5] Another appetizing example is found in the receipt for baked lampreys, where the cook is directed to blow through the crust so that the wind shall "abide within" and "raise up the coffin that it fall not down".[6]

To make herbelade one is directed to boil pork cut in pieces, add various spices, strain the broth of the boiled pork, add the herbs and boil again. Then skim off the herbs and cast them to the pork in the bowl. "Then mince dates small and cast them thereto, and raisins of currants and pines, and draw through a strainer yolks of eggs thereto, and sugar, and powdered ginger and salt, and colour it a little with saffron. And rub *with thy hand* all these together."[7]

Doubtless in ordinary houses baking, especially the baking of meat pies in "coffins", was carried on in the kitchen itself. But where the family, with the servants and retainers, numbered scores, an oven of sufficient size could not find room in the kitchen and had to occupy a separate building.[8] The multitude of receipts in the cookery books for tarts, for pastry, and in particular for "bakemeats", indicate, moreover, that the oven, great or small, must have been in almost constant use.

All in all, the English kitchens of five or six centuries ago differed in few important details from the great kitchens of half a century ago on the Continent,[9] many of which in provincial towns are still in active service.

It remains only to say a word about the chief figure in the kitchen; and we may borrow the interesting comment in *Our English Home* (p. 78): "In early times [the cook] was often a person of rank and wealth. . . . On state occasions he sometimes joined the procession into the hall, and claimed the honour of carrying the first dish to the table; he had the warmest seat in the chimney corner in the kitchen, and, as a mark of his rank, he carried a large wooden spoon, for the double purpose of tasting the soups and chastising those who failed to obey orders."

II

Before considering in some detail the actual preparation of food for the banquets of the late medieval period, it is instructive to note how many articles of food and drink that are the very staples of modern life were utterly unknown four or five hundred years ago. The lack of them at present would cause a considerable domestic revolution, and we can hardly imagine how we could put up with medieval substitutes. For example, England without tea and coffee would be a strangely different country, but neither tea nor coffee came into use before the middle of the seventeenth century. Tobacco, the great consoler, was first introduced near the end of the sixteenth century. Cocoa appeared about the same time. The now omnipresent potato was not known in Europe until after 1550; and the tuber introduced by Sir John Hawkins from Santa Cruz into England in 1553 is said to have been the *sweet* potato. All the so-called "breakfast foods" now widely used were, of course, wholly unknown. Fruit was rarely, if ever, eaten with the early breakfast, and the now inevitable English marmalade was not in use before 1524. Even the bacon that is the mainstay of the modern English breakfast table is strangely different from the coarse product served on the tables of the aristocracy four hundred years ago. Macaroni, which is the most characteristic feature of modern Italian diet, appears to have been wholly lacking on English tables during the period we are studying.[10]

As will be noted later, such beverages as brandy, whisky, champagne, and gin were quite unknown in medieval times. The same is true of all carbonized waters. But without dwelling longer upon food that was unattainable because unknown we may consider what was to be had.

III

In the Middle Ages eating and drinking were among the chief pleasures of life, and a vast amount

1. CARVER AT TABLE

MERLIN LED BY A SPANIEL INTO THE BANQUETING HALL

2. THE ABBOT'S KITCHEN, GLASTONBURY, 1435-40

of time and energy was devoted to the preparation of food. Hence nothing throws more light upon the daily life of four or five centuries ago than a trustworthy account of the food that people ate. And if we can imagine ourselves as sharing the strange dishes once popular, we may perhaps in some degree measure the distance we have traversed since the discovery of America.

Few topics are more welcome to the medieval romancers than feasts, and in describing them they exploit all their conceptions of splendour. But apart from vague indications they tell us little about the actual food that was served. Quite different is it in the old cookery books. There we are introduced to the actual receipts, and are thus able to form some conception of the strange mixtures that found favour in the Middle Ages and, indeed, long after. No more illuminating pages, indeed, are to be found concerning the real life of the upper classes in medieval times than in the books of ancient cookery and in the various Household Books. We there see what is actually provided for an ordinary meal in a great house, or even in a royal palace, and can thus realize the difference between an everyday repast and a feast on a grand scale.

Fortunately, we have also a considerable number of lists of the food served at famous feasts, to say nothing of the descriptions of feasts in the old chronicles. These feasts apparently surpassed in magnificence even those so brilliantly pictured in the old romances.

Among the books most commonly referred to in our discussion of medieval food are the following:

S. Pegge, *The Forme of Cury*, a Roll of ancient English Cookery, compiled about A.D. 1390. London, 1780.

Richard Warner, *Antiquitates Culinariae*, or Curious Tracts relating to the Culinary Affairs of the Old English. This includes a reprint of *The Forme of Cury*, and three other collections of old receipts, one dating from 1381. London, 1791.

Le Ménagier de Paris, composé vers 1393 *par un Bourgeois Parisien.* Paris, 2 vols., 1846.

R. Morris, *Liber Cure Cocorum*, copied and edited from the Sloane MS. 1986. Philological Society, London, 1862.

F. J. Furnivall, *The Babees Book*, pp. cxxxvi, 405 + 132. This contains a great variety of early short treatises relating to food and how to serve it, how to behave at table and elsewhere, etc. London: Early English Text Society, 1868.

Mrs. Alexander Napier, *A Noble Boke off Cookry* [fifteenth century]. London, 1882.

Thomas Austin, *Two Fifteenth Century Cookery Books*. London: Early English Text Society, 1888.

The French origin of the late fourteenth-century *Forme of Cury* is obvious from the names of a large proportion of the receipts, such as Egourdouce, Sawce Madame, Blank Manng, Blank Dessorre, Pynnonade, Payn Fondewe, Douce Ame, Vyannde Ryal, and many more. So, too, if we trace the

PREPARATION OF FOOD 51

antecedents of the *Liber Cure Cocorum*, the *Noble Boke off Cookry*, and of the *Two Fifteenth Century Cookery Books*, we find them betraying their origin in the retention of a multitude of French terms mixed with English, such as *Lange wortys de chare, trype de motoun, soupes dorye, auter brawune en peuerade, autre vele in bokenade, mortrewys de fleysshe, tartes de chare, vyaunde ryal, pome dorres*,[11] and many more.

We turn to the famous *Ménagier de Paris* and we find the same sort of heterogeneous combinations as in the English books. Nothing, indeed, is more instructive than to compare, for example, the sauces in the English cookery books with those described in the *Ménagier de Paris*, II, 229-237, and the hundred and fifty-three *potages* in the *Two Fifteenth Century Cookery Books* with the very similar ones in the *Ménagier*, II, 134-177. Both the French and the English books, whether intentionally or not, appear to follow old Roman traditions. In the Roman cookery book which has come to us under the name of Apicius, the famous epicure, we find the same atrocious combinations of incongruous elements that so strikingly characterize the late medieval cookery books.

IV

As we now turn to the discussion of the old receipts we encounter peculiar difficulty in arrangement, since out of the variety of matters to be discussed it is not easy to determine which should be treated first. Moreover, a certain amount of repetition is almost unavoidable. The greater proportion of the receipts use materials that are employed elsewhere in combination with other materials to make dishes more or less similar. But it is important to single out for discussion various features that constantly reappear and more or less definitely distinguish the old cookery from that of our own day.

In a great number of cases the old name of a dish gives a modern reader no clue to its character. For example, the modern blanc-mange is commonly some sort of simple gelatinous composition served with a sweetened sauce. The blanc-mange of long ago was made of meat or fish boiled with sweetened almond milk and further seasoned with sugar and salt.[12] What we now call custard is a sufficiently familiar dish, but it bears no resemblance to the custards of four or five hundred years ago. A custard like the following was a serious undertaking: "Take veal and smite in little pieces into a pot and wash it clean; then take fair [i.e. clean] water and let it boil together with parsley, sage, savory, and hyssop cut small enough; and when it is boiling take powdered pepper, cinnamon, cloves, mace, saffron, and let them boil together, and a good deal of wine therewith. When the flesh is boiled, take it from the broth all clean, and let the broth cool; and when it is cold, take eggs, the white and the yolks, and cast through a strainer, and put them into the broth, so many that the broth be stiff enough. Then make fair coffins and couch .iij. pieces or .iiij. of the flesh in a coffin. Then take dates and cut them, and cast thereto. Then take powdered ginger and a little verjuice, and put into the broth and salt. And then put the broth in the coffins, bake a little with the flesh before thou put thy liquor thereon, and let all bake together till it be enough [done]. Then [take] it out, and serve forth."[13] The old custard was obviously no more nor less than a meat or fruit pie; now it is a preparation of eggs "beaten up and mixed with milk to a stiff consistency, sweetened, and baked".

V

Modern taste is so different from that of four or five hundred years ago that scarcely one of the favourite dishes served at feasts would now be found eatable. This does not mean that the elements of which most medieval dishes were composed were of inferior quality. On the average, the food served at feasts was probably as costly as that of our time. But the old standards of acceptable food were strangely different from ours. Scarcely anything was prepared in what would now be regarded as a simple and natural fashion. In the strictest sense of the term everything was fearfully and wonderfully made. The ideal, apparently, was that nothing should be left in its natural state, but rather deviled and hashed and highly spiced and mixed with a dozen or a score of other ingredients so that no one might have an inkling of what a dish was composed.[14] One might almost suspect that the cooks were aiming to render food unfit for human consumption.

Some of the food, indeed, according to modern notions, was unfit before it came into the hands of the cook. Perhaps no one in Europe or America would now eat a cormorant. Yet this disgusting bird was often seen on the tables of the well-to-do in the Middle Ages[15]; and the cormorant is typical of a goodly number of foods once served to the wealthy but now utterly discarded even by the poorest classes. On the other hand, medieval appetites made capricious distinctions in the choice of food. "The very men who ate heron, the vulture, and the cormorant did not dare to touch game when it was young. They regarded this sort of meat as immature, and hence indigestible. Thus, for example, they ate the hare and the partridge, but not the young hare and the young partridge."[16] So, too, diners who relished the cormorant found little pleasure in eating the swan or the peacock.[17]

Even more surprising than the choice of the cormorant as a food is the use of the whale, the seal, and the porpoise. Ambrose Paré does indeed say that the flesh of the whale is not at all esteemed, but the tongue, since it is soft and delicious, is salted like pork and eaten in lent with pease.[18] The flesh of the whale itself remains hard and indigestible even after twenty-four hours of cooking. But the whale, and especially the porpoise, were often eaten in the Middle Ages. In the *Noble Boke off Cookry*, a receipt for porpoise with almonds (p. 86) is found, and another for "nombles of porpas"[19]

(p. 90). Sir John Neville was assuredly able to furnish his table as he wished, yet he regarded seal as worthy of a place there, and he was no exception.[20] But food of this type gradually went out of use. From Carter's well-known cookery book (1730) herons, peacock, whale, and seal have already vanished, though lampreys are retained.

It goes without saying that food of the sort just cited is revolting to modern taste. But hardly more attractive are scores of other medieval dishes. Indeed, it is astonishing to run through the receipts found in the *Liber Cure Cocorum*, in the *Two Fifteenth Century Cookery Books*, in Warner's *Antiquitates Culinariae*, and in Mrs. Napier's *Noble Boke off Cookry*, vainly trying to find one that could be served today. Even the best, as a rule, contain one or more ingredients repulsive to modern taste or ingredients which, though palatable when taken separately, are combined in a fashion that would now make them nauseating in the extreme.

Everyone is aware that nothing is more sickening than an oyster sprinkled with sugar. Yet we have more than one old receipt recommending such a combination. One of the briefest is the following: "Oysters in gravy bastard,—Take great oysters and shell them; and take the water of the oysters, and ale, and bread strained, and the water also, and put it in a pot, and ginger, sugar, saffron, powdered pepper, and salt, and let it boil well. Then put the oysters thereto, and serve it forth."[21]

Something equally choice is the following: "Take brawn and cut it thin. Then take the yolks of eggs and some of the white therewith. Then take manchet flour and draw the eggs through a strainer. Then take a good quantity of sugar, saffron, and salt, and cast thereto, and take a fair [clean] pan with French grease and set it over the fire. And when the grease is hot, take the brawn and put in batter and turn it well therein, and then put it in the pan with the grease, and let [them] fry together a little while. Then take it up into a fair [clean] dish, and cast sugar thereon, and serve forth."[22]

Such delicacies are not for our time. But whatever we may think of the food of the Middle Ages there can be no doubt that it was heartily relished by the people who ate it. In the romance entitled *La Patience de la Comtesse d'Anjou* is a long passage (ll. 1104–58) in which "the fugitive countess recalls the delicate food to which she had been accustomed. She enumerates capons, swans, peacocks, partridges, pheasants, and other birds, venison and rabbits, wild boar and other game, many sorts of fish, sturgeon, cod, mackerel, herring, bream, carp, lampreys, great eels in 'paste', pepper, cameline sauce, verjuice, many kinds of cakes, wafers, tarts, and more than a dozen kinds of wine".[23] The food in this list is, in name at least, precisely the same as that described in the English cookery books current in the fifteenth century.

Comparatively little progress towards simplicity in preparing food for the table was made in the sixteenth and seventeenth centuries, but in the eighteenth century a complete revolution was effected. As Alfred Franklin remarks[24]: "Cookery has little by little become simpler and more wholesome, one eats less and better, and at regular hours. ... I will let Mercier speak,[25] who about 1780 wrote as follows: 'One almost dares boast of having a good stomach, something that one would not have dared to do twenty years ago'."

VI

The first impression upon glancing through a medieval cookery book is that a great variety of food was offered to diners in the days before the Reformation. Closer study leads to a different conclusion. When practically every dish was smothered in spices or some other ingredient of sharply pronounced flavour, the general effect must have been monotonous in the extreme, or at least it would now be to the average European or American. But we cannot hope to understand medieval cookery until we realize what the cook was trying to accomplish. Unlike a skilled modern cook, he was not endeavouring to conserve the peculiar quality of a particular meat—of a pheasant as distinguished from a goose or a capon, the individual quality of a rare fruit—but his pride consisted rather in the skill with which he could combine the most disparate elements and thus produce something hitherto unknown. In one sense this tendency is apparently not in keeping with what might have been expected in the age before the discovery of America; for when we consider the amazing complexity of of our own time, with the endless inventions in every department of life, with the astonishing development of modern means of transport, with the news from the remotest corners of the earth served up to us at the breakfast table, with the telephone at our elbow enabling us to converse at will with friends in Australia or China or Japan, we are prone to regard the Middle Ages as a time of painfully simple living. And, as we have already seen, this was in considerable measure true. Even the most luxurious houses were strangely lacking in comfort.

But, however simple life in general may have been, this was far from being true of the diet of the upper classes. As already noted, except in the lower ranks of society, English cookery, particularly in the later medieval period, followed French models somewhat closely. This means, of course, that simplicity was as far as possible avoided and that the cook, like the physician and the apothecary in their prescriptions, aimed to combine as much irreconcilable material in one dish as he could without making it impossible to swallow. Plain food, prepared so as to preserve as far as possible its own peculiar taste, was not greatly esteemed, and a cook of any reputation would have blushed to place such a dish before his guests. His aim seems always to have been to make something appear to be what it is not. Of this we have numerous brilliant illustrations.[26]

At first sight nothing seems less complicated than the preparation of stewed beef, for which we have more than one receipt. I select a relatively simple one: "Take fair ribs of fresh beef, and (if thou wilt) roast it till it be near enough [done]. Then put it in a fair [clean] pot. Cast thereto parsley and minced onions, raisins of currants, powdered pepper, cinnamon, cloves, saunders, saffron, and salt. Then cast thereto wine and a little vinegar. Set a lid on the pot and let it boil 'soakingly' on a fair charcoal till it be done. Then lay the flesh in dishes, and the syrup thereupon, and serve it forth."[27]

Under modern conditions, what can be simpler than a poached egg? But note what had to be done some four centuries or more ago before poached eggs were ready for the table. "Take[28] eggs, break them, and seethe them in hot water. Then take them up as whole as thou mayest. Then take flour and mix with milk and cast thereto sugar or honey and a little powdered ginger, and boil all together, and colour with saffron. And lay thy eggs in dishes and cast the broth above, and cast on powder enough. Blanche powder is best."[29]

The modern method of stewing apples aims to conserve as far as possible the natural flavour; the old receipt left scarcely a trace of the original taste of the fruit: "Take apples and seethe them and sift them through a sieve into a pot. Then take almond milk and honey and cast thereto, and grated bread, saffron, saunders, and a little salt, and cast all into the pot, and let them boil. And look that thou stir it well, and serve it forth."[30]

One who is more tempted by the following receipt may take his choice: "Take apples, stew them, let them cool, pass them through a hair sieve. Put them into a pot, and on a flesh day add good fat beef broth, white grease, sugar, and saffron: on fish days, almond milk, olive oil, sugar, and saffron. Boil it, mess it out, sprinkle on good spices, and serve."[31]

If stewed apples appear to be too simple, one may stimulate a jaded appetite with rissoles of fruit: "Take figs and grind them in a mortar all small with a little oil and grind with them cloves and maces. And then take them up into a dish and cast thereto pines, saunders, currants, minced dates, powder of pepper, cinnamon, saffron, and salt. And then make fine paste of flour, water, sugar, saffron, and salt, and make thereof fair cakes. And then roll the stuff in thy hand and lay it in the cakes. Cut them and so fold them together as rissoles, and fry them in good oil, and serve them forth hot."[32]

Fortunately for the cooks who prided themselves upon the number of incongruous elements they could combine in one dish without making it uneatable, they catered for men and women who were coarse feeders, whose palates were dulled by sharp sauces, by spiced wines, and by the pepper and mustard and ginger and cubebs and cardamom and cinnamon with which the most innocent meats and fruits were doctored and disguised until the cook himself could hardly determine from the taste what had entered into the composition.

What, for example, could be more mystifying than the following composition, selected at random?

PREPARATION OF FOOD

"Take wine and put in a pot, and clarified honey and saunders, pepper, saffron, cloves, mace and cubebs and minced dates and raisins of currants, and a little vinegar, and seethe it on the fire. And seethe figs in wine and draw them through a strainer, and cast thereto, and let them boil all together. Then take good flour, saffron, sugar, and clean water, and make thereof cakes, and let them be thin enough. Then cut them like leechings,[33] and cast them in clean oil, and fry them a little while. Then take them out of the pan and cast into a vessel with the syrup, and so serve them forth, the brindons[34] and the syrup in a dish. And let the syrup be running and not too stiff."[35]

As a rule, one had slight control over the vagaries of the cook, but an occasional protest made itself heard. Froissart complains of a feast at which there were a great number of dishes so strange and so disguised that one could not tell what they were.[36] Evidently, the more difficult a dish was to prepare, the more it was esteemed by the cook who made it.

The practice of mixing all sorts of inharmonious elements in a single dish was paralleled by the fashion of piling a huge platter full of meats of various sorts. This particularly characterized the tables of the French aristocracy. We learn that as early as 1333, and doubtless much earlier, the Dauphin had a dish of twelve chickens, or six cut in half, served on Tuesdays. "This custom of piling in the same platter many pieces at once was not peculiar to him but was common to all the princes and great lords."[37] "*Les Contes d'Eutrapel*, published posthumously in 1587, bears witness that before Francis I, and even still in his time, many families had served on their tables a great platter garnished with beef, mutton, veal, and pork, with a great quantity of greens and cooked vegetables [racines]. Each one selected as he preferred and ate either vegetables or meat or both. The dishes so loaded were called *mets*, whether boiled or roasted. This fashion of piles of meat continued till the time of the Regency. Then began a new type of cuisine, which required a new method of serving."[38]

What gave most satisfaction to the medieval cook was doubtless the combination of ingredients in such fashion as to produce a new dish and at the same time conceal the identity of the chief component.[39] Take, for example, such an astonishing mixture as the following: "Take figs and seethe them till they be neysshe [soft], then bray them till they be small. Then take them up and put them in a pot and ale thereto. Then take bread grated, and whole pines, and cast thereto, and let it boil well. And at the dresser, cast on powdered cinnamon enough, and serve forth. And if thou wilt colour it in three manners, thou might, with saunders, saffron, and himself, and lay on powder enough, and serve forth."[40] But what trace of figs is left in the mixture? Incredibly clever must have been the *bon viveur* whose taste was sure enough to determine the components. One pronounced flavour tended to overpower all the rest.

Most of the receipts are too long to quote in full,

but we note that stewed capons[41] require thirteen ingredients in order to be presentable—among them, spices, dough, wine, herbs, saffron, raisins, sugar; "herbe-blade"[42] has thirteen ingredients besides the "coffins"; a "Vyaunde Furnez"[43] is made up of eighteen ingredients, dough, meat, eggs, bread crumbs, spices, cheese, and so on; and "Grete pyes"[44] are a mixture of beef and "suet of a fatte beste or of Motton", pepper, salt, capons, hens, mallards, coneys, woodcocks, teals, great birds, marrow, hard yolks of eggs, dates, currants, whole cloves, whole mace, cinnamon, saffron, and other things up to twenty-one, besides the "coffin".

VII

One of the most characteristic features of the old receipts is their vagueness. In our own time all cookery books worthy the name prescribe that every ingredient shall be carefully weighed or measured. But, as a rule, in the old books no definite quantity of meat or fish or of anything else is specified, and the proportions are left to the judgment of the cook. As an inevitable result, a cook of experience easily became indispensable and ran no risk of dangerous competition. What, for example, could a novice do with directions like the following, especially with no indication of the number of persons to be served?

One is told, for example, to take "enough of powder of cinnamon, a good quantity, and cast it in red wine, and draw it through a strainer; cast sugar thereto, and put it [in] an earthen pot, and let it boil".[45]

Or, "Take yolks of eggs drawn through a strainer; then take sugar, a good quantity, and cast thereto, and a little salt",[46] etc. With plain food having no pronounced flavour this indefiniteness is of small importance, but where spices are used as freely as in the Middle Ages, a momentary indiscretion might spoil a costly dish.

In order to indicate to what extent the success or the failure of a dish depended upon the experience and skill of the cook I cite without comment a number of typical illustrations, all taken from the *Two Fifteenth Century Cookery Books*. To make white wortes, "take milk of almonds and cast thereto, and honey, not too much, that it be not too sweet", etc. (p. 6). When making fried cream of almonds "cast white sugar enough thereto, and a little salt" (p. 7). So, too, when compounding the so-called *bowres*, "cast thereto ale enough, and sage and salt" (p. 8). For fillets in galantine, "cast thereto powdered pepper, cinnamon, cloves, and mace, and let them boil well together" (p. 8). If drawn gruel "be not brown enough, take a little blood and cast thereto before it be drawn, and make it brown enough, and serve it forth" (p. 10). One is cautioned when preparing a pottage on fish-day "to put sugar a good quantity thereto of honey, but not too much, then heat it a little, and serve it all abroad in the dishes" (p. 15). If, by some miracle, a satisfactory dish resulted from vague directions of this sort, the cook was certainly to be congratulated.[47]

3. POULTRY SERVED WHOLE

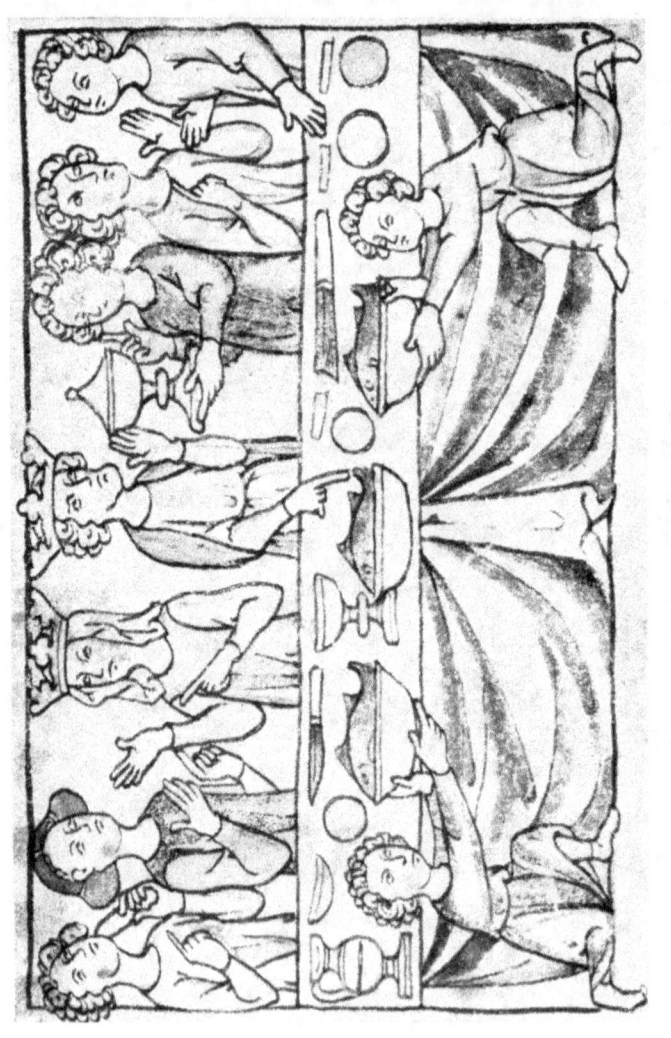

4. A FISH DINNER

In a few cases we find definite quantities specified, and these deserve special mention. For making oil sops one is directed to "take a good quantity of stale ale, as .iij. gallons, and thereto take a pint of oil fried".[48] Very specific is the rule for making "Mammenye bastarde". One is to "take a pottle of clarified honey, and a pound of pines, and a pound of currant raisins, and a pound of saunders, and powdered cinnamon, and two gallons of wine or ale, and a pound of pepper.—Then take three pounds of amidons, and a gallon of wine, and a good gallon of vinegar", etc.[49] For Primrose, "take other half pound of flour of rice, three pounds of almonds, half an ounce of honey and saffron, and take the flower[s] of the primrose, and grind them and temper them with milk of the almonds, and put powdered ginger thereon".[50]

Not only are the old receipts vague, but in many cases the name offers no suggestion of the character of the composition; and occasionally the name is actually misleading. Gingerbread sounds familiar, but when we learn how it is made we see that the name connotes nothing that we have before known[51]: "Take a quart of honey and seethe it and skim it clean. Take saffron, powdered pepper, and throw thereon. Take grated bread and make it so stiff that it will be leched.[52] Then take cinnamon powder and strew thereon enough. Then make it square as though thou wouldst slice it. Take, when thou slicest it, and cast box leaves above, stuck thereon in cloves. And if thou will have it red, colour it with saunders enough".[53] This is gingerbread without ginger!

VIII

One of the native products indispensable for the feast was bread. On a great estate the bread might be baked in one's own oven, but public bakers were common, and their craft was strictly regulated by law. The baker who adulterated his flour or sold a loaf that was under the legal weight was liable to severe penalties. As for millers, the popular opinion was that when they had opportunity they stole what they could of the flour or meal that they ground[54]; and hence the proverb: "An honest miller has a golden thumb."

The bread was naturally of variable quality. Wheat bread was comparatively dear and for the most part too costly for the poor. As a rule, flour was somewhat coarse, and the *Northumberland Household Book* (p. 58) prescribes that "Trencher Brede be maid of the Meale as it cummyth frome the Milne". The finest sort of flour was used in making manchet loaves. The cheat loaf was "wheaten bread of the second quality, made of flour more coarsely sifted than that used for manchet, the finest quality".[55] This sort of bread was the type consigned to the alms dish. Ravel bread was made of unbolted flour, along with bran. The very poor had small choice in the flour they used, and they eked out their supplies by using oats, rye, barley, or even peas and beans.[56]

As for the grain used for bread during the period we[57] are discussing, we may note the conclusions of Sir William Ashley, undoubtedly the foremost authority on the subject. He observes: "Firstly, that a complete transition to a wheat bread diet on the part of the people was only effected during the eighteenth century; secondly, that there is reason to believe that the culture of rye was relatively more extensive the farther back we go in time; thirdly, that during the Middle Ages rye was cultivated to some extent in almost all the arable districts, and that in some it preponderated over wheat; and fourthly, that throughout the Middle Ages it was a very important element in the rural life of the country, in the food of the people, and in the policy of the government."[58]

The cookery books appear to assume that ordinary bread is too well known to require directions for making it. They refer familiarly to brown bread and white. Paindemain[59] "is apparently the same as manchet bread", i.e. bread of fine quality.[60] Payne puffe is identified with pety pernauntes[61], and appears to be another name for *pain perdu* or *fondu*, that is, a fried brioche. The French origin of these kinds of bread is evident.

For making the finer types of bread specific directions are obviously necessary; and the cookery books prescribe exactly what to do. "To make 'payn pardieu' take paynmayne or fresh bread and pare away the crust. Cut them in shives and fry them a little in clarified butter. Then take yolks of eggs, draw through a strainer as hot as ye may, and lay the bread therein and turn it therein that they may be covered in batter, and serve and strew on sugar enough."[62]

Trenchers were slices of coarse bread used instead

of a plate. After the trencher had served its purpose and had been saturated with the sauce and the juice of the meat laid upon it, it was often eaten, if not by the guest, at least by a servant or by the poor. In Wynkyn de Worde's *Boke of Kervynge* the Carver is told that all of his first year he must be butler and panter,[63] and that he must have three knives, one knife to square the trencher loaves, another to be a chipper, and the third sharp, so as to make smooth trenchers. Trencher bread is to be four days old,[64] so as to give a sharp edge when cut. In some households, as for example that of the Earl of Northumberland, the trenchers were of wood.[65]

Particular emphasis is laid upon the fact that bread served at the table is to be cut, not broken, and that it is to be pared. Whether the dislike of the crust, now esteemed by many persons as the most desirable part of the loaf, was due to the fact that it was ill suited for sops or to a distrust of the cleanliness of those who may have handled it, is not easy to decide. The prejudice may have been due to dietitians. For example, Andrew Boorde says[66]: "Burnt breade, and harde crustes and pasty crustes doth ingendre color,[67] aduste,[68] and melancholy humours; wherefore chip[69] the upper crust of your bread. And who so doth use to eate the seconde cruste after meate it maketh a man leane." In any case, we read in the *Modus Cenandi*: "Let an upper slice of fine bread be taken off for the master. Let it be cut through the middle, but not entirely cut."[70] Children, when taught their manners, are directed to cut their bread with a knife and not break it, and, moreover, to lay a clean trencher before them.[71]

It is interesting to note that in the last quarter of the sixteenth century the bread used in England was essentially the same as that of generations earlier, as we see from the comments of Harrison in his famous contemporary description of England: "The bread throughout the land is made of such grain as the soil yieldeth; nevertheless the gentility commonly provide themselves sufficiently for their own tables, whilst their household and poor neighbours in some shires are forced to content themselves with rye, or barley, yea, and in time of dearth, many with bread made either of beans, peas, or oats, or of altogether and some acorns among, of which scourge the poorest do soonest taste, sith they are least able to provide themselves of better. . . . Of bread made of wheat . . . the most excellent is the manchet, which we commonly call white bread. . . . The second is the cheat or wheaten bread, so named because the colour thereof resembleth the grey or yellowish wheat, being clean or well dressed, and out of this is the coarsest of the bran (usually called gurgeons or pollard) taken."[72]

IX

An essential element in modern cookery is a certain amount of fat. So it was also in medieval cookery, but the solution of the problem was different. In France, the marrow of veal and beef was then among the dishes greatly esteemed by the people. Beef marrow was put into apple tarts, and also used to spread on slices of bread.[73] Throughout England swine were plentiful, and lard was freely used, even for butter.[74] But the early cookery books make comparatively small use of butter.[75] In the *Two Fifteenth Century Cookery Books*, containing more than four hundred and sixty receipts, only seven prescribe the use of butter.[76] In Dickenmann's carefully prepared discussion of food in England from the twelfth to the fifteenth century, he remarks that although butter, cheese, and cream were an important part of the food of the poorer middle classes, they were not utterly despised on the tables of the rich. There, indeed, they were by no means among the chief articles of diet, but together with fruit were eaten before meals and afterwards, as a sort of dessert.[77] The *Northumberland Household Book* (p. 12) mentions oil[78] for frying fish, and the *Two Fifteenth Century Cookery Books* four times prescribe the use of oil, once with apples, and three times in making sops. The medieval choice of fats would doubtless in our time fail to win universal approval, but, all in all, with cream, mutton tallow, beef suet, the fat of domestic fowls, and the ever-abundant pork, the Middle Ages managed to find sufficient fats for their daily needs.

X

Among European nations the English of our time have not been notable for their soups. But the old English cookery books offer numerous receipts, mostly borrowed from the French, for various soft compositions that might pass for soup. For example, in the first of the *Two Fifteenth Century Cookery Books*, some thirty pages are taken up with directions for making various *potages*. These include a great variety of dishes, most of which contain meat or fish or eggs, some herbs, and nearly all a quantity of spices. Many would now hardly be classed as soups, but if so classed, they would be exceedingly thick. The range of the titles is very wide, including not less than a hundred and fifty-three different receipts— sturgeon in broth, oysters in gravy, stewed partridge, rabbits in gravy, goose in hotchpotch, meat jelly, fish jelly, and so on.

There are also various forms of *bonet* or broth, some made up with almonds, some made of "boiled cream, boiled again with brayed curds, honey, and butter, thickened with yolks of egg", and sliced. An occasional receipt, with slight modification, might even pass muster to-day. Such, for example, is the following, called "Hens in bonet", which is a rather simple chicken broth. This is made by stewing hens and fresh pork together, grinding pepper, bread, and cummin, seasoning it, tempering it with the hens' broth, colouring it with saffron, adding salt, and serving it.[79]

A so-called German broth[80] is compounded as follows: "Take conies[81] or kids and hew them small into morsels or pieces. Parboil them with the same broth. Draw [make] an almond milk and put the flesh therein. Cast thereto powder of galingale [cypress root] and of ginger, with flour of rice and colour it with alkenet [bugloss]. Boil it and mess [serve] it forth with sugar and powder-douce."

Two more specimen receipts for broth will sufficiently illustrate this comparatively innocuous type of medieval diet. For making roe broth: "Take the flesh of the deer or of the roe-buck; parboil it in small pieces. Seethe it well, half in water and half in wine. Take bread and bray [grind] it with the self [same] broth, and draw [add] blood thereto, and let it seethe together with powder-fort [strong] of ginger or of cinnamon and mace, with a great portion of vinegar and currants."[82] Cold brewit (broth), according to one receipt,[83] is extremely simple: "Take pulp of almonds, dry it in a cloth, and when it is dried put it in a vessel; add thereto salt, sugar, and white powder of ginger, and juice of fennel with wine. And let it well stand. Lay full and mess, and dress it forth." This contrasts strikingly with another cold brewit[84] made of almonds, wine or vinegar, with anise, sugar, and green fennel mixed together. To these is to be added powder of cinnamon and ginger, with cloves and whole maces. Then kid or chickens or other flesh is to be chopped small and boiled. When all the flesh is boiled it is to be laid in a clean vessel, and the liquor boiled and salted. Then all this is to be cast into the pot with flesh and served.

XI

Among the materials employed in medieval cuisine, without doubt spices and condiments occupy the first place. The modern kitchen requires a small amount of pepper, a nutmeg or two, a little cinnamon, ground or in sticks, a few cloves, some mustard, and possibly a little ginger and allspice.

In the medieval kitchen spices were used far more lavishly than in our day. They were, of course, rare and costly, and brought from the Far East. Commonly they were transported across country by caravan, and then brought by Venetian or Genoese[85] vessels from various seaports, especially from Alexandria or Aleppo. During the early Middle Ages spices were prized like jewels. When the Venerable Bede approached his end he distributed his few treasures among his brethren, and divided a little parcel of pepper as one of his choicest possessions. With the growth of commerce spices naturally became more common and less costly. But they were never cheap, and the constant use to which they were put imposed one of the heaviest charges upon the purveyor for the kitchen.[86] Every great establishment kept a quantity of spices in store,[87] some of the inventories of which have been preserved to our time. Quite naturally, the French were as addicted to spices as the English, if not more so. A considerable number of spices and condiments are enumerated among the household expenses of Richard de Swinfield, 1289-90. These comprised "cloves, cubebs, mace, saffron, sugar [always included among spicery], garingale [galingale], cinnamon, ginger, raw and preserved, pepper, cummin, liquorice, buckwheat, aniseed, gromil and coriander".[88] There was no lack of spices in the kitchen of the Earl of Northumberland, as may be inferred from the space given to them in the *Household Book*.[89] In the sixteenth-century Losely

MSS. (p. 12), ginger, cinnamon, cloves, mace, pepper, raisins and prunes are enumerated, together with the quantities in the spicery, and their cost. We learn that in one year spice and pepper in the household of Sir Thomas Cawarden cost £10, and that wine, Rhenish, red, white, sack, claret, and malmsey, cost a similar amount.

A large proportion of the receipts in all the cookery books prescribe spices, even for food which, according to modern taste, would be far better without them. Practically all ordinary meats and game, fish and poultry, as well as stewed fruit and desserts of every description, were so loaded with cinnamon, ginger, cloves, cubebs, pepper, galingale (cypress root), mace, and nutmeg, one or all, that whatever had been taken as the basis of the dish was made practically unrecognizable.

A few illustrations will make this clear. Fillets of pork in galantine are spiced with powdered pepper, cinnamon, cloves, and maces, tempered with vinegar, blood, and ale, or with saunders and salt.[90] Giblets of chicken are flavoured with pepper, saffron, mace, cloves, and a little verjuice and salt.[91] Boiled venison requires the addition of parsley, sage, powdered pepper, cloves, mace, vinegar, and a little red wine.[92] Numbles of venison are to be seasoned with wine, powdered pepper, and cinnamon, followed by powdered ginger and a little vinegar and salt.[93] Conies boiled or roasted are to be improved by adding ground almonds, then coloured with saffron and sprinkled with rice powdered, after which the whole should be seasoned with powdered ginger, galingale (cypress root), cinnamon, sugar, cloves, and mace.[94] Typical in all its details—excess of spices, the grinding in a mortar, the complicated mixing—is the following: Sturmye. "Take good milk of almonds drawn with wine. Take pork and hew it small. Put it in a mortar and grind it right small. Then cast it into the same milk and cast it into a pot. Take saunders and rice flour, mix them with the milk, draw them through a strainer and cast into a clean pot. Look that it be stiff enough. Take sugar and put thereon, and honey. Put it over the fire and let it boil a great while. Stir it well. Take eggs hard boiled. Take the white[s] and hew them as small as thou might. Cast them into the pot. Take saffron and cast thereto, with powdered ginger, cinnamon, cloves, and look that thou have powder enough. Cast it into the pot, temper it with vinegar. Take salt and add thereto, mix them well together. Make a syrup, the half part shall be wine and the half part sugar or honey. Boil it and stir it clean. Therein wet thy dishes and serve and skim forth."[95]

In varying degrees the practice of smothering ordinary meats with spices was followed in the preparation of poultry[96] and fish,[97] and even of fruit for the table. Quinces are not merely boiled but flavoured with rose water, brayed in a mortar, strained, treated with milk of almonds, white wine, and vinegar, besides powdered cloves, ginger, grains of paradise, sugar, salt, and saffron.[98] Strawberries are to be washed in red wine, strained through a cloth, put in a pot with almond milk tempered with amidon or rice flour, and made stiff and boiled, after which raisins, saffron, pepper, great plenty of sugar, powdered ginger, cinnamon, and galingale are to be added. Then the mess should be made acid with vinegar and a little white grease put thereto. Then it is to be coloured with alkenade, "planted" with grains of pomegranate, and served forth.[99] One may be permitted to inquire what trace of strawberry is left in the mixture.

Cherries receive similar treatment: "Take cherries, and pick out the stones, wash them clean in wine, then wring them through a cloth, and put them in a pot, and put thereto a quantity of white grease and a portion of rice flour, and make it stiff. Add thereto white honey or sugar, make it acid with vinegar. Season it with strong powder of cinnamon and cypress root, and temper it with a great portion of yolks of eggs. Colour it with saffron or saunders, and when thou servest it in, plant it with cherries, and serve forth."[100]

The highly spiced dishes that one encounters in India, in northern Africa, and in out-of-the-way districts of Italy and Spain to-day differ in no essential particulars from those that chiefly characterize medieval cookery. Even in England two or three generations ago many dishes still retained a strikingly medieval character, and were spiced far beyond what the average modern appetite can easily endure.

Not only were all possible dishes highly spiced, but, as a climax to the feast, spices were served with wines.[101] Spice plates of gold or silver, often richly

PREPARATION OF FOOD

gilt, were divided into compartments and loaded with spices, sugar plums, and various other sweetmeats. The great spice plate was, however, as a rule not presented indiscriminately to the guests but only to the donor of the feast and such others as he might designate.

The reason for the immoderate use of spices may be found in part in the current opinions on diet in the Middle Ages. Most men knew that the enormous amount of meat served for a feast, or even for an ordinary meal, imposed a heavy burden upon the digestion, and hence they used cinnamon and cardamon and ginger and many other spices to whip up the action of the stomach. Even when not at table they made free use of spiced comfits, partly for the sake of aiding digestion and partly to gratify the appetite. One may well believe, too, that at a time when overkept meats and fish were freely used, spice was employed to cover up the incipient decay. At all events, whatever the reason, most dishes were smothered in spices, whether needed or not.

As a rule, possibly because of its provenance from the East, sugar was classed with spices. But honey made a very tolerable substitute, and from early times it had been freely used, especially for making mead and metheglin. Needless to say, no sugar was produced in England, and it had to be imported, mainly from Syria, Rhodes, Cyprus, Candia, Alexandria, Sicily.[102] For families of moderate means the price was prohibitive. An ordinary quality was retailed up to the close of the fifteenth century at from 1s. 6d. to 3s. a pound, or, on an average, at a price equivalent to about thirty shillings or more at present.[103]

"Western Europe", we are told, "used sugar at first almost wholly as medicine. Not till it became less dear did the use of fruit comfits and other sweet things become more general, and it never was an article of daily consumption as in our time."[104] Even a well-to-do family like the Pastons used sugar very sparingly. Margaret Paston requests John Paston to "Bye for me 1 *li.* of almonds and 1 *li.* of sugyr",[105] since obviously it could not be procured where she lived. In another letter she says, "ther is non gode in this town".[106] We need not enumerate the various receipts that require sugar,[107] but we note in passing the fondness of our ancestors for dishes like "Whyte mortrewys of Porke", made of lean pork, finely ground and boiled with ground almonds and rice flour, after which one is to "throw thereto sugar enough and salt, and at the dresser to strew thereon powdered ginger mixed with almonds".[108]

XII

While illustrating some of the features of medieval cookery we have already incidentally discussed various meat dishes. We must now consider them in somewhat more detail.

It is hardly an exaggeration to say that the food of the Middle Ages consisted of meat and fish— meat for ordinary days and fish for fast-days.

There was, of course, a certain amount of other food, along with accessories such as eggs and bread and spices and almonds and sweetmeats. But in comparison with meat and fish everything else may almost be left out of the reckoning.

Foreigners were astonished at the vast supplies of beef, pork, veal, mutton, venison, rabbits, capons, swans, partridges, peacocks, pheasants, pigeons, and other birds provided for a single English banquet. The favourite meat of all classes was pork, and swine were easily maintained on the mast in the oak forests.

The *Regimen Sanitatis*, translated by Thomas Paynell in 1528, highly commends pork as the most wholesome meat. We note, for example: "Porke is better than any other fleshe, fyrste for the lyknes unto man's fleshe." Pork is, indeed, so like man's flesh, "that many have eaten man's fleshe instede of pork, and coude not perceive neither by the savour nor the taste but that it had bene porke" (C^{iii}). Galen is cited as saying, "One can eate no fleshe that nourisheth more than porke." Moreover, according to Avicen, "Christen men and their followers say that the best wylde fleshe, that is of a wyldeswyne, and in wynter there can be no better fleshe" (C^{iiii}).

In the later Middle Ages sheep were abundant and required little attention beyond ensuring that they should not stray too far from the fold which sheltered them at night. Goats were in the same category as sheep, though far less numerous. Cows and oxen afforded a sufficient supply of beef, though for the most part the quality was coarse and tough. Not unnaturally, veal, which was almost invariably tender, was prized along with pork as one of the most satisfactory meats. But in the Middle Ages the principles of breeding were imperfectly understood and the flesh of most domestic animals was little adapted to the needs of a delicate appetite.

With the approach of winter, when pasturage was no longer available, the days of slaughter began, and great quarters of beef and pork were salted[109] and kept in vats or casks until needed.[110] Throughout the cold season a monotonous and unwholesome diet of salted meat or fish was the rule, since the expense of keeping animals over the winter was felt to be prohibitive. A limited number were, of course, maintained for the sake of obtaining milk and butter and for breeding purposes. The natural result of a regular diet of salt meat and the scarcity of vegetables was that scurvy was practically universal. And although some persons pretended to find satisfaction in that their systems were relieved by means of their skin diseases, their gratification must have been slight.

Most kinds of meat that we now eat were eaten in the olden days, but with singular additions and modifications. Many of the receipts prescribe that the meat shall be ground to a paste or minced, and nearly all add a quantity of spices. Meats were supposed to be improved by the addition of various liquids of sharp taste, wine, vinegar, and, particularly, verjuice. This is the juice of various fruits, crabapples, green grapes, gooseberries, sometimes, though not always, fermented, and used for flavouring meat, fish, and eggs.[111] Sometimes the juice of oranges, especially Seville oranges, was used. When verjuice was made from grapes the practice arose of putting the juice into barrels and salting it when it had fermented.[112] The consumption of verjuice in France appears almost incredible. In 1385-6 Jean de Neele declared that his household used in one year between six and seven "queues" of verjuice or between 2,346 and 2,737 litres.[113]

Some meat was boiled in the mass. For example, the entire carcass of a swine was boiled in a great caldron after being disembowelled. Whole oxen were roasted on the spit. With a view to the difficulty of the guest in cutting his meat without the aid of a fork to hold it firmly, nearly all meat that was not minced or ground was cut into small pieces before being served.

When the cook had done his work the simple meat with which he started was commonly so disguised that it was practically impossible to decide exactly what one was eating. This appears particularly in so apparently simple a dish as stewed beef.[114] "Take fair beef of the ribs of the fore quarters and smite in fair pieces and wash the beef in a fair pot. Then take the water that the beef was sodden in, and strain it through a strainer and seethe the same water and beef in a pot, and let them boil together. Then take cinnamon, cloves, mace, grains of 'parise' [ginger], cubebs, and onions minced, parsley, and sage, and cast thereto, and let them boil together. And then take a loaf of bread, and steep it with broth and vinegar, and draw it through a strainer, and let it be still. And when it is near enough [done] cast the liquor thereto, but not too much, and then let [it] boil once, and cast saffron thereto in quantity. Then take salt and vinegar and cast thereto, and look that it be poignant [piquant] enough, and serve forth."

In this case the beef is not ground to a paste, but that after all these additions there could be any of the original flavour left is not to be imagined. Another receipt for stewed beef adds parsley, raisins of currants, powdered pepper, cinnamon, cloves, saunders, saffron, and salt, together with wine and a little vinegar.[115]

If in place of beef one prefers veal, kid, or chicken, one may proceed as follows: "Boil in clean water or in fresh broth, and cut into pieces, and pick them clean. Then draw the same broth through a strainer and cast thereto parsley, sage, hyssop, mace, cloves, and let [it] boil till the flesh be [cooked] enough. Then set it [away] from the fire and mix it with raw yolks of eggs, and cast thereto ginger, verjuice, saffron, and salt, and then serve it forth for a good meat."[116]

Hares were exceedingly common in the Middle Ages, and were prepared for the table in a variety of ways. A typical method is the following: "Take a hare and flay him clean. Then take the blood and bread and spicery and grind them together, and draw it up with the broth. Then take wine or ale,

PREPARATION OF FOOD

and cast thereto, and make gobbets, and then serve it forth."[117]

The liking for hare has somewhat diminished in England and America, but it is still very active in Germany. One of the familiar sights of my student days in Germany was a brace of hares hanging outside a window, safely out of reach of dogs or sneak thieves. There they hung in sun, wind, and rain, until sufficiently "high" to suit the taste. An infallible test of the ripeness was to shake the hare over a sheet or an outspread newspaper, and to note the vitality of the surface.

A welcome addition to the list of ordinary meats was afforded by venison. From early Norman times the chase had been strictly reserved for royalty and the privileged classes,[118] and a fat buck or doe could, as a rule, be easily run down in the then widely extended forests. Various methods of preparing venison for the table are found in the cookery books, most of which would now be regarded as nauseating. A venison steak would be treated as follows:

"Take venison or beef and slice and grill it up brown. Then take vinegar and a little verjuice and a little wine, and put powdered pepper thereon enough and powdered ginger. And at the dresser strew on powdered cinnamon enough, that the steaks may be all covered therewith and but a little sauce. And then serve it forth."[119]

In preparing meats for the table medieval cooks made great use of pastry. Innumerable receipts prescribe that the meat or fish or the fruit or the custard is to be placed in what is picturesquely termed a coffin. This, however, has none of its modern implications. It is nothing more nor less than a pastry crust designed to hold a meat or fish or fruit pie. The crust that contains meat is, in the quaint language of Andrew Boorde, a "bake meate,[120] which is called flesshe that is beryd, for it is buryd in paast". He adds that it "is not praysed in physycke".[121] One reason for the popularity of the "coffin" may have been that the meat or fish or fruit when put therein, along with the strange medieval accompaniments, cooked more satisfactorily than when merely jumbled together and stewed over a fire. Moreover, it is evident that the pastry itself was an attraction, as it is to many persons to-day. England shared with France the liking for meat pies, which were very commonly made by professional cooks. Ordinary cakes, we are told, were made in the household.[122] Le Grand d'Aussy adds that in the Middle Ages "all pastry containing meat or fish was called a pie; the name of tart was reserved for that which contained milk, fruits, herbs, or preserves".[123] This distinction was abandoned before the end of the eighteenth century.

Many of the bakemeats are extraordinarily complicated, but a simple type will serve our purpose. To make "Pies of Paris": "Take and smite fair butts of pork and butts of veal together, and put it [them] in a fair pot, and do [add] thereto fresh broth and a quantity of wine, and let all boil together till it be enough [done]. Then take it from the fire and let [it] cool a little. Then cast thereto yolks of eggs and powder of ginger, sugar, and salt, and minced dates, and raisins of currants. Then make fair paste and coffins and do [put] therein. Cover it and let [it] bake, and serve forth."[124]

Venison in a pasty—the favourite type of food for aged hermits in modern historical romances—was prepared as follows: "Take haunches of venison, parboil it in fair water and salt. Then take fair paste and lay thereon the venison cut in pieces as thou wilt have it, and cast under it and above it powder of ginger, or pepper and salt mixed together. And set them in an oven and let them bake till they be enough [done]."[125]

A curious instance of a type of cookery popular in the old books appears in the receipt for Yrchouns or hedgehogs: "Take pigs' maws and scald them well. Take ground pork and knead it with spices, with powdered ginger, and salt and sugar. Put it in the maw, but fill it not too full. Then sew it with a fair thread and put them on a spit as men do pigs. Take blanched almonds, and carve them long, small, and sharp, and fry them in grease and sugar. Take a little prick and prick the 'yrchouns' and put in the holes the almonds, every hole half, and each [separated] from the other. Lay them then to the fire. When they are roasted, glaze them, some with wheat flour and milk of almonds, some green, some black with blood, and let them not brown too much, and serve forth."[126]

Medieval diners were extraordinarily fond of fried meats. As is well known, food plunged into boiling fat and removed as soon as cooked is comparatively wholesome. But quite likely this procedure was not uniformly followed in the medieval kitchen.[127] At all events the medieval dietitians agree in warning against the use of meat that is fried, though doubtless their admonitions had little effect.

In the *Two Fifteenth Century Cookery Books*[128] there is a list of more than sixty "leche" meats, not all of which were meats in the modern sense. A leche is merely something cut in slices. The dishes run from brawn, gingerbread, and stewed pears, to a variety of meats and fish and fruits, pigs' maws, haggis, fritters. A good number of these compositions are compounded of the most diverse materials and then fried. John Russell, in his *Boke of Nurture*, wisely admonishes the reader to avoid fried meats, "for they are fumose[129] indede" (l. 500). Cooks with their chopping, stamping, and grinding tempt people to excesses and hasten their end. But when one sees what one had to choose from who would avoid the dangerous fried meat one can only sympathize with those who were condemned to live on a medieval diet.

We cannot here make a complete catalogue of all the meats[130] consumed on the medieval table, but one famous dish deserves a word of mention. The boar's head was for some reason especially esteemed, particularly at Christmas, and was brought to the table with stately ceremonial, attended by music. This custom is still maintained on Christmas Day at Queen's College, Oxford.

XIII

Although for an everyday diet beef, mutton, and pork were deemed quite sufficient, for a banquet something more dainty was sought. If we glance through the bills of fare of the feasts of olden time, we find a great variety of poultry, small birds, and game birds, some of which would now be regarded as unfit for food. Small birds, stewed, or roasted on spits, are very common. At the coronation feast of Henry IV, in 1399, cygnets, fat capons, pheasants, and herons were served as a part of the first course. In the second course appear peacocks, cranes, and bitterns, and in the third course aigrettes,[131] curlews, partridges, pigeons, quails, snipe, and "small birds".[132] At the wedding feast of Henry IV at Winchester, among other birds we note plover and woodcocks and fieldfares.[133] At the installation feast of John Stafford, Bishop of Wells, in 1425, swans, fat capons, herons, cranes, peacocks, pheasants, teal, chickens, curlews, pigeons, aigrettes, partridges, plover, quails, snipe, small birds, and even gulls were served.[134] Gulls appear likewise, along with swans, peacocks, ducks, and other birds, at the wedding feast of the Earl of Devonshire,[135] the date of which is not exactly known. Enormous supplies of poultry of all sorts were provided for a feast given to King Richard II in 1387 at the palace of the Bishop of Durham.[136]

Although, as we have seen, most meats were cut into small pieces[137] or even ground in a mortar, the peacock, the crane, the pheasant, and some other birds were commonly roasted whole. The peacock, in particular, was carefully flayed, and when roasted was dressed once more in its plumage as though it were alive. As a table decoration, few ornaments can have been more effective. Detailed directions for preparing a peacock for roasting are found in the old cookery books:[138] "Take a peacock, break his neck, and cut his throat. And flay him, the skin and the feathers together, and the head still to the skin of the neck. And keep the skin and the feathers whole together. Draw him as a hen, and keep the bone to the neck whole, and roast him, and set the bone of the neck above the broach [spit], as he was wont to sit alive, and above the legs to the body, as he was wont to sit alive. And when he is roasted enough, take him off and let him cool. And then wind the skin with the feathers and the tail about the body and serve him forth as he were alive, or else pull him dry, and roast him, and serve him as thou dost a hen."[139]

Pheasants were enormously popular on the tables of the rich in medieval times. At certain seasons of the year the Prince of Condé was said to have served not less than one hundred and twenty pheasants a week. This handsome bird was commonly put upon the table in its feathers like the peacock.[140]

As for poultry in general, the birds that were roasted were first filled with a stuffing and not infrequently breaded. The directions for stuffing a capon or a goose are as follows: "Take parsley and swine's grease, or suet of a sheep, and parboil them together till they be tender. Then take hard yolks of eggs and chop forthwith. Cast thereto powdered pepper, ginger, cinnamon, saffron, and salt, and grapes in time of year, and cloves enough. And for lack of grapes—onions, first well boiled and afterward all chopped, and so stuff him and roast him, and serve him forth. And if it please thee, take a little boiled pork and chop it small among the other; for it will be better, and especially for the capon."[141]

If the capon is to be stewed, the directions are even more extraordinary than for stewing beef: "Take parsley, sage, hyssop, and thyme and break it between thy hands, and stuff the capon therewith. Colour him with saffron, and lay him in an earthen or brass pot, and lay splints underneath and all about the sides [so] that the capon touch nothing of the pot. Strew good herbs in the pot, and put thereto a pottle[142] of the best wine that thou mayest get, and none other liquor. Cover the pot with a close lid, and stop it about with dough or batter, so that no air come out. And set it on the fair charcoal, and let it seethe easily and long till it be enough. And if it be an earthen pot, then set it on the fire when thou takest it down, and let it not touch the ground for [fear of] breaking. And when the heat is overpast, take out the capon with a prick.[143] Then make a syrup of wine, raisins of currants, sugar, and saffron, and boil it a little. Mix powder of ginger with a little of the same wine and add thereto. Then take away the fat of the broth of the capon, and add the syrup to the broth, and pour it on the capon, and serve it forth."[144]

If one prefers stewed partridge, one may try the following: "Take fair marrow, broth of beef or of mutton and, when it is well sodden, take the broth out of the pot and strain it through a strainer, and put it in an earthen pot. Then take a good quantity of wine, as though it were half, and put thereto. Then take the partridge and stuff him with whole pepper and marrow, and then sew the vents of the partridge, and take cloves and mace and whole pepper, and cast it into the pot, and let it boil together. And when the partridge is boiled enough, take the pot off the fire, and when thou shalt serve him forth cast into the pot powdered ginger, salt, saffron, and serve forth."[145]

For another delectable dish, note the following: "Take small birds, and pluck them, and draw them clean, and wash them well, and chop off the legs, and fry them in a pan of fresh grease right well. Then lay them on a fair linen cloth, and let the grease run out. Then take onions, and mince them small, and fry them in fair fresh grease, and cast them in an earthen pot. Then take a good portion of cinnamon and wine, and dry through a strainer, and cast into the pot with the onions. Then cast the birds thereto, and the cloves and mace, and a little quantity of powdered pepper thereto, and let them boil together enough. Then cast thereto white sugar, and powdered ginger, salt, saffron, and serve forth."[146]

Singular illustrations of the occasional whimsical perversity of medieval cookery appear in the following receipts: "Cokyntryce,—Take a capon and scald him, and draw him clean and chop him in two across in the waist: take a pig, and scald him, and draw him in the same manner, and chop him also in the waist. Take a needle and a thread and sew the fore part of the capon to the after part of the pig, and the fore part of the pig to the hinder part of the capon, and then stuff them as thou stuffest a pig. Put him on a spit and roast him. And when he is done, glaze him with yolks of eggs and powdered ginger and saffron, then with the juice of parsley without. And then serve it forth for a royal meat."[147]

"To make two capons of one, take a capon and scald him clean, and keme [scrape] off the skin by the back. Then flay off the skin, but keep it whole. Then grind figs and fresh pork with powder of ginger and cinnamon, and stuff the skin and sew it fast and roast it sokingly [thoroughly] and serve it."[148]

Popular as were most of the birds served on the tables of the rich, the dietitians found them worthy of censure, though if they had been prepared in reasonable fashion the decision might have been different. Says Andrew Boorde: "A crane is harde of dygestyon and doth ingender evyll blode. . . . All maner of wylde fowle the which lyveth by the water, they be of dyscommendable nowrysshement." Likewise, "Gose-flesshe and ducke-flesshe is not praysed, except it be a yonge grene goose. Yonge peechyken of halfe a yere of age be praysed. Olde pecockes be harde of dygestyon." But he adds, "Al maner of smale Byrdes be good and lyght of dygestyon, excepte sparowes, whiche be hard of dygestyon."[149]

XIV

In these modern days of all varieties of religious belief and practice, one cannot easily find entire communities that regulate their diet in accord with the dictates of the Church. But pre-Reformation Englishmen, with negligible exceptions, conformed to the rule prescribing abstinence from meat on Fridays and during Lent. Naturally, the only satisfactory substitute was fish, the consumption of which was enormous.

Pretentious feasts consisting almost wholly of fish were not uncommon in the Middle Ages. A royal banquet in the time of Henry IV consisted of three courses and over thirty dishes, all of which, with the exception of the sweets and the subtleties, were made up of fish.[150] A feast of three courses and over thirty dishes, given by Lord de la Grey, likewise was wholly of fish except for the sweets and the "potage".[151] A similar feast was given at the funeral of the Bishop of Bath and Wells in 1424.[152] A goodly number of menus for all-fish dinners are suggested in the *Ménagier de Paris*,[153] written at the close of the fourteenth century.

For this extraordinary consumption of fish the lakes, swamps, and streams in the neighbourhood of a great house commonly afforded abundance of eels and pike and tench and other freshwater fish, while cod and herring, to say nothing of lobsters and crabs, were brought from the sea. Most great houses, as well as monasteries, maintained a fish-pond ready to supply at a moment's notice whatever might be needed. To ensure the preservation of fish brought from a distance, such as herring, mackerel, and cod, they were salted and kept in readiness for the requirements of the kitchen.

A partial list of the fish—or what passed for fish—eaten in the later Middle Ages includes halibut, cod, codling, haddock, perch, carp, ray, sole, flounders, sturgeon, pike, luce, salmon, whiting, minnows, plaice, rockfish, mullet, trout, turbot. The unscientific age included among fish porpoises, seals, and whales, together with mussels, whelks, shrimps, crayfish, and oysters. Stockfish, which is frequently mentioned, "seems to have been made of all sorts of cod, and even of porpoise".[154] As for frogs, which might compete with the whale and the porpoise for a place among fish, they were rarely, if ever, eaten in England, and even in France the liking for frogs appears not to have been common before the sixteenth century.[155]

In the various cookery books, and particularly in John Russell's *Boke of Nurture* (c. 1450), a great variety of fish are enumerated. But Russell, like others of his time, includes among fish the beaver (the tail of which was "accounted a very delicate dish"),[156] the porpoise, the whale the seal, the crab, the crayfish, the oyster, the shrimp, the whelk. Eels were particularly esteemed for fish pies. Russell's list thus includes some fifty varieties.[157]

The smaller fish were often served whole, as may be seen in more than one of the illustrations of feasts in medieval manuscripts. Larger fish, such as sturgeon and turbot, to say nothing of the seal and the porpoise, were, as a rule, too bulky to be placed upon the table, and hence were cut into pieces. The directions for preparing some of these delicacies are as follows:

To boil whelks: "Take whelks and cast them in cold water, and let them boil but a little. And cast them out of the vessel and pick them out of the shell, and pick away the horn of them, and wash them and rub them well in cold water and salt, in two or three waters. And serve them cold, and cast upon them leaves of parsley wet in vinegar. And sauce to them is vinegar."[158]

Notably simple, too, are the directions for boiling crabs, lobsters, and shrimps. "Take a crab or a lobster, and stop him in the vent with one of their claws, and seethe him in water, and no salt. Or else stop him in the same manner, and cast him in an oven, and bake him, and serve him forth cold. And his sauce is vinegar."[159]

"Take shrimps and seethe them in water and a little salt, and let them boil once or a little more. And serve them forth cold; and no manner sauce but vinegar."[160]

Seal and whale and porpoise do not appeal to the average modern taste, and in the period that we are discussing the flesh of the whale was little esteemed, though the tongue when salted was counted delicious.[161]

"Of all blubber dainties, porpoise", however,

"was deemed the most savoury. The Saxons called it sea-swine, and the ecclesiastics of the Middle Ages *porco-marino*. This coarse animal was esteemed as food until late in the sixteenth century; it was often on the table of Henry VIII; and Wolsey, Somerset, and other Lords of the Star Chamber, having in 1509 a snug little official dinner together, feasted sumptuously off a porpoise which cost 8s. Even Queen Elizabeth, who was rather choice in her appetite, had porpoises among her Friday diet."[162]

Anyone with a liking for porpoise might have it served as a pudding:

"Take the blood of him and the grease of himself, and oatmeal and salt and pepper and ginger, and mix these well together, and then put this in the gut of the porpoise and then let it seethe easily, and not hard, a good while. And then take him up and broil him a little, and then serve forth."[163]

Typically medieval is the receipt for baked lampreys, which is worth quoting in full: "Take and make fair round coffins of fine paste, and take fresh lampreys, and let them bleed four fingers within the tail, and let them bleed in a vessel, and let them die in the same vessel in the same blood. Then take brown bread, and cut it, and steep it in the vinegar, and draw through a strainer. Then take the same blood, and powder of cinnamon, and cast thereto until it be brown. Then cast thereto powdered pepper, salt, and wine a little, that it be not too strong of vinegar. And scald the lampreys, and pare them clean, and lay them round on the coffin, till it be covered. Then cover it fairly with a lid, save a little hole in the middle, and at that hole blow in the coffin with thy mouth a good blast of wind. And suddenly stop the hole, that the wind abide within, to raise up the coffin that it fall not down. And when it is a little hardened in the oven, prick the coffin with a pin stuck on a rod's end for [fear] of breaking of the coffin, and then let it bake and serve forth cold. And when the lamprey is taken out of the coffin and eaten, take the syrup in the coffin and put in a charger, and cast wine thereto and powdered ginger, and let boil on the fire. Then take fair paindemain wet in wine, and lay the sops in the coffin of the lamprey, and lay the syrup above, and eat it so hot, for it is good lords' meat."[164]

XV

We can hardly exaggerate the importance of sauces in medieval cookery, for many dishes appear to owe most of the character that they have to the sauce. In French kitchens sauces have always played a prominent part, and in modern French cuisine some threescore are said to be still in vogue.[165] The old French cooks had "a special sauce for poultry and for ordinary meat, roast or boiled—often two or three, one more complicated than the other";[166] and the French[167] passed on to the English most of their culinary methods.

Our ancestors, as we have found, did not highly esteem simple dishes, and a cook of any reputation aimed as far as possible, by grinding and mixing, to transform one thing into another quite different,

PREPARATION OF FOOD

since as a rule it was beneath his dignity to offer food that had cost but slight effort. The most effective way to remove the stigma of simplicity, apart from smothering a meat or a vegetable in a complex mass of incongruous ingredients, was to employ a sauce made hot with spices and condiments. Such a sauce was regarded in effect as an integral part of the meat or the fish for which it was intended, and the more pronounced the flavour, the more it was esteemed. Chaucer's Frankelyn, whose house was never without bakemeat, evidently maintained a high standard for his table, and

> Wo was his cook, but if his sauce were
> Poynaunt and sharp, and redy al his gere.[168]

What these terms must have meant to Chaucer's readers we may judge by examining a few receipts for sauces in the old standard cookery books. A typical example is that for making "Chaudoun", a sauce for various meats:

"Take gizzards, and livers, and heart of swan; and if the guts be fat, slit them, and cast them thereto, and boil them in fair [clean] water. And then take them up, and hew them small, and then cast them into the same broth (but strain it through a strainer first); and cast thereto powdered pepper, and vinegar, and salt, and let it boil. And then take the blood of the swan, and fresh broth, and bread, and draw them through a strainer, and cast thereto, and let [them] boil together. And then take powder of ginger, when it is almost enough [done], and put thereto, and serve forth."[169]

To make a sauce for a goose, a bird very popular in the olden time: "Take parsley, grapes, cloves of garlic, and salt, and put it in the goose, and let it roast. And when the goose is enough [done], shake out what is within, and put all in a mortar, and add thereto hard yolks of eggs. And grind all together, and temper it up with verjuice, and cast it upon the goose in a fair [clean] charger, and so serve it forth."[170]

More than once we find in the cookery books two or more receipts bearing the same name. But that the "same thing" might be very different we may see by comparing with the following receipt another of a generation or two later:

Sauce Madame

"Take sauce, parsley, hyssop, and savoury, quinces and pears, garlic and grapes, and fill the geese therewith, and sew the geese that no grease come out. And roast them well, and keep the grease that falleth thereof. Take galantine and grease and do [put] it in a posnet [skillet]. When the geese be roasted enough, take and smite them in pieces and that that is within, and put in a posnet, and put therein wine, if it be too thick. Put thereto powder of galingale, powder-douce, and salt, and boil the sauce, and dress the geese in dishes, and lay the sowe [liquor] onoward [upon it]."[171]

But note the directions of the later receipt:

"To make sauce madame, take the tharmes [intestines] of a goose and slit them, and shave them clean. Then take the gossern [?], the wings, the skin, and the soul[172] of the goose, and put them all in a pot with minced onions, minced wardens [pears] and grapes roasted. Then roast her and smite her in pieces and lay her in a charger, and put the farser [stuffing] in a pot. Put thereto wine and season it up with powder and salt and vinegar. If thou wilt, thou mayst take yolks of eggs boiled hard and crumbed small and put thereto. And let it be salt, and pour it on the pieces and serve it."[173]

In the *Two Fifteenth Century Cookery Books*,[174] from which we have so frequently quoted, is a typical list of nineteen sauces, all but two or three of which contain vinegar or spices or both together. Out of all these probably not more than one in six would now be found tolerable. The three simplest are the following:

"Surelle,—Take sorrel, wash it, grind it, put a little salt thereto, and strain it, and serve forth."[175]

"Percely,—Take parsley, and grind it with vinegar, and a little bread and salt, and strain it through a strainer, and serve it forth."

"Gauncile,—Take flour and cow's milk, saffron well ground, garlic, and put into a fair little pot. And seethe it over the fire, and serve forth."

John Russell, in his *Boke of Nurture* (ll. 853 ff.), suggests that much use be made of mustard, since it is best for every dish. Other sauces are served to sovereigns at great feasts, but mustard will satisfy ordinary guests.

XVI

In our study of medieval food we are struck with the enormous supplies of meat and fish and the liberal provision of wine and ale, but the limited variety of vegetables. The principal vegetables grown in medieval England are mentioned in *The Forme of Cury*, where they are included among the ingredients in various dishes. We note that onions are far in the lead, appearing in no less than twenty-nine receipts. Leeks appear five times; pease, three times; cabbage, twice; and a number of other vegetables once each. The few vegetables that were known were "valued more for soups than for their own sake."[176] In the Household Book of Richard de Swinfield, 1289-90, only "onions, leeks, garlic, peas, beans, and potherbs" are mentioned, "and in one instance salted or pickled greens." So, too, in the Roll of the Countess of Leicester, "dried peas and beans, parsley, fennel, onions, green peas, and new beans are the only species named. . . . If any other vegetables were in general use at the time, they were, perhaps comprised under the name *potagium*. . . . Even in the fifteenth century the general produce of the English kitchen garden was contemptible when compared with that of the Low Countries, France, and Italy." Gilbert Kymer[177] can enumerate only, besides a few wild and forgotten sorts, "cabbage, lettuce, spinach, beetroots, trefoil, bugloss [oxtongue], borage, celery, purslane, fennel, smallage [wild celery], thyme, hyssop, parsley, mint, a species of turnip, and small white onions. According to him, all these plants were boiled with meat. He observes also that some were eaten raw, in spring and summer, with olive oil and spices, but questions the propriety of the custom."[178]

In *The Forme of Cury* we find frequent mention of parsley, sage, and garlic, occasional notice of mint, savory, bugloss (oxtongue), hyssop, and several others rarely used. Not infrequently "herbs"[179], without further explanation, are suggested. Obviously, these serve no other purpose than to season a soup or some other dish.

The English used salads to a certain extent, though never in such profusion as the French and the Italians, who were favoured by having oil as a native product. But we may well believe that from very early times water-cresses, onions, leeks, lettuce,[180] mint, sorrel, and other herbs were eaten with a sprinkle of salt and a dash of wine or vinegar or verjuice.[181] The Oxford Dictionary cites from the *Howard Household Book* (p. 398) under the years 1481–90 the entry: "Item, for erbes for a salad." The next mention of salad is in 1553. In *The Forme of Cury*, No. 76, occurs the only receipt for salad that I have found in the ancient English cookery books, but if this may be regarded as typical we can hardly doubt that there were many others far simpler, improvised without the assistance of professional cooks. This one prescribes: "Take parsley, sage, garlic, chibollas,[182] onions, leek, borage, porrectes,[183] and cresses, rue, rosemary, purslain. Lave and wash them clean. Pick them, pluck them small with thy hand and mix them well with raw oil. Lay on vinegar and salt and serve it forth." This, except for the extraordinary mixture of components, is not very unlike an ordinary salad of our time.

In striking contrast with the English, the French devised many ingenious types of salad, one of which even Le Grand d'Aussy found most extraordinary.[184] This was made with parsley and mint, "and the feet, combs, heads, and livers of poultry, seasoned with pepper, vinegar, and cinnamon." Another salad containing lettuce, fennel, chervil, mint, borrage, and other plants was appropriately named "salade de plusieres herbes", and the warning was given that one who ate it needed good teeth. The English cooks were capable of producing some atrocious mixtures, but, possibly for lack of opportunity, they offended less in their salads than in the meat dishes that we have considered.

XVII

The cooks of the Middle Ages were not at all indifferent to the appearance of their food when served. They had that instinctive feeling for colour now most obvious in eastern lands, and they even coloured their food so as to make a more brilliant display. The most popular colouring material was saffron, which for a long time was one of the most lucrative crops grown in the county of Essex.[185] In *A Noble Boke off Cookry*[186] not less than seventy-six receipts within eighty pages prescribe saffron for dyeing food yellow. Similarly, in the *Liber Cure Cocorum*, within fifty-two pages, forty-five receipts suggest the use of saffron. In one cookery book the author piously urges, "For hen in broth, colour it with saffron for God's sake!"[187] But the cook was by no means limited to saffron. The yolks of eggs were employed for "endoring" food, and saunders and blood for colouring it red. Saffron and saunders were used together in making "lesk lombard".[188] To prepare roast hens for the table, one is directed to roast them and then "endore them yellow or green".[189] When making gingerbread, "if you will have it red, colour it with saunders enough".[190] So-called urchins get their name from being made bristly with almonds, "and they are to be coloured some green, some black with blood, and let them not brown too much".[191] For glazing rissoles, the cook is directed to "dore them with some green thing, parsley, or yolks of eggs together, that they be green".[192]

Pomegranates, so called from their shape, are only a sort of meat-ball to be covered with two sorts of batter, one green and the other yellow—the green of parsley.[193] Yellow and green are recommended for colouring a combination of pig and capon with yolks of eggs, powdered ginger, and saffron, "then with the juice of parsley without".[194] A pottage on a fish-day[195] is to be coloured with saunders and saffron in variegated streaks like marble. And in preparing a "capon in Salome" the cook is to "take a little saunders and a little saffron and make it a marble colour".[196] Cherries, after being stoned, washed in wine, mixed with white grease, rice flour, and white honey or sugar made piquant with vinegar, are then to be flavoured with strong powdered cinnamon and galingale and blended "with a great portion of yolks of eggs."

This precious medley is then to be coloured with saffron or saunders, and when served, to be planted with cherries.[197]

Blood is freely used. When killing a swan, for example, one should "keep the blood to colour the chaudron".[198] When cooking "Nombles", "colour it with brown bread or with blood". And when making "Rose", "colour it with saunders and blood". Roe in a "sewe" is to be coloured "with blood or saunders".

The cooks, however, were not satisfied with one or two colours, as we shall at once see. Three colours were obtained by using saunders, saffron, and "a third in another degree".[199] If they wished to make a "sew", that is, a broth, without fire,[200] they were to "let one part be white, another part yellow with saffron, and make a third part green with the juice of mint and parsley". "Ledlards of iij colours" were produced by using saffron for yellow, saunders for red, and herbs for green.[201] "Braun ryalle" (royal brown) was made with saffron, green leaves, and saunders.[202] The following receipt shows how the colour was laid on:[203]

> Endore hit with yolkes of egges, then
> With a fedyr at fyre as I the kenne;
> Bothe grene and rede thow may hit make,
> With juse of herbs I undertake.

One of the most elaborate of the coloured dishes is the following formidable composition, a meat dish, with the meat not specified[204]: "Take flour, almond milk, and saffron, and fry thereof four strips in oil. Take thy almonds, and draw thereof milk right thick. Take mace, cubebs, and flour of rice, cinnamon, galingale. Then take haddock, crayfish, perch, tench, and boil them. When they are sodden, take thy fish from the bones, and bray it right small with thy spicery together, and make thereof thy stuffing. When it is made, divide it into four parts, one part white, the second yellow, the third green, the fourth black colour, with figs, raisins, and dates. Take the first course of the fish of all the four courses, and lay on thy cyvey [stew] above thy fish, in four quarters, as a checker, as broad as thy cake, and cast above sugar of Alexandria, and thereupon thy slice. Take another course, and lay on thy four quarters as broad as thy slice, and thereupon thy sugar. Take the third course of thy fish, and lay on four quarters, and cast above sugar and a slice. Take the four courses accordant to thine other, pinched [?] together, and above, a hole as a rose, and so forth."[205]

XVIII

We have already noted the lavish use of spices in the old cookery. Not less remarkable is the amazing consumption of almonds. They are boiled and stamped and sugared and served cold.[206] They are blanched and ground, mixed with ale and water, strained, boiled, flavoured with saffron, sugar, and salt, and served hot.[207] Almond milk, caudle of almond milk, almond butter, fried cream of almonds, are frequently mentioned as dainties to be served separately.[208]

The native production of nuts in England was practically limited to hazel-nuts, or filberts, and acorns,[209] which latter were highly prized by the keepers of the swine that for a good part of the year roamed the vast medieval forests. Foreign nuts were imported in great quantities, chiefly pines, walnuts, chestnuts, and, above all, almonds. Coconuts, pecans, brazil-nuts are never mentioned. Pines appear to be pine cones containing edible kernels such as are still common in Italy.

Almonds are in a class by themselves. The extent to which they were employed in medieval cookery is almost incredible, especially since they can never have been notably cheap. If we examine, for example, the *Two Fifteenth Century Cookery Books* and tabulate the dishes in which almonds are the chief or an important component, we get a surprising result. The first book, from Harleian MS. 279, is divided into three groups. The first group contains 153 receipts for "potage" of various sorts (pp. 1–34). The second group is taken up with *Leche vyaundes*, or sliced meats, 64 receipts (pp. 34–46). The third group consists of bakemeats of *vyaunde furnez*, 16 receipts (pp. 47–56). Of the 153 receipts in the first group no less than 60 make some use of almonds; of the 64 receipts in the second group, 13 use almonds; and of the 41 in the third group, 10 use almonds. We have then an aggregate of 258 receipts, of which 83, or nearly one-third of the entire number, contain this nut in one form or another.

Besides those dishes in which almonds are a

minor factor, we find a variety of receipts in which almonds are the principal, if not the only, ingredient. Thus we have "Froyde Almaundys", "Fryit creme of Almandys", "Cawdel de Almaunde",[210] "Hagas de Almondes", "Froyte de Almondes", "Cheaut de Almondes."[211]

In the *Noble Boke off Cookry*, edited by Mrs. Napier, we find "creme of almonds", "hoot mylk of almondes", "cold mylk of almondes", "cawdelle of almondes", "bruet de almondes", "gruell dalmond", "joutes dalmond", "pese de almonds".[212]

Almond milk plays so large a part in the old cuisine that we may well present a specimen receipt[213]: "To make Cold Milk of Almonds, put fair [clean] water in a pot with sugar or honey clarified so that it be douce [sweet], then salt it and set it on the fire, and when it is at boiling [point], skim it and let it boil a while. Then take it from the fire and let it cool. Then blanch your almonds and grind them, and temper them with the same water into a good thick milk, and put [add] it to wine that it may have a good flavour thereof, and serve it. Then cut bread and toast it, and baste it, and toast it again, that it be hard, and serve them in one dish and the milk in another dish."

Lastly, we may note the picturesque directions for preparing "Fride Creme of Almaundys"[214]: "Take almonds, and stamp them and draw it [them] up with a fine thick milk tempered with clean water. Throw them on and set them in the fire, and let [them] boil once. Then take them down and cast salt thereon, and let them rest a furlong way[215] or two, and cast a little sugar thereto. And then cast it on a fair linen cloth, fair [clean] washed and dry, and cast it all abroad on the cloth with a fair ladle. And let the cloth be held abroad [stretched out], and let all the water underneath the cloth be had away [taken away], and then gather all the cream in the cloth and let [it] hang on a pin, and let the water drop out two or three hours. Then take it off the pin, and put it in a bowl of tre [i.e. wood] and cast white sugar enough thereto, and a little salt. And if it wax thick, take sweet wine and put thereto that it be not seen. And when it is dressed [for the table] in the manner of mortrews,[216] take red anise in comfit or the leaves of borage, and set them on the dish, and serve forth."

As a dish not notably digestible we may cite "Sardeynez", which consists almost wholly of spices, on a basis of almonds: "Take almonds, and make a good milk of flour of rice, saffron, ginger, cinnamon, mace, cubebs. Grind them small in a mortar, and temper them with the milk. Then take a clean vessel and a moderate amount of sugar and boil them well, and rinse thy dish all about within with sugar or oil, and then serve forth."[217]

It is interesting to note that in some countries the use of almonds in cookery is still very extensive. This is particularly true of the Balearic Islands and of Sweden. The skilled Swedish cooks employ them in a great variety of dishes and also use them freely for decorating puddings and cakes and custards.

XIX

In the chapter on Serving the Feast a section is devoted to the dessert, with mention of some of the delicacies that were offered to the guests. We have here to note how a few of the most characteristic dishes were prepared. But although we may select certain compositions that would seem to belong at the close of a banquet, we cannot certainly decide at what point medieval diners would have preferred them. Uncooked fruit, for example, if eaten at all, would probably find a place comparatively early in the course of a meal, but we cannot be too certain as to just where. But cooked fruits, as far as we can see, are, as a rule, included among delicacies to be eaten after the heavy meat dishes are mostly disposed of.

As compared with many other countries more favoured in climate, England in the later Middle Ages produced, and still produces, a limited amount of fruit. There was, however, an abundance of apples, pears, plums, sloes, cherries, quinces, and wardens, which were much like quinces, but brown and spotted. Grapes could ripen only in favoured localities, and oranges and lemons had, of course, to come from abroad. Strawberries were plentiful, and so were mulberries. But English gooseberries, which in our day are unsurpassed anywhere, do not appear before the sixteenth century. Currants, as we know them, "were introduced into English cultivation sometime before

1578", and raspberries in 1623. Such tropical fruits as bananas and pineapples were, of course, entirely unknown. The apricot is first mentioned in the sixteenth century, the muskmelon in the last quarter of the sixteenth century, and the watermelon in the first quarter of the seventeenth.

The old dietitians, as we shall see later, had a singular prejudice against raw fruit, much of which they regarded as injurious to health unless eaten at carefully chosen times. But the old books prescribe various elaborate receipts for cooking or preserving "chare de warden",[218] "pears in compost",[219] "apple muse",[220] "quynade"[221] (quinces), and quinces or wardens in paste, "apple mayle",[222] "applade ryal", mulberries,[223] strawberries, and cherries,[224] any one of which receipts would apparently have wrought more damage than an indefinite amount of raw fruit.

In the customary medieval cookery, the aim of which seemed to be to obliterate the natural taste of everything that passed through the kitchen, the characteristic flavour of the fruit could rarely survive treatment at the hands of the cook. By way of illustration we may select two receipts, one for quinces or wardens in paste[225] and the other for pears in compost. The first is comparatively simple. Raw quinces are to be pared and the cores cut out. "Then take sugar enough and a little powdered ginger and stop the hole full. And couch [lay] two or three wardens or quinces in a coffin, and cover them, and let them bake, and for defaut [lack] of sugar, take honey; but then put powdered pepper thereon, and ginger, in the manner before said." To make warden pears in compost: "Take wine and canel [cinnamon] and a great deal of white sugar, and set it on the fire and heat it hot, but let it not boil, and draw it through a strainer. Then take fair dates, and pick out the stones, and leche [slice] them all thin, and cast thereto. Then take wardens, and pare them and seethe them, and slice them all thin, and cast thereto into the syrup. Then take a little saunders and cast thereto, and set it on the fire, and if thou hast charde quince, cast thereto into the boiling, and look [that] it stand well [stiff] with sugar, and well allayed with canel, and cast salt thereto, and let it boil. And then cast it in a treen [wooden] vessel, and let it cool, and serve forth."[226]

A comparatively simple but horrible example of what to avoid appears in the directions for making charewarden: "Take warden pears and boil them in wine or clean water. Then take and grind them in a mortar and draw them through a strainer without any liquor, and put them into a pot with sugar and clarified honey and cinnamon enough, and let them boil. Then take them from the fire and let them cool, and cast thereto yolks of raw eggs till it be thick. And cast thereto powdered ginger enough and serve it in the manner of fish. And if it be in lent, leave out the yolks of eggs and let the remnant boil so long till it be thick, as though it had been tempered with the yolks in the manner of charde quince. And so serve them in manner of rice."[227] Could anyone imagine from the taste that this jumble of incongruities was a preparation of a choice fruit?

Although we cannot always determine whether this or that composition would have been served as the concluding delicacy of a formal meal, we may be reasonably certain that "Doucetys", such as are described in the following receipt, would have found favour: "Take cream a good cupful and put it in a strainer. Then take yolks of eggs and put thereto, and a little milk. Then strain it through a strainer into a bowl. Then take sugar enough and put thereto or else honey for lack of sugar. Then colour it with saffron. Then take thy coffins and put in the ovens empty and let them be hardened. Then take a dish fastened on the peel's end,[228] and pour thy mixture into the dish, and from the dish into the coffins. And when they do arise well, take them out, and serve them forth."[229]

As another dish suitable for a dessert we may select "dariolles", for which we have a considerable choice of receipts: "Take wine and fresh broth, cloves, mace, marrow, powder of ginger, and saffron, and let all boil together. And take cream (and if it be clots draw them through a strainer) and yolks of eggs, and mix them together, and pour thereto the liquor that the marrow was boiled in. And then make fair coffins of fine paste, and put the marrow therein, and minced dates and strawberries, if it be in [the] time of [the] year, and set the coffins in the oven, and let [them] bake a little while, and take them out, and put the liquor thereto, and let them bake enough."[230]

A sort of tart, not unlike a simple modern custard, is the "Flathon": "Take milk and yolks of eggs, and draw it through a strainer with white sugar or black sugar; and melt fair butter and put thereto, and salt. And make fair coffins, and set them in the oven till they be hard. Then take a peel[231] with a dish on the end, and fill thy dish with thy mixture, and pour into the coffins, and let [it] bake a little while. Then take them out into a fair [clean] dish, and cast thereto white sugar thereon, and serve forth."[232]

As for "Rapeye", one hesitates to say what is most characteristic in its composition: "Take almonds, and draw a good milk thereof, and take dates and mince them small, and put thereon enough. Take raw apples and pare them, and stamp them, and draw them up with wine or with draff of almonds, or both. Then cast powder of ginger, canel [cinnamon], maces, cloves, and cast thereon sugar enough. Then take a quantity of flour of rice, and throw thereon, and make it chargeant [stiff], and colour it with saffron, and serve forth: and strow cinnamon above."[233]

The following faintly suggests a modern type of receipt: "Take pears, and seethe them, and pick and stamp them, and draw them through a strainer, and mix them with Bastard [wine]. Then cast them into a pot with saffron, and boil with mace, cloves, powdered cinnamon, cubebs, and a little powdered pepper, and roll them up with bread, the crumbs within thy hands, and serve forth."[234]

Various other dishes doubtless regarded as

delicacies are cream boiled,[235] "cryspes",[236] "leche lumbarde",[237] made of dates, spices, eggs, cream, bread and wine, "risshewes",[238] made of fruit, flour, spices, and sugar, to say nothing of the numerous compositions of almonds, sugar, and spices. But we already have before us sufficient to indicate the general character of a medieval dessert.[239]

XX

Although, as we have observed, great occasions like a royal wedding, the installation of a bishop or an archbishop, a coronation, brought vast numbers of people together, and afforded opportunity for an elaborate feast, the overwhelming majority of people throughout Europe during the Middle Ages lived simply enough, and the English were no exception. Even the wealthy classes could not always be consuming rich and indigestible food. The breakfasts in the royal household would not now be regarded as extravagant in a day labourer's family, and they make a striking contrast with the lavish display at the feasts.[240] The mother of the luxurious King Edward IV might be expected to maintain a table much above the average. But we find that on ordinary days the following dishes are prescribed: "For dinner on Sundays, Tuesdays, and Thursdays, boiled beef and mutton and one roast; for supper, 'leyched' [sliced] beef and mutton roast; on fasting days, salt fish and two dishes of fresh fish. Upon fatter days at dinner, salt fish, one fresh fish and butter: at supper, salt fish and eggs."[241]

As typical of the first meal of the day in the house of a great nobleman we may take the data that we find in the *Northumberland Household Book*. For the household of the Earl of Northumberland at least ten breakfasts were served daily, the best naturally for the Earl and Countess, and the others shading down to something very ordinary.[242] The *Household Book* names in detail for 1510–11 the food designed for "ii Meas of Gentilmen o' th' Chapel" and a "Meas of Childeren". The allowance is surely simple enough. It consists of three loaves of bread, a gallon and a half of beer, and three pieces of salt fish, or four white herrings to a mess. In 1511 the allowance of food for the breakfast of the "Gentylmen o' th' Chapel and a Meas of Childer" is three loaves of household bread, a gallon and a half of beer, and a piece of salt fish. In place of the fish there might be three pieces of beef boiled. Singularly enough, in the various allowances for breakfast there is no mention of butter. But in dealing with supper for the gentlemen and children of the chapel on Tuesday in the Rogation Days[243] there is the following entry: "Item, to every Mess a Loaf of Bread, a pottle of Beer, Half a Dish of Butter, and a piece of Salt-fish—viii Dishes."

If this type of food was deemed adequate for a great house like the Percys', we may perhaps imagine the simplicity of the breakfasts and other meals in the average household.[244]

At all events, the members of the royal household

fared no better. In the seventeenth year of Henry VIII we find the following breakfast prescribed for the Queen's maids: "For their bouch in the morning, one cheat loaf, one manchet, and one gallon of ale."[245] And we may well believe that there were innumerable occasions when plain bread, boiled meat, fish boiled or baked, a vegetable or two, along with some slight relish, took the place of the interminable banquets so frequently described in the old romances. This is probable for many reasons. The rarer types of food had to be brought from afar, and, as elsewhere remarked, transportation of any sort was slow and costly. Medieval roads, particularly in England, were frequently almost impassable after heavy rains or during the spring floods, and, as for food products brought from overseas, the merchant vessels were commonly small and unseaworthy, and so dependent upon wind and tide that they were often held up for weeks while awaiting an opportunity to cross the Channel.

The cookery books prepared for the use of wealthy families offer an occasional dish as simple as one could desire. Here is a sort of milk soup that could hardly disturb a confirmed dyspeptic:

"Lyode [steeped] Soppes,—Take milk and boil it, and then take yolks of eggs y-tryid [separated] from the white and draw them through a strainer, and cast them into the milk, and set it on the fire and heat it, but let it not boil. And stir it well till it be somewhat thick. Then cast thereto salt and sugar, and cut fair paindemains in round sops, and cast the sops therein, and serve it forth for a pottage."[246]

And one would with difficulty find anything simpler than the following[247]: "Take an haddock or codling, and draw him in the belly. And make sauce of water and salt. And when it beginneth to boil, skim it clean, and cast the fish thereto, and seethe it in his sauce. His sauce is garlic or verge-sauce [verjuice]. Then serve him forth."[248]

In view of the simplicity of the average meal in the household of the Earl of Northumberland and other great personages, we are not surprised to see that small savings are made at every possible point. In the *Household Book* the most insignificant items are carefully recorded. The expense of each meal is calculated down to the last penny. If anyone is absent from table where he might normally have been expected to be present, accounts must be made to balance accordingly.[249] Keeping the accounts of the Percy estate was something like keeping the accounts of a great manufacturing corporation in our day, where all purchases are duly checked and all waste products as far as possible profitably disposed of.[250]

Very suggestive is the entry: "Yearly. Item. That from henceforth there be no herbs bought, seeing that the cooks may have enough in my Lord's gardens."[251] And also: "Item. It is thought good that my Lord's swans be taken and fed to serve my Lord's house, and to be paid for as they may be bought in the country, seeing that my Lord hath swans enough of his own."[252]

At the end of every year a list was to be made out of all the household stuff bought during the year and not used up, with the names of parcels, every parcel by itself, with the price it was bought for, and the day of the month that it was bought on, with more details as to the recording of the same.[253] A specimen monthly record is that for the expense of all manner of victuals for the household during the month of November in the eighth year of the reign of Henry VIII. This takes account of the bread, wine, beer, ale, beef, mutton, wax, spices, salt, oatmeal, sauces, fuel, horsemeat, and all manner of other things procured for the household. The record, it is interesting to observe, includes "the strangers (all the vacants deducted), and what every person stands in a meal a day, a week, and a month, as hereafter followeth in this book."[254] Obviously, if the household of the great Earl of Northumberland may be regarded as typical of noblemen's establishments at the beginning of the sixteenth century, living on ordinary days in ordinary families must have been somewhat drab and monotonous.

Since the sixteenth century the art of cookery has undergone a complete revolution, and few contrasts are more startling than that between the average table of a well-to-do English family to-day and that of a family of similar station four or five hundred years ago. For the most part the food of that time was lacking in delicacy; and everybody was practically condemned to be a gross feeder. The mutton was likely to be rank and to taste of the fell, and the beef to be tough and stringy. During the colder months most meat was strongly salted and during the warmer months unsalted meat rapidly became "high".

Whatever the conclusion that may be drawn, it is a striking fact that practically every one of the dishes that satisfied the palates of our ancestors should have disappeared from the modern table except in the "unchanging East". But considering the innumerable digestive disorders that were the direct result of the diet of centuries ago, we have no reason to regret that our habits of living are different.

Yet it is notable that the transition to modern taste was exceedingly slow. The Middle Ages did not suddenly come to an end in the year 1500, nor did medieval cookery vanish until long after the discovery of America. This is amply evidenced by Charles Carter's book, published at London in 1730 under the title *The Complete Practical Cook*. The medieval character of the book appears at every turn in the excessive use of spices, in the jumbling together of all sorts of ingredients after the fashion of the fifteenth century. This appears notably in Olio Podrida or Spanish Olio (p. 3), with some fifty kinds of materials—poultry, vegetables, herbs, spices, beef, ham, pork, veal, mutton, and so on. With this may be compared hotchpotch (p. 4) and the stupendous Terrene la Savoy (pp. 5–7), with its vegetables and spices, its mixture of meats, some whole, some beaten in a mortar, bones and all, and so on through two pages of gastronomic absurdity. The various pottages (pp. 9-34) follow the same pattern. Scarcely anything in the book is simple if it can be made complicated; and in true medieval fashion, wherever possible, the mortar is put into play.

Very different is *The Art of Cookery Made Plain and Easy, by a Lady*, published in London in 1748 (148 pages, folio). There is, indeed, a brief chapter devoted to French dishes (pp. 53-54), but on the whole it is commendably free from the atrocious compounds that appear at every turn in the old cookery books, and except for a few dishes that hardly appeal to modern taste it could safely be used to-day.

XXI

After our study of the diet of the fifteenth century it is instructive to read the comments of a representative Englishman a hundred years later upon the food of the sixteenth century. William Harrison was doubtless thoroughly familiar with conditions in his time, and writes as follows: "The gentlemen and merchants keep about one rate, and each of them contenteth himself with four, five, or six dishes, when they have but small resort, or peradventure with one, or two, or three at the most, when they have no strangers to accompany them at their tables. . . . To be short, at such times as the merchants do make their ordinary or voluntary feasts, it is a world to see what great provision is made of all manner of delicate meats, from every quarter of the country, wherein, beside that they

PREPARATION OF FOOD

are often comparable herein to the nobility of the land, they will seldom regard anything that the butcher usually killeth, but reject the same as not worthy to come in place. In such cases also, jellies of all colours, mixed with a variety in the representation of sundry flowers, herbs, trees, forms of beasts, fish, fowls, and fruits, and thereunto marchpane wrought with no small curiosity, tarts of divers hues and sundry denominations, conserves of old fruits, foreign and home bred, suckets,[255] codinacs,[256] marmalades, marchpane, sugar-bread, gingerbread, florentines,[257] wild fowls, venison of all sorts, and sundry out-landish confections, altogether sweetened with sugar (which Pliny calleth *mel ex arundinibus*), a device not common nor greatly used in old time at the table but only for medicine, (although it grew in Arabia, India, and Sicilia) do generally bear the sway, besides infinite devices of our own not possible for me to remember.

"But among all these, the kind of meat which is obtained with most difficulty and costs is commonly taken for the most delicate, and thereupon each guest will soonest desire to feed."

Going on to speak of the excess of wine consumed, Harrison remarks: "Neither do I mean this of small wines only, as claret, white, red, French, etc., which amount to about fifty-six sorts, according to the regions from whence they came, but also of the thirty kinds of Italian, Grecian, Spanish, Canarian, etc., whereof vernage, catepument, raspis, muscadell, romnie, bastard lire, osy, caprie, clary, and malmesey, are not least of all to be accompted of, because of their strength and valour. . . .

"The beer that is used at noblemen's tables in their fixed and standing houses is commonly a year old, or peradventure of two years tunning, or more; but this is not general. . . . Our drink, whose force and continuance is partly touched already, is made of barley, water, and hops, sodden and mingled together, by the industry of our brewers in a certain exact proportion."[258]

CHAPTER IV

MEDIEVAL DRINKS

A CENTURY or two ago the consumption of intoxicants was practically universal, and water served mainly for bathing and cooking. The doctor on his rounds was treated as a matter of course to a friendly glass from the sideboard, and the minister received the same consideration. As we go back two, three, four, five hundred years we find an occasional protest from some dietitian[1] who had noted the results of excess, but of any organized effort to check the evils of drink there is no trace, and although the Church included gluttony and drunkenness among the Seven Deadly Sins, the average man appears to have paid little heed to clerical interference with his food and drink.

Fortunately for the Middle Ages, distilled liquors were as yet practically unknown—brandy,[2] rum, whiskey, gin, and the so-called cordials coming into use after the close of the period we are discussing.

Mead was common in Anglo-Saxon times and was made by fermenting a mixture of honey and water, continuing a practice inherited from the ancients.[3] Metheglin was much like mead, but with the addition of herbs, boiled with the honey and water.[4] Both gradually went out of fashion.[5] Cider was easily produced whenever apples were plentiful, and perry was made from the fermented juice of pears. Before the sixteenth century ale was the practically universal drink of the poorer classes—

though by no means confined to them—being made from malted grain and not from hops.[6] The process was simple, and the ale was commonly brewed by the household, though great breweries were in London as early as the reign of Henry III.[7] Wheat, barley, or oats were ordinarily used, though we are told the French brewed from vetches, lentils, rye, and darnel. "The art of brewing did not arrive at any degree of perfection until the fifteenth century"; even at the table of royalty beer "was often brought in so thick that the guests were obliged to filter it through their teeth".[8] When hops were imported into England from Flanders in the sixteenth century "ale was the name exclusively applied to malt liquor, the term beer being gradually introduced to describe liquor brewed with an infusion of hops".[9] But the more bitter drink was not at first popular, though it gradually won its way to a foremost place.

As Andrew Boorde quaintly remarks: "Ale is made of malte and water; and they the which do put any other thynge to ale than is rehersed, except yest, barme or godesgood[10] do sophysticat theyr ale. Ale for an Englysshe man is a naturall drynke. Ale must have these propertyes: it must be fresshe and cleare, it must not be ropy nor smoky, nor it must have no weft nor tayle. Ale should not be dronke under .v. dayes olde.[11] . . . Beere is made of malte, of hoppes, and water: it is a naturall drynke for a Dutche man. And now of late dayes [1542] it is moche used in England to the detryment of many Englysshe men."[12]

"The following receipt for beer, taken from Arnold's *Chronicle*, published in 1521, reminds us that by this time hops were in use—'ten quartets of malt, two of wheat, two of oats, with eleven pounds of hops for making eleven barrels of single beer.' This is the first I can find with hops as an ingredient. . . . But there is a difficulty here, inasmuch as the use of this plant in brewing was known long before, and Henry VIII, who interfered in everything from religion to beer barrels, forbade his subjects to put hops in their ale."[13]

Since it was possible here and there in England to raise tolerable grapes in favoured localities, so in a few districts in the south a small amount of wine was produced. But the native wine could not rival in amount or quality that imported from abroad, and we may regard it as negligible. Vast quantities were brought from France, from the Rhine, and from the East. The marriage of Henry II with Eleanor of Aquitaine made a large part of southern France an English possession and led to extensive importation of a variety of French wines. Froissart remarks that in 1372 a fleet of some two hundred ships laden with wine arrived in England.[14] Genuine French wines came principally from Guienne, Anjou, Poitou, and other well-known regions, "but a great proportion, though bearing foreign names, were manufactured by the butler".[15] But whether false or genuine the prices appear astonishingly low, even when we make allowance for the greater value of money five or six centuries ago. "In 1342 the price of Gascon wines in England was 4d. and that of Rhenish, 6d. per gallon; and in 1389 foreign wine was only 20s. per tun for the best, and 13s. 4d. for the second, that is, about three halfpence a dozen."[16]

We cannot here enumerate the bewildering varieties of wine in use in England and Western Europe during the fourteenth and fifteenth centuries. Wynkyn de Worde names nineteen,[17] but these are only a small part of those actually in use.[18] Harrison in the sixteenth century counts fifty-six sorts of "small wines", besides thirty kinds of Italian, Grecian, Spanish, Canary, and so forth.[19] More important is it to note the amounts of drink consumed at public banquets. When George Neville was installed as Archbishop of York, in 1464, three hundred tuns of ale and one hundred tuns of wine were drunk by the company. In the household of Archbishop Booth, his predecessor, about eighty tuns were consumed annually.[20]

The expense books detailing the annual outlay by great households for various intoxicants are very suggestive. The *Northumberland Household Book* covers the period from about 1511 to 1525 and the annual allowance of wine was forty-two hogsheads, although economy was rigidly enforced.[21] The Lady Anne of Cleves did not live extravagantly, yet in 1556 she had on hand Gascon wine at 18s. the tun, to the value of £6. In the cellar, three hogsheads of Gascon wine at £3 the tun; of malmsey, ten gallons at twenty pence the gallon; and of muscadel eleven gallons at 2s. 2d. the gallon.[22]

At the feast held at Canterbury in 1504 "when

William Warham was enthroned as archbishop" wine, ale, and beer were provided in vast quantities: "six pipes of red wine, four of claret, one of choice wine, one of white for the kitchen, one butt of Malmsey, one pipe of wine of Osey, two tierces of Rhenish wine, four tuns of London ale, six of Kentish ale, and twenty of English beer."[23] The name malmsey is very common in the older literature. "Malmsey was a strangely generic term for sweet wines from almost every vine-growing district; Candia, Chios, Lesbos, Tenedos, Tyre, Italy, Greece, Spain, all yielding the Malmsey."[24]

The wines consumed in such enormous quantities were by no means always of a sort that would appeal to modern taste. Not infrequently they were crude and sharply acid and required softening to render them palatable. Hence they were commonly mixed with honey and spices and then called piments. Hippocras, compounded of wine, red or white, ginger, cinnamon, "grains" of pomegranate, sugar and "turesole",[25] was thus prepared for people of high station. For common people the wine was flavoured with ginger, cinnamon, long pepper, and clarified honey.[26] Clarry, or claret, differed in no essential particular from hippocras and both were made up with honey and spices.[27] The old claret was not the same as modern claret wine, but was a kind of liqueur. According to medieval tradition, hippocras was invented by Hippocrates. Wines of various kinds were liberally supplied during the progress of the feast, but after the last course, when the cloth was removed, the wine with spices was served.[28] No feast was supposed to be complete without it; and the elaborate ceremonial foolery with which it was presented testifies to its social importance, both in England and on the Continent.

A favourite combination of food and drink was the wine sop, so prized by Chaucer's Franklin. Its virtues are extolled by the famous *Regimen Sanitatis Salerni* in a sixteenth-century version (1528)[29]: "Here are declared .iiij. commodites of wyne soppis. The fyrst is / they purge the tethe / by reason they stycke longer in the tethe / than wyne alone or bread alone: therfore the fylthynes of the tethe is the better consumed / and the tethe the better purged. The .ij. comodite is / that it sharpeth the syghte: for it letteh[30] the yll fumes to ascende to the brayne: which by th[e]yr mynglynge together / darke[31] the syghte. And this is by reason that hit digesteth all ill matters beynge in the stomake. Thyrdly / hit digestethe perfectly meates nat well digested: for it closeth the mouthe of the stomake / and conforteth digestion. Fourthly / hit reducethe superfluous digestion to meane. All this is of trouthe / so that the breade sopped in wyne / be fyrste tosted or dryed on imbers."

4. A FISH DINNER

5. THE GREAT HALL, HAMPTON COURT PALACE

CHAPTER V

THE SCENE OF THE FEAST

FROM the earliest times the hall of the English house was the common meeting-place of the family, since it was the only room where all could assemble.[1] With the passing of centuries and the increase of wealth and security it developed into a stately apartment far larger and more important than any other in the house or castle. A typical early example is the famous Norman hall of Oakham Castle (c. 1180) in Rutlandshire,[2] with pillars supporting the high roof. The semi-monastic life at the universities of Oxford and Cambridge made necessary for each college a common meeting- and dining-room, a brilliant example of which is the hall of Christ Church at Oxford, founded by Wolsey. Cardinal Wolsey was also the builder of the vast palace of Hampton Court, the hall of which, added by Henry VIII, was one of the largest in England.[3] But the noblest hall in the kingdom was Westminster Hall, the great hall of William Rufus, with its vast roof supported by tie-beams of Irish oak, brilliantly reconstructed by King Richard II toward the end of the fourteenth century. This hall witnessed innumerable banquets, and must have been constantly in service in the latter days of the extravagant King Richard, of whom we are told that every day ten thousand men sat down to meat in the king's house.

The various halls[4] throughout the kingdom

naturally differ somewhat in detail, but certain features were regarded as obligatory. "There is no better way of realizing the appearance and arrangement of an ancient hall than by inspecting those of the colleges of Oxford and Cambridge. There can be seen the hall, the screens, and in some cases the buttery too, occupying the same relation to each other and answering the same purpose as they did in large houses of five centuries ago."[5]

At one end of the hall the dais, a platform raised a step or two above the main floor, was the place where were seated the host and the most distinguished guests. At the other end of the hall was the screen, behind which were the buttery and the passage leading into the cellar. The screen "was often panelled into compartments, enriched with carvings or emblazoned with shields and armorial bearings, and affixed to it were branched lights or candelabra of laten or 'tre', which on great occasions were filled with Paris wax. The minstrels' gallery, sometimes called the oriel, was erected above the screen."[6] Under the musicians' gallery were commonly two doorways through which the servants passed in going to and from the kitchen and the buttery. During the Norman period and much later the fire for warming the hall was as a rule near the centre, and the smoke that did not get into the eyes of the guests found its way out through the louvre or open hole in the roof.[7]

Furniture was not abundant. The most distinctive piece was the buffet or cupboard, where the richest plate was exhibited. To serve at the cupboard on the occasion of a great feast was an honour to which nobles of high rank aspired; and the books of courtesy are full of directions for the proper behaviour on such occasions.

It is to be noted that with the increase of wealth and luxury even the great hall of the old English castle was not sufficiently commodious for the ambitious banquets of the sixteenth century. Hence "in new erections" it was "divested of its ancient importance and merely formed the stately approach to a wide and decorated staircase, which led to sumptuous banqueting rooms, and endless galleries on the upper floor; in which were celebrated those magnificent entertainments which far surpassed all the festive wonders of the Gothic age".[8]

Pictures, properly so called, found no place in the old English hall. But with the growth of Eastern trade tapestries rich in colour and design were imported. For the most part these were deemed too precious to be trodden upon and were hung conspicuously upon the walls. In exceptional cases a short strip of carpet was spread under the feet of the most important guest. Naturally, the finest decorations found their place behind the chief table on the dais, and to this point all eyes would be directed.[9]

In the famous representation of a medieval feast taken from a monumental brass in the Church of King's Lynn, Norfolk, the guests sit on only one side of the table, while behind them rises what appears to be the back, in Gothic style, of the long seat, which is occupied by twelve persons. Musicians play their instruments standing at each end of the table, while two attendants bring at each end what may be a peacock, roasted whole. A kneeling attendant in front of one of the guests also presents what seems to be a fowl.[10] In the later fifteenth century arras became the normal decoration of a medieval hall. Twelfth-century tapestry is very simple, with narrow borders, and good examples are not common. Thirteenth-century tapestry also is comparatively rare. But in the course of the fourteenth and fifteenth centuries, and especially the sixteenth, tapestry was in general use and the art of the tapestry maker had developed so as to include the most varied scenes taken from romance or ancient mythology or everyday life. In the early sixteenth century tapestries representing allegorical scenes are seldom lacking. The spaces on the wall not covered by tapestry were commonly adorned with antlers and the heads of wild boars, while from the tie-beams of the roof fluttered banners, emblazoned with the coat of arms of the lord of the castle. High on a perch in the hall were the favourite hawks, and wandering freely from table to table were the hounds, which from time to time caught the scraps thrown to them by the guests.

A word remains to be said about the floor of the hall. This was commonly covered with rushes, which in course of time were naturally worn to shreds. When the covering was worn thin new rushes were laid upon the old, until the accumulations of bones, scraps of meat and other food, expectorations, and the nameless contributions of cats and dogs, along with fleas, beetles, and other vermin, made the filthy mass an offence to the eye and the nose and a serious menace to health. Erasmus, in a famous description too specific for modern delicacy, has left us an unforgettable picture of this abomination.[11]

As already noted in an earlier chapter, a matter of considerable difficulty was the lighting of the hall. Indeed, one of the most striking differences between the olden time and our own is the abundance of light that we enjoy and the lack of it in the time of our ancestors. At best, the illumination of a medieval feast, if held after nightfall, must have been comparatively dim, though doubtless very picturesque. At the high table wax candles found their place, and the soft, clear flame lit up the gold and silver vessels and the scarlet and ermine robes of the guests. In other parts of the hall blazing cressets and smoking torches at least rendered darkness visible. But the ordinary dinner hour in the fifteenth century ranged from ten o'clock to noon, and even a long feast would, as a rule, come to an end before sunset. Feasts that began in the evening were often followed by dancing, with supplementary refreshments, and continued till the early hours of the morning.

Halls such as we have enumerated were the show-places of the kingdom, but it is hardly possible to exaggerate the simplicity of the ordinary hall and its furnishings. The tables were rough, heavy planks hewn by the labourers on the estate and laid when required upon primitive trestles and removed when the meal was over.[12] Chairs were conspicuous by their absence. Throughout the hall the seats were commonly mere benches without backs, as they still are in the halls of the Inner and the Middle Temples and in the college halls at Oxford and Cambridge. In some cases settles with high backs appear to have been used, but only upon the dais. The name banquet itself is due to the fact that the feasters sat upon benches.[13] The walls of the hall when constructed by the local masons were rude and wholly unadorned, with the broad bands of mortar showing white and rough as the workmen had left them. Any covering for the walls must have been an improvement, and the tapestries so enthusiastically described in medieval romances doubtless deserved all the praise they received.

On ordinary occasions the halls of the more important castles were more than equal to the demands placed upon them, and fully justified the reputation of the English for lavish hospitality. But even the largest structures must have proved inadequate when thousands were to be fed, and we may therefore trust the romances as truly representing the practice of medieval times when the feasts were on such a scale that tables had to be placed in the open fields. Tents of linen or costly stuffs were reared, adorned with the armorial bearings of the visiting knights, while above the tables awnings were spread as a protection against sun and rain.

One of the most brilliant descriptions of such a feast is found in the famous prose romance

THE SCENE OF THE FEAST

of *Merlin*. The French original dates from the thirteenth century, and the English version here followed belongs to the middle of the fifteenth century.[14] No details concerning the eatables are given, but many features doubtless accurately represent essential features of actual feasts in the fourteenth and fifteenth centuries.

"Grete[15] was the feeste that the Kynge [Arthur] hilde[16] on the even of the assumpcion to the riche baronye[17] that to hym were come. When the kynge and the barouns hadde herde eve[n]songe at the mynster of seynt Stephene, the tables were sette in teintes and pavelons,[18] ffor thei myght not alle in to the town; and on that othir side was the Quene Gonnore, and the ladyes and damesels with soche[19] joye that merveile it were to reherse, ffor in all the londe of Breteigne, ne in all the power of Kynge Arthur, ne lefte mynstrall ne jogeloure ne oon ne other, but all were come to that feeste; and at that soper were thei served so well as was convenient[20] to so myghty a prince as was the Kynge Arthure, and thus endured thei in joye and myrthe till tyme was to go to reste till on the morowe. And on the morowe a-roos the Kynge Arthure and the riche barouns, and the Quene, and wente to hire masse at the mynster of Seint Stephene, and the servise was honourably seide in the worship and reverence of that high feste, and grete and riche was the offrande;[21] and the Kynge Arthur and alle other Kynges and Quenes that day bar[22] crownes in worship[23] of the day, and so ther wer LX crownes, what of kynges and quenes;

and whan the masse was seide, and the servise ended, the Kynge Arthur lepe[24] on his palfrey, and alle the other Kynges after hym I-crowned, and so dide the quene Gonnore and alle the other quenes, and everyche[25] of hem[26] a crowne of golde on theire heedes[27]; and the Kinge Arthur satte at the high deyse,[28] and made all the xij kynges sitte at his table downward a renge[29]; and also in honour of the high feste of oure lady, he made the Quene Gonnore sitte by hym crowned, and so dide all the other xij quenes by-fore theire lordes; and at other tables satte other princes, Dukes, and Erles, and othir knyghtes were sette richely thourgh the medowes in tentes and Pavelouns with grete ioy and melodye that never was seyn gretter in no Court."

CHAPTER VI

SERVING THE FEAST

I

WE may fitly preface the account of the serving of the feast with a brief outline of what was deemed necessary upon festal occasions as far back as the thirteenth century.[1] This anticipates in many features the essentials of the feasts of the fourteenth and fifteenth centuries.

"Meat and drink are ordained and convenient[2] to dinners and feasts, for at first meat is prepared and arrayed[3]; guests are called together; forms and stools are set in the hall, and tables, cloths, and towels are ordained, disposed, and made ready. Guests are set with the lord in the chief place of the board, and they sit not down at the board before the guests wash their hands. Children are set in their place, and servants at a table by themselves. First, knives, spoons, and salts are set on the board, and then bread and drink, and many divers messes. Household servants busily help each other to everything diligently, and talk merrily together. The guests are gladdened with lutes and harps. Now wine and now messes of meat are brought forth and departed.[4] At the last cometh fruit and spices, and where[5] they have eaten, board, cloth and relief[6] are borne away, and guests wash and wipe their hands again. When all this is done, at the threshold[7] men take their leave, and some go to bed and sleep, and some go home to their own lodgings."

After this account of what constitutes a normal supper offered to guests in a well-to-do household the author, in medieval fashion, points out parallels with the feast of Ahasuerus described in the first chapter of the book of Esther. We need concern ourselves only with the supper. He advises, in the first place, that it is convenient that a supper be served "in due time, not too early nor too late. Many things are necessary and worship the supper.[8] The second is convenable[9] place, large, pleasant, and secure.[10] The third is the heart and glad cheer of him that maketh the feast. The fourth is many divers messes, so that who will not of one may taste of another. The fifth are divers wines and drinks. The sixth is courtesy and honesty of servants. The seventh is natural[11] friendship and company of them that sit at the supper. The eighth is mirth of song and instruments of music. Noblemen use not[12] to make suppers without harp or symphony. The ninth is plenty of light of candles and of prickets[13] and of torches. For it is shame to sup in darkness, and perilous also, for flies and other filth. Therefore candles and prickets are set on candlesticks and chandeliers; lanterns and lamps are necessary to burn. The tenth is the deliciousness of all that is set on the board. For it is not used at supper to serve men with great meat and common, as it is used at dinner, but with special light meat and delicious, and namely[14] in lords' courts. The eleventh is long during[15] of the supper. For men use, after full end of work and of travail, to sit long at the supper. For meat eaten too hastily grieveth against[16] night. Therefore at the supper men should eat by leisure and not too hastily. The twelfth is sureness. For without harm and damage every man should be prayed[17] to the dinner. After supper that is freely given it is not honest to compel a man to pay his scot. The thirteenth is softness and liking of rest and of sleep. After supper men shall rest, for then sleep is sweet and liking.[18] For, as Constantine saith, when smoke of meat cometh into the brain, men sleep easily."

II

We have already briefly described the medieval hall in some of its aspects, but a few additional comments are necessary. When used for a feast the hall was quite transformed according to the taste of the time, which was certainly picturesque and strangely fantastic. The Middle Ages were in many respects far more primitive than our own time, but they by no means affected simplicity in dress or in the appointments of the household, and they did not shun the expense of costly mantles of velvet and silk, of rare foods and wines, and the conventional adornments of a great feast.[19]

The popular romances quite outdo themselves in describing royal palaces hung with gorgeous Eastern tapestries, princesses in silken robes wrought with gold and silver thread and studded with jewels, and knights scarcely less brilliant in heavy gold chains and robes of red samite lined with fur and bordered with ermine. Garments of this sort lent splendour to every great feast; and the most extravagant description in the romances hardly surpasses the accounts of actual feasts recorded by the English chroniclers.

The Crusades had made Western Europe familiar with many features of Oriental life and had stirred the West to emulation of the East.[20] As wealth increased, the houses of an earlier time, with their cramped quarters and simple domestic arrangements, were gradually replaced by more pretentious edifices. The early Norman keep and the primitive living-apartments had long been superseded by the concentric Edwardian castle, where at least the great hall afforded ample opportunity for all the magnificence that one could afford to exhibit. All up and down England lordly castles, many of which are now in ruins, bear witness to the luxurious standard of living of the nobility of four or five centuries ago. With the dawn of the sixteenth century, which was far more medieval than we are at first inclined to think, houses on a still grander scale began to be reared all over England. Hampton Court, with its long galleries and its lofty hall, was an early anticipation of the vast mansions of the English nobility of which William Harrison speaks with pride in his famous account of Elizabethan England.

At this moment we are concerned only with the hall as the usual place for serving the feast. Obviously, the tables in the hall were not of equal importance. Notable guests always sat upon the dais and were thus raised somewhat above the level of ordinary diners. The tables, at least the more important, were covered with a cloth laid with ridiculous solemnity and ceremony[21] and decorated in the taste of the time. On the dresser stood gold and silver plates and vases and tankards, while similar vessels adorned the table. Besides the vessels of gold and silver there were also cups and vases of glass or rock crystal. Not uncommonly there were miniature fountains spouting wine. Flowers were employed in great profusion, spread upon the tables and strewn about the room. In France, at all events, the flowers sometimes took the place of the cloth.[22] For a time there was even a fashion of wearing flowers on the head at a feast.[23]

But the gold and silver vessels were not wholly for ostentation, and not even a proof of extravagance, but rather of economy. In the Middle Ages the lack of opportunity for safe investment encouraged the lavish use of gold and silver for the table and for various household purposes. It was, indeed, the simplest form of banking, for in any emergency the vessels could be thrown into the melting-pots and the metal used for exchange. We are told, in fact, that "the ransom of Richard of the Lion Heart was not made up with coin, but by contributions of baronial goblets and salvers".[24] As years went on the display at feasts became more and more impressive. Harrison gives a striking picture of the array of precious metal upon the tables of the rich in the sixteenth century. "The chief part... of their provision is brought in before them (commonly in silver vessels, if they be of the degree of barons, bishops, and upwards) and placed on their tables.... As for drink, it is usually filled in pots, goblets, jugs, [and] bowls of silver in noblemen's houses; also in fine Venice glasses of all forms: and, for want of these elsewhere, in pots of earth of sundry colours and moulds, whereof many are garnished with silver, or at the leastwise with pewter."[25] How magnificent some of the vessels were upon medieval tables may be realized from the exquisite gold cup of the Kings of France and England in the British Museum, "the sole surviving example of a kind itself unique".[26]

We cannot here detail all the adornments of the table, but a few are in a sense obligatory and recur so frequently that they deserve at least a word or two. If the feast were at all pretentious one of the most conspicuous ornaments was likely to be the *nef*, a vessel in the form of a medieval ship with a high prow and stern. In some households this held the saltcellar,[27] small towels for wiping the hands and mouth, and sometimes knives and spoons. Of individual dishes there was a surprising lack. There was, indeed, a drinking-cup shared by the guest with his table companion; but, except perhaps for a knife or a spoon, the only strictly individual feature of the equipment of the table was the trencher. This was made of wood or of coarse bread cut in small slices and placed before each guest to serve as a sort of plate. With moderate care this gave some protection to the table-cloth, though, since the trencher had no rim, a juicy sop or a piece of meat swimming in sauce laid upon it must often have been a source of embarrassment to the guest. The trencher, when well saturated with sauce, was sometimes eaten by the guest. Otherwise, all trenchers left upon the tables were swept into a basket and given to the poor.

Far more spectacular than the gold and silver vessels were the stuffed peacocks and the allegorical devices arrayed upon the board. A peacock selected as a decoration for the feast was carefully flayed, roasted, once more dressed in his gorgeous plumage,[28] and then toward the end of the feast brought ceremoniously with music to the table to be placed before the most valiant knight. If we may believe the old accounts, when the fantastic ceremony of taking the vow of the peacock was performed the bird was brought to the table late in the progress of the feast by a lady distinguished by birth, rank, or beauty and followed by a train of ladies marching to music played before the master of the feast. When the banquet followed a tourney the knight who had won had the honour of carving the fowl, and he endeavoured to give every guest a piece. If the knight took the peacock vow he placed his hand on the bird and swore he would be the first to plant his standard upon the walls of a besieged city, the first to strike a blow against the enemy; that he would defend the honour of his lady, and so on. Other knights in their turn made wild promises.[29]

Whatever the truth of the legendary vow of the

peacock, the performance is quite in harmony with the general temper of the Age of Chivalry. At all events, the Middle Ages, though strikingly sober and conventional in many particulars, appear almost childish in their fondness for bright colours, for processions, for disguises, for allegorical figures. Allegory was the most characteristic form of expression in the fourteenth, fifteenth, and sixteenth centuries, and a great feast afforded ample opportunity for displaying the most fantastic devices, each with its special meaning. As we have elsewhere noted, food of all sorts was coloured, but it was also shaped to represent flowers, fruits, birds, fish, and animals. Sugar was easily moulded into the forms desired and later could be used again in the cuisine. Philippe de Commines tells us that "when Queen Charlotte of Savoy, wife of Louis XI, made her entry into Paris in 1467 the citizens presented to her a beautiful stag, made of sweetmeats, which had the arms of that noble queen hung on its neck".[30]

III

As the descriptions just presented clearly indicate, the Middle Ages, though singularly indifferent to many matters now deemed essential, laid much stress upon conventional usages. A formal feast had therefore to be served with elaborate ceremony in accordance with what we may call an established ritual; and this involved a great retinue of attendants. At a time when the wages of menials were trifling, mighty lords took pride in surrounding

6. THE GOLD CUP OF THE KINGS OF FRANCE AND ENGLAND

STEWARD. SERVANTS BRINGING DISHES.
15th Century. In M. du Sommerard's Mediæval Art. Wright, p. 151.

SERVANTS BRINGING IN DISHES, PRECEDED BY MUSIC. Early 14th Century.
MS. Reg. 2, B. vii. Brit. Mus. Wright, p. 152.

KING HEROD AND HIS DAUGHTER HERODIAS. Early 14th Century. MS. Reg. 2, B. vii.
Wright, p. 167.

7. CEREMONIAL BRINGING OF DISHES TO THE TABLE IN A PROCESSION BY SERVANTS HEADED BY THE STEWARD BEARING HIS OFFICIAL STAFF

SERVANTS BRINGING IN DISHES, PRECEDED BY MUSIC

SERVANT OFFERING A ROYAL CUP

SERVING THE FEAST

themselves with troops of servants dressed in the resplendent livery of the house. In order that each servant might nominally have something to do, the labours of the household were divided and subdivided to such a degree that without special instruction a stranger was at a loss to know to whom to apply. A partial excuse for the multiplicity of servants was the fact that on great estates, like that, for example, of the Earl of Northumberland, nearly all the essentials of living had to be produced at home. His household was managed with close economy, but it numbered 166 persons,[31] sixteen of whom had to attend at table daily. According to modern standards, the hours of service were inhuman. I note one or two entries relating to the kitchen. The Clerk Comptroller is to call every day at 4 a.m. upon the Clerks of the Counting House. The second Clerk of the Kitchen with his book is to make up the rating of meals daily. The Clerk of the Spicery is daily to go about with the Emption book in hand. Every morning the Clerk Comptroller has to call up the cooks after four o'clock has struck. He has to look after the keys of the larder, to call the cooks to him and "to strike owt the Measses [messes] which shal be apointed to be spende for that day". Among other things, he has to see that meals are served at the appointed hours, and that the bread is of full weight, to have an eye to the slaughter-house, and to ensure that the suet is honestly brought into the storehouse.[32]

Vastly more extravagant than the somewhat old-fashioned household of the Earl of Northumberland was that of the great Cardinal Wolsey, which, with refinements unknown in the castle of the powerful Earl, continued the traditions of the fifteenth century.[33] In the words of George Cavendish, long in Wolsey's service: "First, ye shall understand that he had in his hall, daily, three special tables furnished with three principal officers; that is to say, a steward, which was always a dean or a priest; a treasurer, a knight, and a controller, an esquire, which have always within his house their white staves. Then had he a cofferer, three marshals, two yeoman ushers, two grooms, and an almoner. He had in the hall-kitchen two clerks of his kitchen, a clerk comptroller, a surveyor of the dresser, a clerk of his spicery. Also there in his hall-kitchen he had two master cooks, and twelve other labourers, and children as they called them; a yeoman of his scullery, and two other in his silver scullery; three pages; of purveyors, two and two yeoman of his pastry, and two grooms.

"Now in his privy kitchen he had a Master Cook who went daily in damask, satin, or velvet, with a chain of gold about his neck; and two grooms, with six labourers and children to serve in that place; in the Larder there, a yeoman and a groom; in the Scaldinghouse a yeoman and two grooms; in the Scullery there, two persons; in the Buttery, two yeomen and two grooms, with two other pages; in the Pantry, two yeomen, two grooms, and two other pages; and in the Ewery likewise; in the Cellar, three yeomen, two grooms, and two pages;

beside a gentleman for the month; in the Chaundery, three persons; in the Wafery, two; in the Wardrobe of beds, the master of the wardrobe and two other persons; in the Laundry a yeoman, a groom and three pages; of purveyors, two, and one groom; in the Bakehouse, a yeoman and two grooms.³⁴ . . . Then had he of Gentlemen, as cupbearers, carvers, sewers, and Gentlemen daily waiters, forty persons; of yeoman ushers he had six; of grooms in his chamber he had eight; of yeomen of his chamber he had forty-six daily to attend upon his person; he had also a priest there which was his Almoner, to attend upon his table at dinner."³⁵

As compared with the troops of servants in Wolsey's household, the number of officials in the establishment of Edward III seems almost beggarly.³⁶

The special duties of the hosts of servants deemed essential to one's dignity in the Middle Ages need not be enumerated in detail. But some of the more important officials require a few words of comment.

The Marshal, who carries a wand of office, is responsible for the preparation of the hall. He sees that the hangings and other decorations are properly attended to and that the tables are firm upon their trestles. He has also general supervision of the feast; attends to the lodging of the guests, and, as we shall presently note, he seats the guests in the hall. Under the supervision of the Marshal are the Butler, the Panter, and the cooks, whose duties are elaborately described in the *Boke of Curtasye*, and need not be detailed here.³⁷

We must, however, devote a few words to one

man without whom the feast could not proceed at all—the Carver. In view of the enormous quantities of meat consumed at the average banquet and the inability of the guest to supply himself from the joint, the Carver is obviously an indispensable official. His duties are set forth in detail in Wynkyn de Worde's *Book of Carving*, first published in 1508 and again in 1513, a book which merely summarizes the practice of the greater part of the later medieval period.[38] The Carver was in the first place expected to know the terms of his profession and to use the technical phrases known only to the expert. Hence, instead of using the vague terms employed by the uninitiated he should say "splat a pike", "spoil a hen", "unbrace a mallard", "fin a chub", "untache a curlew", "barb a lobster", "border a pasty", "thigh small birds".[39] The Carver, we are told, "must know the carving and the fair handling of a knife", and he should put only two fingers and a thumb on his knife. Moreover, upon "fish, flesh, beast, or fowl" he should never set more than two fingers and a thumb to keep them in position, and in particular he should not smear the table-cloth with his knife but wipe it upon his napkin.[40] Two directions for carving may serve as specimens:

Dysplaye that Crane

Take a crane, and unfolde his legges, and cut of his wynges by the joyntes: then take up his wynges and his legges, and sauce hym with poudres of gynger, mustard, vynegre, and salte.

Dysmembre that Heron

Take an heron, and reyse his legges and his wynges as a crane, and sauce hym with vynegre, mustarde, poudre of gynger, and salte.[41]

Carving was by no means regarded as a menial service, and even great lords counted it an honour to carve at a royal feast. Joinville, for example, makes special mention of the occasion of his carving before King Louis IX.[42] Chaucer's Squire, we see therefore, really occupied a post of distinction when he "carf byforn his fader at the table". To be a skilled carver required not only dexterity but considerable strength, since sheep and oxen were boiled entire[43] and often roasted whole. And to win approval the carver must perform his duties in accordance with recognized conventions, infraction of which brought unkind comment.

Since meat in various forms was the principal food and forks as we know them were not in use,[44] the carver or his assistants came into direct contact with the guests. Singularly enough, the ordinary fork was a late addition to the furniture of the table, and, as is well known, it did not come into use in England until the beginning of the seventeenth century, after the eccentric traveller Thomas Coryat had brought one up from Italy, where forks were already common. The lack of forks compelled the use of the fingers, and since without a fork extensive use of a knife is difficult, most dishes were more or less liquid, to be eaten with a spoon, or soft messes to be scooped up with the fingers. Serviceable in such cases was the sop, a morsel of bread about the size of two fingers, which was dipped in the sauce, and as Chaucer tells us of his Prioress, perhaps so skilfully conveyed to the mouth that no drop fell upon the table or elsewhere.[45] When the carver wished to offer a slice of meat he held it out on the point of his knife and the guest received it with his fingers. Not unnaturally, in the absence of forks, the knife was often employed where we now use a fork, as is still not uncommon in some circles to-day.[46]

Serviettes or small towels appear to have been used for wiping the hands before and after meals at least as early as the last quarter of the fifteenth century. They are mentioned in the *Liber Niger*, (1483) along with basins, ewers, and cups,[47] and also in Wynkyn de Worde's *Boke of Kervynge* (1513): "Laye your Knyves & set your brede, one lofe by an other / your spones, and your napkyns fayre folden besyde your brede." How extensively napkins were used as they are to-day is difficult to decide. Le Grand d'Aussy (1783) appears to think that both mouth and hands were wiped with the tablecloth. And he quietly adds: "Comme font aujourd'hui les Anglois, qui n'usent point de serviettes."[48]

IV

We are now prepared to begin the feast, but before that can be served we note the elaborate preliminaries prescribed by custom. The food is almost lost sight of amidst the stately ceremony with which it is presented at the table. "When the guests had entered the hall, and not before, the sewer (whose office combined the functions of taster and head waiter) ascertained whether the cooks were ready, and, if so, the carvers, having first washed at the 'ewrie', (a sideboard specially furnished with jugs and basins for this purpose) were accoutered with long towels passed over the right shoulder and the left arm; and each having been furnished besides with a couple of napkins, was ready for his several duties.

"Then after much elaborate ceremony and many bows the pantler [panter] first came forward and tasted the bread and the salt. Next, water previously 'assayed' or tasted, to avoid suspicion of poison, was brought by the cupbearer for the lord of the feast to wash in, the towel on which he was to dry his hands being kissed as a similar precaution. Thereupon the rest of the company also washed, either at the ewrie, or at a lavatory at the lower end of the hall, before taking their places."[49]

This washing of hands before and after meat was by no means a perfunctory matter, for since owing to the lack of forks the guest had to dip his fingers into the common dish, his greasy and sticky hands at the end of the meal must have been intolerable. Furthermore, a knight and a lady often had to share a dish with each other, and in such cases a modicum of cleanliness was desirable. Sometimes the guests were formally conducted to an adjoining lavatory accompanied by the music of a minstrel, but ordinarily they remained in the hall and received from the ewer the warm water, often perfumed with rose leaves, thyme, lavender, sage, camomile, marjoram, or orange peel, one or all. The water and the towels were, of course, presented in the order of the social standing of the guests, and it was esteemed a signal honour thus to serve a king or a great noble. In accord with the dignity of the ceremony the water-jug and the basin in great houses were often of gold or silver curiously wrought and enamelled.[50]

After the guests had washed their hands they had to be conducted to their seats at the table, the places being assigned according to their rank. Throughout the Middle Ages people of any standing strenuously insisted upon due consideration of their social position. Chaucer notes how the Wife of Bath would allow no one to precede her when making the offering in church. In order, therefore, to ensure the proper seating of the guests at the feast, manuals indicating the order of precedence were written for the use of the marshal of the hall. In the volume called *Queene Elizabethes Achademy*[51] is a *Booke of Precedence* (pp. 13–28) giving minute directions as to the order in which guests may go in a procession or sit at table, of which the following are fair specimens:

"A Barron must go after his Creation, so that the Eldest barron goe uppermost; and the barronesse his wife must goe according to the same; and they may have there gownes borne upp with a man in the presence of a viscountesse. And a barron may have the Cover of his cupp holden underneath when he drinketh" (p. 18). "A Baronesse may have no trayne borne; but haveing a gowne with a trayne, she ought to beare it herself" (p. 26).

With the guests in their seats all is in readiness for serving except that the food and drink must be tasted for persons of royal blood and of the higher nobility.[52] The Middle Ages had a wholesome dread of poison, a favourite means, particularly in Italy, of putting an enemy or a rival out of the way. Hence arose the institution of the taster, whose duty it was to partake of the food and drink before it was served to persons of high rank. In France the food remained covered until the guests had taken their places, so that the table was loaded with dishes without anyone knowing what was therein.[53] The credulity of the age imagined that an infallible preservative against poison of every sort was to touch the food with a "serpent's tongue" —really a shark's tooth; with the horn of a "unicorn"—actually the horn of a narwhal; with toadstone, serpentine, agate, and so on.[54]

After all the tedious preliminaries, the actual serving begins. The trumpet sounds, and the steward, bearing his wand of office, enters the hall followed by the servants carrying covered dishes, which are duly presented to the guests in the order of their importance. But notwithstanding the pretentious character of the medieval feast the courses are as a rule ill defined and ill arranged. An Order of Courses is given in the *Modus Cenandi*,[55] but there is no discernible system, except that fried dishes are put into the last course, followed by wafers, spices, fruits, and light cakes.

In many cases fish were served in the same course with meat. At the coronation feast of Henry IV at Westminster, in 1399, pikes and sturgeons were included in the first course, along with a boar's head, swans, capons, pheasants, and herons.[56] At his wedding feast no fish except sturgeon is served, and it appears at the end of the third course. As for poultry and game birds, they are in all three courses.[57]

At one of the dinners served at the enthronization of Archbishop Neville, in the sixth year of the reign of Edward IV,[58] pike in harblet is served in the first course, along with poultry and roast haunches of venison; in the second course, bream in harblet, along with poultry and baked venison; in the third course, tench in jelly, and baked venison, with rabbits and various birds, notably a "peacock with gylt neb".

It is interesting to find that in the *Ménagier de Paris*, dating from the end of the fourteenth century, the courses outlined in the menus suggested for dinners and suppers include fish along with meat. A model menu puts eels and other fish into the second course[59] and carp into the third, evidently following no rule except convenience. Another dinner[60] includes eel broth as part of the second course, fresh- and salt-water fish as part of the third, and baked fish as part of the fifth. In a so-called *meat* dinner, beef was served along with

SERVING THE FEAST

eels, loaches, and sea-fish, for the first course, while fresh-water fish formed a part of the second course, and lampreys, sturgeon, and jelly a part of the third.[61] Elsewhere we have noted that fish were a constant feature of medieval diet. In the lenten season entire banquets consisting of fish were served in great houses,[62] and in feasts of that type the order was a matter of small importance.

England, in general, followed the lead of France, but even in France for a long time little attention was given to the orderly succession of dishes. Olivier de la Marche, however, states[63] that in general the soup was served at the beginning, then the eggs, the fish, and the meats. Following these came the entremets, swan, peacock, or pheasants, each dressed in their plumage, and the *pattes gilded*. The dessert followed the entremets. Then the cloth was again taken up, or the guests passed into another room, and the wines and spices were served, much as one to-day serves coffee. There was claret or hippocras, there were sugar plums, sugar made up with roses, comfitures of fruit, sage, ginger, cardamon, fennel, anise, coriander, cinnamon, powdered saffron, and so on.[64]

In England also, in the course of the two or three centuries after the period we are studying, banquets came to be served according to a generally accepted formula, beginning with soup and proceeding by regular stages through fish, meats, poultry, salad, and dessert to the end.[65]

V

Table Manners

We have followed the progress of the feast through the substantial portions of the repast. Before taking up the dessert we shall do well to consider what behaviour was expected of the feasters, for in theory, at all events, the feast was not merely an occasion for vulgar feeding but a school of manners.

Very little was left to chance. In the *Boke of Curtasye*[66] the guest is instructed as to how he is to eat. First, he is to pare his loaf and cut it in two, from the bottom to the top. Then he is to divide the top crust into four parts and the bottom crust into three. After this he is to put his trencher in front of him and to wait until his mess[67] is brought from the kitchen; otherwise he will be thought to be starving or a glutton. He must have his nails clean or else he will disgust his table companion who has to dip into the dish where the dirty nails have been. He should not bite his bread and then lay it down, but rather break off as much as he requires and leave the rest for the poor.

At the table he should avoid quarrelling and making grimaces. Moreover, he should not stuff his mouth with morsels of bread; otherwise, when he has his cheeks full, men will say he has a mouth like an ape. He must not eat on both sides of his mouth, and especially he should refrain from talking or laughing when his mouth is full. He is not to make a noise in supping his pottage, not to let his spoon stand in his dish or to lay it at the side, but he should clean it properly, whether by licking it or by rubbing it on the cloth we are not informed. In any case, he should not leave finger-marks on the table-cloth. If he has once wet his bread he is not to put it again into the dish. Then follows a variety of useful admonitions. A guest should not call back a dish that has been removed from the board. He should not spit upon or over the table. He should not scratch or claw his dog, and if he has to blow his nose he should remember to clean his hand, wiping it unobtrusively with his skirt or passing it through his tippet. He should not pick his teeth at the table with a knife, straw, or stick, or drink with his mouth full of food; otherwise he may get choked and lose his life by having his wind stopped. He must not tell unseemly tales at the table, not soil the cloth with his knife, not blow on his meat or drink, not put his knife in his mouth,[68] not wipe his teeth or his eyes with the table-cloth. If he hands his cup to anyone he should turn towards the one who receives it. He should not lean on his elbow, not dip his thumb into his drink or touch the salt in the common salt-cellar with his fish or his meat. Lastly, when washing after the meal he should not spit in the basin he washes in, and in the presence of a man of God he should take especial heed where he spits!

That the *Boke of Curtasye* substantially represented the general standard of polite behaviour at table during the first half of the fifteenth century is obvious from a comparison with various other brief manuals of deportment belonging to the same century.[69] What is more surprising is that Hugh Rhodes's *Boke of Nurture*, or *Schoole of Good Maners*, published in 1577, not only repeats several of the most obvious admonitions of the *Boke of Curtasye*, but suggests others that indicate a general crudeness of manners in the mid-Elizabethan period. A few of the more elementary cautions offered to diners will afford abundant illustration: If any man eat of your dish, crumble you therein no bread, lest that your hands be found sweaty: thereof take ye good heed.[70] Burnish no bones with thy teeth, for that is unseemly. Rend not thy meat asunder, for that swerves from courtesy.[71] Belch thou near to no man's face with a corrupt fumosity.[72] Defile not thy lips with eating much, as a pig eating draff.[73] Scratch not thy head with thy fingers when thou art at meat.[74] If that your teeth be putrefied, methinks it is no right to touch the meat another should eat: it is no cleanly sight.[75] Blow not your nose on the napkin where you should wipe your hand; but cleanse it in your handkerchief.[76] Fill not thy mouth too full, lest thou perhaps of force must speak; nor blow out thy crumbs when thou doest eat.[77] If thou must spit, or blow thy nose, keep thou it out of sight; let it not lie upon the ground, but tread thou it out right.[78] Blow not thy pottage nor drink, for it is not commendable; for if thou be not whole of thy body, thy breath is corruptible.[79] Scratch not thy head, nor put thou not thy finger in thy mouth:[80] blow not thy nose, nor look thereon; to most men it is loath.[81]

However useful such advice may have been, and we may assume that the author knew the weaknesses of those for whom he wrote, it indicates at least that, although formal manners may have been elaborate, the standards of propriety and of cleanliness were not particularly high in the last quarter of the brilliant sixteenth century.[82] And as for the beginning of the sixteenth century, behaviour certainly left something to be desired, if we may trust the picture that Alexander Barclay paints in one of his Eclogues of the haste of the servers at feasts to remove a savory dish and of the guests to secure their share before it was too late:

> Slowe be the servers in serving in alway,
>   But swift be they after, taking thy meate away;
> A speciall custome is used them amonge,
>   No good dish to suffer on borde to be longe:
> If the dish be pleasaunt, eyther fleshe or fishe,
>   Ten handes at once swarme in the dishe:
> And if it be fleshe, ten knives shall thou see
>   Mangling the flesh, and in the platter flee:
> To put there thy hands is perill without fayle,
>   Without a gauntlet or els a glove of mayle.[83]

VI

We have just noted the lack of fixed order in serving the multifarious dishes of the medieval banquet. We have, furthermore, to note that the place assigned to the dessert, in so far as it existed, appears to have been a matter of indifference. A few illustrations will make this clear. "Doucettys" are mentioned in the list given for the third course of Henry IV's coronation feast,[84] though not at the end. And "quincys in comfyte" are listed near the beginning of the third course. Possibly this means that sweets might be served at any time when wanted. Quite likely the appetite for sweets was as keen in the fifteenth century as it is to-day, but, except when influenced by considerations of health, medieval diners appear to have been relatively unconcerned as to the order in which they were fed.

At the wedding feast of Henry IV at Winchester each of the three courses ends with a "sotelte", and the only other items that suggest dessert are mentioned at the beginning of the third course—cream of almonds and pears in syrup.

It would seem that diners gradually came to prefer to end a feast with the taste of a sweet in their mouths rather than with that of fish or meat. At all events, the feast of Bishop Flemming, of Lincoln, ends with "doucetys"; the installation feast of John Chandeler, Bishop of Salisbury, ends with "payn puffe" (buns?), jelly, and a "sotelte"; but the funeral feast of the Bishop of Bath and Wells, in 1424, apparently has no dessert unless "payn puffe" be counted as such. On the other hand, the installation feast of John Stafford, Bishop of Wells, in 1425, ends with a "sotelte", fruit, wafers, and a sweet.

In 1458 Gaston, Count de Foix, and Prince de Viane gave a great feast in seven courses to the

8. MEDIEVAL TABLES

9. FOUR MEN AT TABLE

SIX AT TABLE

King of France and his Court. After enormous quantities of game and poultry there came in the fifth course tarts, custards, plates of cream, oranges, and "citrons comfits". Then in course six were wafers with red hippocras, and, lastly, in the seventh course, spices and confections made in the form of lions, swans, stags, and other sorts of animals. On each piece were the arms and the device of the King.[85] This indeed was a French feast, but in matters of cuisine and the regulation of the table the English looked upon the French as masters.

Precisely what sorts of cakes[86] the English ate at their feasts is not easy to determine. There is a sort of tansy-cake made of eggs, tansy, and butter mentioned in the *Liber Cocorum* (p. 50), but it is not a cake in our sense. In fact, the Oxford English Dictionary cites nothing before 1683 in any way corresponding to the modern conception of cake. In that year Tryon's *Way to Health* (p. 233) remarks: "Observe the composition of Cakes, which are frequently eaten. . . . In them are commonly Flour, Butter, Eggs, Milk, Fruit, Spice, Sugar, Sack, Rose Water, and Sweetmeats, as Citron, or the like."

There were indeed wafers, regarded in the fifteenth century as a delicacy, but singularly unlike any modern wafers. The old receipt directs:[87] "Take the belly of a pike and seethe it well, put it in a mortar, add cheese thereto, and grind them together. Then take flour and white of eggs and beat together; then take sugar and powder of ginger, and put all together, and look that thy eggs be hot, and lay thereon thy paste, and then make thy wafers and serve in."[88]

In general, among the dainties served, at whatever time seemed most convenient, appear to have been fruits in some form, raw, dried, or preserved in syrup; nuts, chiefly almonds; various comfits in sugar; spices, and sweet wine. But fruits, it was thought, should be eaten with circumspection,[89] and since they were supposed to be "cold" in their nature they were best disposed of as early as possible in the meal. "Melons in particular, on account of their 'cold' nature, were recommended to be eaten only at the beginning of a meal."[90] We note further: "Up to the end of the seventeenth century it was generally believed that fruits, especially those that easily decay, should be eaten at the beginning of a meal when the stomach was empty, for one should always begin a meal by eating the things most difficult to digest."[91] But Le Grand d'Aussy himself says of feasts in the twelfth and thirteenth centuries that "when the entertainments were over the fruit was brought on, which was not counted as making a part of the meal and passed as a sort of *hors-d'œuvre*. . . . In the fourteenth there was some change. The fruit was transferred to the meal itself."[92]

Since fruits were to be used only with fear and trembling, one should counteract their "frigidity" and aid the natural heat of the stomach by the use of ragouts and other strongly spiced dishes, ending the meal with spiced wines and spiced comfits.[93]

SERVING THE FEAST

Fresh fruits form so large a part of a modern diet, especially in America, that one can hardly realize how rare they were in the medieval period. In the Oxford English Dictionary lemons are only twice mentioned before 1500. About the end of the fifteenth century they were cultivated "in the Azores and largely shipped to England".[94] Oranges were also a rare and late addition to an English feast and naturally expensive. The climate in most parts of England has never favoured extensive fruit raising, but small fruits, such as gooseberries, strawberries, mulberries, as well as apples, cherries, plums, peaches, pears, and quinces, were grown in considerable quantities.[95] In the *Northumberland Household Book*[96] are cited dates, Corinth raisins, figs, great raisins, almonds—all, of course, imported. Andrew Boorde in the sixteenth century mentions in his Dyetary[97] (pp. 282-6), figs,[98] raisins, currants, grapes, peaches, medlars, services (a kind of pear), strawberries, cherries, whortleberries, pears, apples, pomegranates, quinces, dates, gourds, cucumbers, pepones (pumpkins), prunes, damsons, oranges. Perishable fruits such as pineapples (not mentioned in England before 1664) and bananas (not mentioned before the sixteenth century) were never seen on English tables.

Because only a few fruits like oranges, lemons, and pomegranates could survive transport by sea, the greater part of the fruits coming from various parts of the East and South were dried, either with or without sugar.[99] These were mainly dates, raisins—especially from Greece—and figs. Dates, it is interesting to note, were regarded throughout the seventeenth century as a medicament.[100] The English dried fruits included apples, cherries, dogberries, apricots, quinces, early peaches, pears. Warner prints[101] receipts for preserving in sweet syrup flavoured with spice a variety of fruits, pippins—red, white, green—apricots, myrobalans (a sort of plum), cherries, and red *rose leaves*!

Although fresh fruits were eaten with caution, the appetite for sweets was strong, and it was gratified by the use of comfits, nougat, and marchpane, to say nothing of the "sotelties" made of sugar. Comfits were also made of sugar, enclosing a nut, a savory seed like the caraway, the coriander, or a rolled leaf of anise or fennel. Nougat was a sort of marchpane made with sugar or, for the sake of economy, with honey. Marchpane itself early won popularity, and already in the thirteenth century was made of pistachio nuts or almonds, with sugar.[102] At the end of the sixteenth century it was composed of whites of eggs, white honey, or sugar, beaten together and heated over a fire. Then peeled sweet almonds were thrown in. Marchpane was much used for making fancy figures at feasts, and moulded and coloured to represent fruit and animals.

All in all, at the old feasts there appears to have been no lack of dainties, but of ices and of confectionery of the modern type, such as chocolates and other sweets now provided in almost infinite variety, there is no trace. At most, after a feast, one finds, particularly in France, what are known

SERVING THE FEAST

as dragées[103] or sugar plums, served with sweet spiced wine at the conclusion of the repast.

The same vitiated taste that demanded dishes loaded with pepper and cardamon and cinnamon naturally required wine highly spiced and sweetened with honey or sugar at the end of the repast. The jaded appetite demanded continual stimulation. This spiced wine was served with much ceremony according to the ritual for such occasions. A modern reader might imagine that the drink consumed at the ordinary banquet would be sufficient to ensure sleep, but in any case spiced wine was commonly served before repairing to the bed-chamber for the night.

In the elaborate English feasts of which we have detailed accounts we find in some cases, as for example the coronation feast of Henry IV, each of the three huge courses ending with a "sotelte", or device to deck the table. This ornament served a double purpose, and, since it was commonly made of sugar, it was often divided among the guests after being sufficiently admired.

Allegorical subtleties have long since ceased to be in vogue, for, to the modern observer, the subtleties, with their obtrusive and not particularly inspired mottoes, appear indeed quite the reverse of *subtle* and seem more adapted to interest and amuse children than full-grown men—especially men who were the foremost representatives of the kingdom. But in one form or another subtleties were in fashion throughout the fifteenth and sixteenth centuries and were indispensable decorations of the feasts of kings and princes. Putting aside the mottoes we must admit, if we may trust the contemporary descriptions, that the miniature castles and cathedrals and the figures of birds and animals equalled or surpassed any of the achievements of modern confectioners.[104]

The subtleties displayed at the coronation feast of Henry V may serve as types of all the others of the fifteenth century. For the first course was a great swan as a "suttelte" sitting upon a green stock, displayed with a writing in his bill: "Regardez Roy, la droyt voy", and six cygnets on the same stock, each bearing a motto. Then twenty-four swans, each of them with the motto in their mouths, "Noble honour and joy". For the second course there were antelopes, as subtleties with the motto, "Un sauvez plus maynteyn dieus". The subtlety for the third course consisted of eagles of gold with the motto in their bills: "Dest jour notable est honourable."[105]

On November 6, 1429, Henry VI was crowned in St. Peter's at Westminster, and, as the quaint old chronicler tells us, "after that solempnyzacion in the sayd churche fynysshed, an honourable feest in the great halle of Westmynster was kepte, where the kinge, syttinge in his astate, was servyd with .iii. coursys, as hereunder ensureth[106] [ensueth]. Frument with venyson, Viand royall plantyd losynges of golde. Bore hedes in castellys of golde and enarmed. Beef with moton boyled. Capon stewyd. Signet rosted. Heyroun rostyd. Great pyke or luce. A rede leche with lyons corvyn therin.

Custarde royall with a lyoparde of gold syttynge therein, and holdynge a floure delyce. Frytour of sunne facion, with a flour delyce[107] therin. A sotyltie of Seynt Edwarde and Seynt Lowys armyd, and upon eyther his cote armoure, holdynge atwene them a figure lyke unto kynge Henry, standynge also in his cote armour, and a scripture passynge from them both, sayinge: 'beholde .ii. parfyght kynges under one cote armour', and under the fete of the sayd seyntes, was wryten this balade:

> Holy seyntes, Edwarde and seynt Lowyce
>   Concerve this braunche, born of your blessyd blode,
> Lyve amonge Christen, moste soveraygne of pryce.
>   Inherytour of the flour delyce so gode:
> This sixte Henry to reygne and to be wyse,
>   God graunte he may, to be your mode
> And that he may resemble your knyghthode and vertue
>   Praye ye hertely unto our Lorde Ihesu.
> Viand blank barryd with gold
>   Gely party wryten and notyd with Te Deum laudamus.

Pygge endoryd. Crane rostyd, Byttore. Conyes. Chekyns endorid. Partryche. Pecok enhakyll. Great breme. A whyte leche plantyd with a rede antelop; a crowne aboute his necke, with a chayne of golde; flampayne powderyd with leopardes, and flower delyce of golde. A frytour, garnysshed with a leopardes hede, and .ii. estryche[108] feders. A sotyltie: an emperoure and a kynge, arayed in mantellys of garters, whiche fygured Sygysmunde the emperoure and Henry the .V.; and a fygure lyke unto Kynge Henry the VI. knelynge to fore theym, with this balade takked by hym:

Agayne myscreants the emperour Sygysmunde,
  Hath shewyd his myght, whiche is imperyall.
And Henry the V. a noble knyghte was founde,
  For Christes cause in actes marcyall
Cherysshed the churche, to Lollers gave a fall,
  Gyvynge example to kynges that succede
And to theyr braunche here in especyall,
  While he doth reygne to love good and drede.

Quynces in compost. Blaund sure, powderyd, with quarter foyles gylt. Venyson rosted. Egrettes. Curlew, Cok and partryche. Plover. Quayles. Snytes. Great byrdes. Larkys, Carpe, Crabbe. Leche of .iii. coloures. A bake mete lyke a shylde, quarteryd red and whyte, set with losynges gylt, and floures of borage. A frytour crispid. A sotyltie of our Lady, syttynge with her childe in her lappe, and she holdynge a crowne in her hande. Seynt George and seynt Denys knelynge, on eyther syde, presentyd to her Kynge Henryes fygure, berynge in hande this balade, as foloweth:

O blessyd Lady, Cristes moder dere,
  And thou seynt George, that called art her knyght;
Holy Seynt Denys, O master most entere,
  The sixt Henry here present in your syght
Shedyth, of your grace, on hym your hevenly lyght;
  His tender youth with vertue doth avaunce,
Borne by discent, and by tytle of ryght
  Justly in reygne in Englande and in Fraunce.[109]

As might be expected, the table decorations at Archbishop Warham's enthronization feast, in 1504,[110] were of an elaborate character, and one deserves special mention. Before the serving of the first course a huge "warner", a sort of subtlety, was brought in representing in the first stage a battlemented castle with eight towers, all made of flowers, with a beadle displaying his staff on each tower; then the King sitting in Parliament with his lords about him in their robes, and St. William like an Archbishop sitting on the right hand of the King: then the Chancellor of Oxford, with other doctors, presenting the said Lord William kneeling in a doctor's habit unto the King with Latin verses, to which the King responds in the same tongue.

Particularly worth noting is the "third board of the same warner", where "the holy Ghost appeared, with bright beams proceeding from him of the gifts of grace, toward the said Lord of the feast", and offering the following flattering verses:

> Gratia te traxit donis, coelestibus aptum:
> Perge, parata manent uberiora tibi.

And then proceeded the course of service under this order:

> Ordo servitii.

The Lord Archbishop sitting in the middle of the high board alone, which was served in this order:
First the Duke on horseback. ii. The Heralds of armes. iii. The sewer. iv. The service, every dish in his order.

We need not reproduce the menu, which consisted almost wholly of fish, but we note that each of the two main courses was followed by elaborate subtleties, of a religious character.

The account of the third course is worth transcribing in full.

"The said Archbishop was solemnly served with Wafers and Ipocras, and immediately after the Sewer with the two Marshals, with great solemnitie from the Ewrie board, the Sergeant of the Ewrie plikyng[111] and foldyng it with great diligence, brought the Surnappe through the Hall to the hygh boorde, and the said Surnappe so brought well pliked to the boorde, one of the Marshals without hande laying thereto drew it through the board with great curiosity, after the old courtesy:[112] and so the said Lord washed and said grace standing. And after this standing at the void,[113] the said Lord Archbishop was served with Consertes, Sugar plate, Fertes[114] with other subtilties, with Ipocras. And so departed to his chamber.

Et sic finitur solemne servitium domini in prandio pro praedicto die."[115]

Not to be classed with the "sotelties", but to our practical age a very juvenile type of entertainment, are pies full of live birds which fly out when the crust is removed.[116] The tradition preserved in the nursery rhyme of the four-and-twenty blackbirds baked in a pie doubtless recalls an incident of a feast. Even as late as the seventeenth century Jeffrey Hudson, the famous dwarf of the Duke of Buckingham, was served at table in a cold pasty out of which he stepped brandishing a sword and saluted King Charles I and his newly wedded queen Henrietta Maria, in whose honour the dinner was given.[117]

VII

Entertainments

We must bear in mind that the medieval feast was not wholly devoted to eating and drinking, though food and drink were consumed in enormous quantities, but was an occasion of varied entertainment,[118] not always of the most refined type. When the feast was proclaimed, all sorts of professional wastrels flocked to the place with the hope of sharing some part of the golden shower along with the minstrels of the household.

The regular accompaniment of a medieval feast was music, or what in the Middle Ages passed for such. At the beginning of the feast the sound of the trumpet announced the first course; and various manuscript illuminations[119] show a minstrel sitting behind a gentleman and lady at table and warming his hands at an open fire, or minstrels in the musicians' gallery or standing beside the festal table blowing their pipes or playing the harp or other instruments.[120] We see then that the minstrels in their own sphere held a recognized place in medieval social life.[121]

In the fourteenth[122] and fifteenth centuries the English kings[123] and the heads of great families[124] regularly maintained, as a part of their household, a certain number of minstrels.[125] "Edward IV, as it appears from his Black Book, 1478, kept thirteen minstrels and a wait in his household. Of the former, one was verger, or chief, 'that directeth them all in festival days' [says Pegge, in his *Curalia*, 1818] 'to their stations, to blowings and piping to such offices as must be warned to prepare for the King and his household, at meats and suppers, to be the more ready in all services; and all these, sitting in the Hall together, whereof some use trumpets, some shawms and small pipes, and some are strange-men coming to this court at five feasts of the year, and then to take their wages of Household after fourpence halfpenny a day, if they be present in Court; and then they to avoid the next day after the feasts be done."[126]

Besides the three minstrels who formed a part of the household of the Earl of Northumberland various strangers appear as players and minstrels, to say nothing of the king's juggler and bearward.[127] And the household of the great Earl may be taken as typical of his class throughout the kingdom at the end of the fifteenth century.

The musicians in their gallery, if they did not pipe continuously throughout the long meal, at least performed actively between courses. As for the guests themselves, they were not silent. Alexander Barclay, in his fourth Eclogue, refers to the singing of songs at the table. At some French banquets the guests used to sing in their turn and the company sang the refrain.[128] Or, they would be expected one after another to tell entertaining tales,[129] doubtless often those of the type found in the *Decameron*, the only type, according to tradition, that King Louis XI cared to hear.

But the burden of the entertainment regularly fell upon the professional performers, who seldom failed to win applause. Invariably the antics and jests[130] of the Court fool, with his cockscomb, his shaven head, his cap and bells, his motley coat and his bauble, were welcomed with hilarity. Jugglers performed tricks that excited astonishment; acrobats tumbled and wrestled; and trained birds and animals imitated the feats of the acrobats, one animal riding upon the back of another, or dancing upon tight-ropes, and in various ways clumsily impersonating human beings. Professional dancers were popular, particularly the young women, not overclad, who stood with their feet in the air and walked about on their hands, after the traditional fashion of Salome at Herod's feast.[131]

Especially popular as entertainers were the professional reciters of romances, of which they commonly had an extensive repertory, gathered it may be in distant lands and jealously treasured for great occasions. The tale might be in prose, but as a rule it was in verse and chanted to the accompaniment of the harp.

One of the most brilliant pictures of such entertainment at a feast is found in the romance of *Merlin* where Merlin appears disguised as a harper: "And as thei were in this joye, and in this feste, and Kay the stiward that brought the firste mese before the Kynge, ther com in the feirest forme of man that ever hadde thei seyn before, and he was clothed in samyte, and girte with a bawdrike of silke harnysshed with golde and preciouse stones, that all the paleys flamed of the light, and the heir of his hede was yelowe and crispe with a crowne of golde theron as he hadde ben a kynge, and his hosen of fin scarlet, and his shone[132] of white cordewan orfraied,[133] and bokeled with fin golde; and hadde an harpe abowte his nekke of silver richely wrought, and the stringes were of fin golde wire, and the harpe was sette with preciouse stones; and the man that it bar was so feire of body and of visage that never hadde thei sein noon so feire a creature; but this apeired[134] moche his bewte and his visage for that he was blinde, and yet were the iyen[135] in his heed feire and cleir; and he hadde a litill cheyne of silver tacched to his arme, and to that cheyne a litill spayne[136] was bounde as white as snowe, and a litill coler aboute his nekke of silk harneysed with golde; and this spaynell ledde hym streight before the Kynge Arthur; and he harped a laye of Breteigne full swetely that wonder was to here, and the refraite[137] of his laye salewed the kynge Arthur, and the Quene Gonnore, and all the other after; and Kay the stiward that brought the firste cours taried awhile in the settyng down to beholde the harper intentifly."[138]

The guests themselves in ordinary festal garb or in masquerade often took advantage of the opportunity offered at feasts for a dance, either between courses or after the dessert; and it will be recalled that, at a dance following a banquet, Henry VIII is said first to have been attracted to Anne Boleyn. Once the dancing had begun it was

SERVING THE FEAST

likely to continue through the night and to end only at daybreak. Then the hosts who were in accord with French fashion served the usual wine and spices and the company dispersed.

In some cases jousting was a notable feature of a great feast, especially of a feast that continued for several days. We read in Froissart that in the last year of Richard II's reign a feast was held of the type described in medieval romances:

"Thus anone after the retourne of the erle of Salisbury out of Fraunce, kyng Richarde caused a justes to be cryed and publysshed throughe his realme, to Scotlande, to be at Wynsore, of xl. knyghtes and xl. squyers, agaynst all commers, and they to be aparelled in grene with a whyte faucon, and the quene to be there, well accompanied with ladyes and damosels. This feest thus holden, the quene beying there in gret noblenes, but there were but fewe lordes or noble men."[139]

How persistent were medieval traditions and practices in the early years of the sixteenth century is obvious when we take account of some of the features of banquets in which royalty participated. Beyond question, in many respects the men of the period we are studying were, even in the highest circles, youthful, not to say childish, in many of their amusements to a degree that has long been out of fashion. Practical jokes, horseplay, were in favour to an extent that seems strangely out of keeping with the dignity of royalty.

Particularly was this true at the beginning of the reign of Henry VIII. He had come to the throne as a youth of eighteen and he took delight in a perpetual round of hunting, jousting, mumming, dancing, and banqueting. A typical example is the following, which occurred in the first year of his reign. It will be noted that the mere feasting is only incidentally touched upon, while the supplementary entertainment is described at length. Upon its juvenile character it is hardly necessary to comment:

"On Shrove Sunday the same yere the Kyng prepared a goodly banket, in the Parliament Chambre at Westminster, for all the Ambassadours which there wer here out of diverse realmes and countreis. The banket beyng ready, the Kyng leadyng the Quene, entered into the Chambre, then the Ladies, Ambassadours, and other noble menne, followed in ordre. The Kyng caused the Quene to kepe the estate, and then satte the Ambassadours and Ladies as they were Marshalled by the Kyng, who would not sit, but walked from place to place, makyng chere to the Quene and the straungers: Sodainly the Kyng was gone. And shortly after, his grace with the Erle of Essex came in appareled after Turkey fasshion, in long robes of Bawdkin, powdered with gold, hattes on their heddes of Crimosyn Velvet, with greate rolles of Gold, girded with two swordes called Cimiteries, hangyng by greate bawderikes of gold. Next, came the lorde Henry, Erle of Wilshire, and the lorde Fitzwater, in twoo long gounes of yelowe satin, travarsed with white satin, and in every bend of white was a bend of crimosen satin after the fashion

10. FEAST GIVEN BY RICHARD II IN WESTMINSTER PALACE

11. PEACOCK IN HIS PLUMAGE PRESENTED TO BE SERVED AT THE TABLE

of Russia or Ruslande with furred hattes of greye on their hedes, either of them havyng an hatchet in their handes, and bootes with pykes turned up. And after them, came Syr Edward Haward, then Admyral, and with him Syr Thomas Carre, in doblettes of Crimosin velvet, voyded lowe on the backe, and before to the cannell bone, lased on the breastes with chaynes of silver, and over that shorte clokes of Crimosyn satyne, and on their heades hattes after dauncers fashion, with feasauntes fethers in theim: They were appareyled after the fashion of Prusia or Spruce. The torchbearers were appareyled in Crymosyn satyne and grene lyke Moreskoes, their faces blacke: And the Kyng brought in a mommerye. After that the Quene, the lordes, and ladyes, such as would, had played, the sayd mommers departed, and put of the same apparel, and sone after entred into the Chamber, in their usuel apparell. An so the kyng made great chere to the Quene, Ladyes, and Ambassadours: The supper or Banket ended, and the tables avoyded, the kyng beeyng in communicacion with the ambassadors; the Quene with the ladies toke their places in their degrees. Then began the daunsyng, and every man toke much hede to them that daunsed. The kyng perceyving that withdrew hym selfe sodenly out of the place, with certayn other persons appoynted for that purpose. And within a litle whyle after there came in a drumme and a fife appareiled in white Damaske and grene bonettes, and hosen of the same sute; than certayn gentlemen folowed with torches, apparayled in blew Damaske purseled with ames grey, facioned lyke an Awbe, and on their heddes hodes with robbes and longe tippettes to the same of blew Damaske visarde. Than after them came a certayn number of gentelmen, whereof the kyng was one, apparayled all in one sewte of shorte garments, litle beneth the poyntes, of blew velvet and Crymosyne with long sleves, all cut and lyned with clothe of golde. And the utter parte of the garmentes were powdered with castels, and shefes of arrowes of fyne doket gold. The upper partes of their hosen of lyke sewte and facion, the nether partes were of Scarlet poudred with tymbrelles of fyne golde, on their heades bonets of Damaske, sylver flatte woven in the stole, and thereupon wrought with gold, and ryche fethers in them, all with visers. After them entred .iv. ladyes wherof twoo were appareyled in Crymosyn satyne and purpull, embrowdred with golde, and by vynettes ran flour delices of golde, with marveylous ryche and straunge tiers on their heades. Other two ladies in Crymosyne & purpull, made like long slops enbroudered and fret with gold after antike fashion: and over that garment was a short garment of clothe of golde scant to the knee, facioned like a tabard all over, with small double rolles, all of flatte golde of Damaske, fret with frysed golde, and on theyr heades skayns and wrappers of Damaske golde with flatte pypes that straunge it was to beholde.

"The other two ladies were in kyrtels of Crymosyne and purpul satyn enbroudered with a vynet of Pomegraneltes of golde, all the garmentes cut compasse wyse, havyng but demy sleves, and naked doune from the elbowes, and over their garmentes were vochettes[140] of Pleasauntes,[141] rouled with Crymsyne velvet and set with letters of golde lyke Carectes, their heades rouled in pleasauntes and typpers lyke the Egipcians embroudered with gold. Their faces, neckes, armes & handes covered with fyne pleasaunce blacke; some call it Lumberdynes, which is merueylous thine,[142] so that the same ladies semed to be nygrost[143] or blacke Mores. Of these foresayed .vi. ladyes, the lady Mary, syster unto the king, was one, the other I name not. After that the kynges grace and the ladies had daunsed a certayne tyme they departed every one to his lodgyng."[144]

CHAPTER VII

NOTABLE FEASTS

AFTER the preceding discussion of the characteristic features of typical medieval banquets we may well give attention to some of the contemporary descriptions of feasts that appeared sufficiently notable to be remembered. And we may begin with a brief extract from a fifteenth-century romance describing a private dinner strikingly like a public feast in the richness of the food and the adornment of the table. To this we may add a few descriptions of famous banquets taken from early chronicles. These descriptions are for the most part written so soon after the events they picture that they are full of colour characteristically medieval. Moreover, the actual feasts often equal or surpass in splendour those described in the romances.

In the romance of *Sir Degrevant*, after the hero has overcome his foe, the lady of the castle welcomes him and gives directions for his entertainment. She orders a wood fire to be built in a chimney, and then has a "board of ivory"[1] set upon trestles and covered with towels, "white as sea foam", with surnaps[2] of the same, along with a gilded saltcellar and a basin and ewer filled with rose-water, in which the two wash. From the pantry she brings paindemain and a shoulder of a wild swine, with the viscera in sauce; then plover in paste, fat coneys, pheasants, and curlews. For wine there are vintages of Italy and Crete.

NOTABLE FEASTS

And the romancer adds, "To tell of the meats served at their supper, no dainty was too dear, and no spices were spared." For the doughty young warrior the maiden often drew the wine, Rochelle, Rhenish, and Malvoisie, and when she herself was not partaking of the feast she played sweetly on the harp and sang love-songs.[3] For an improvised meal this must be admitted to be very creditable, but it is altogether eclipsed by the actual banquets served in great houses.

In 1257 the Scotch King Alexander with his queen Margaret came to Westminster, and on August 28th John Mansel, the King's chaplain, "besought the two kings and other states[4] to dine with him on the morrow following, which they granted, and so he made a marvellous great dinner. There were seven hundred messes served up, but the multitude of guests was such that scarce the same sufficed; his house was not able to receive them all, and therefore he caused tents and booths to be set up for them. The like dinner had not been made by any chaplain before that time. All those that came were worthily received, feasted and entertained, in such sort as every man was satisfied."[5]

Froissart devotes a few words to the feasting upon the occasion of the marriage of Edward III to Philippa of Hainault, in 1329. "And Sir John of Hainault, Lord Beaumont, her uncle, did conduct her to the city of London, where there was made great feast, and many nobles of England, and the queen was crowned. And there was also great jousts, tourneys, dancing, caroling, and great feasts every day; the which endured the space of iii weeks."[6] It is interesting to note that on this and other occasions the supplementary entertainments receive as much attention as the actual feast.

Royalty, in the fourteenth century as in the thirteenth, had no monopoly of feasting. Sir Walter Besant reminds us[7] that about 1348, the year before the Black Death in England, "Henry Picard, the Vintner, gave that most famous of all the City banquets, at which he entertained the King of England, the King of France, the King of Scotland, the King of Denmark, and the King of Cyprus, as well as the Black Prince."

During the long reign of Edward III there were doubtless many notable feasts, but in the voluminous pages of Froissart we find a detailed account of only a few. In 1342, "for the love" of the Countess of Salisbury, and "for the great desire that the King had to see her", he "caused a great feast to be cried and a jousting to be holden in the city of London in the midst of August". The "cry was also made in Flanders, in Hainault, in Brabant, and in France. . . . This was a noble feast; there was the Earl William of Hainault and Sir John of Hainault his uncle, and a great number of lords and knights of high lineage; there was great dancing and jousting the space of XV days. . . . All ladies and damosels were freshly beseen,[8] according to their degrees, except Alice countess of Salisbury, for she went as simply as she might, to the intent that the King should not set his regard on her, for she was fully determined to do no manner of thing that should turn to her dishonour nor to her husband's."[9]

Of exceptional interest is the account of the founding of the Order of the Garter. In 1343 "the King of England took pleasure to new reedify the Castle of Windsor" which, by tradition, was "begun by King Arthur. Then King Edward determined to make an order and a brotherhood of a certain number of knights, and to be called knights of the blue garter; and a feast to be kept yearly at Windsor on Saint George's Day. And to begin this order, the King assembled together earls, lords, and knights of his realm and shewed them his intention; and they all joyously agreed to his pleasure, because they said it was a thing much honourable, and whereby great amity and love should grow and increase. Then was there chosen out a certain number of the most valiantest men of the realm, and they swore . . . to maintain the ordinances, such as were devised; and the King made a chapel in the castle of Windsor of Saint George, and established certain canons there to serve God and endued[10] them with fair rent. Then the King sent to publish this feast, by his heralds, into France, Scotland, Burgundy, Hainault, Flanders, Brabant, and into the empire of Almayne, giving to every knight and squire that would come to the said feast XV days of safe conduct before the feast and after; the which feast to begin at Windsor on Saint George day next after, in the year of our Lord Mcccxliiii, and the queen to be there accompanied with iiiC ladies and damosels, all of noble lineage and apparelled accordingly."[11]

Richard II carried to still greater heights the luxury that had characterized the Court of Edward III and organized his household on a more than regal scale, as the well-known lines in Hardynge's *Chronicle* indicate. Robert Ireleffe, Clerk of the Green Cloth, reports that in the King's household almost every day were ten thousand folk, and in the kitchen three hundred servitors, many occupiers in each office:

> And ladies fair with their gentlewomen,
> Chamberers also and lavenders,[12]
> Three hundred of them were occupied then.
> There was great pride among the officers,
> And of all men far passing their compeers,
> Of rich array and much more costious[13]
> Than was before or sith,[14] and more precious.
> Yeomen and grooms in cloth of silk arrayed,
> Satin and damask, in doublets and gowns.
> In cloth of green and scarlet, for unpaid
> Cutwork[15] was great both in courts and towns,
> Both in men's hoods and also in their gowns.
> Brouder[16] and furs and goldsmith work aye new[17]
> In many a wise each day they did renew.[18]

In 1390 King Richard II was twenty-three years old, and he, along with his three uncles, "ordained a great feast to be holden at the city of London; where there should be jousts and lx. knights to abide all comers, and with them lx. ladies freshly apparelled to keep them company. . . .

"This noble feast whereof I make mention was published and cried in divers places, whereby knights and squires and other advanced themselves to go thither. . . . And on the Sunday next after the feast of Saint Michael this feast and triumph should begin, and that day to be done in Smithfield jousts called the challenge." The feast continued until Friday, with daily jousting and banqueting. "On the Saturday the King and all the lords departed from London to Windsor", along with the visiting earls and all other knights and squires who desired to accompany him. "Then there began again great feasts, with dinners and suppers given by the King." This feast was especially designed to do honour to the young Earl of Ostrevant, who there received the Order of the Garter. Not unnaturally, the French King, his brother, and his uncles were sore troubled and grievously displeased with the Earl of Ostrevant, since the extravagant outlay of King Richard had won him the promise that the Earl would never bear arms against the crown of England.[19]

Especially interesting is the account of the first banquet in Westminster Hall after King Richard had largely rebuilt the hall of William Rufus:

"This hall being finished in the year 1399, the same King kept a most royal Christmas there, with daily joustings, and runnings at tilt, whereunto resorted such a number of people that there was every day spent twenty-eight or twenty-six oxen, and three hundred sheep, besides fowl without number: he caused a gown for himself to be made of gold, garnished with pearl and precious stones, to the value of 3000 marks: he was guarded by

Cheshire men, and had about him commonly thirteen bishops, besides barons, knights, squires, and other more than needed: insomuch, that to the household came every day to meat 10,000 people, as appeareth by the messes told out from the Kitchen to 300 servitors."[20]

In the reign of Henry V at least two feasts deserve brief mention. The first was held two years after the memorable battle of Agincourt:

"In this year also [1417] Sigismund Emperor of Almayne came into England, and in the month of May by the King's commandment, and Vii day of the said month, the mayor and brethren met him upon Blackheath; and at Saint George's met him the king and his lords in great number, and so conveyed him unto Westminster with great honour, and lodged him in his own palace. And shortly after was the feast of Saint George holden at Windsor, which before was deferred for his coming, in time of which solemnity, during the divine service, the King kept the estate,[21] but in sitting at the feast the Emperor kept the estate; the service and subtleties of which feast, with sitting of the lords after their degrees I pass over."[22]

Equally notable, if not more so, was the feast on February 24, 1420-21, at the coronation of Catherine, queen of Henry V. The young queen was solemnly crowned in Westminster Abbey.[23] "After which solempnization in the church ended, she was conveyed into the great hall of Westminster, and there set to dinner; upon whose right hand sat, at the end of the same table, the Archbishop of Canterbury and Henry, surnamed the rich Cardinal of Winchester; and upon the left hand of the queen sat the King of Scots in his estate,[24] the which was served with covered mess like unto the forenamed bishops, but after them. And upon the same hand and side, near to the board end, sat the Duchess of York, and the Countess of Huntingdon. The Earl of the March, holding a sceptre in his hand, kneeled upon the right side. The Earl in like manner kneeled upon the left hand of the queen. The Countess of Kent sat under the table[29] at the right foot, and the Countess Marshall at the left foot. The Duke of Gloucester, Sir Humphrey, was that day overlooker, and stood before the queen bareheaded. Sir Richard Neville was that day carver to the queen."

At this coronation feast, adds Holinshed (p. 579), "the Earl of Worcester was that day Earl Marshal in the Earl Marshal's absence; who rode about the hall upon a great courser with a multitude of tipped staves about him to make and keep room in the said hall". The chronicler also gives the menu of the feast.

Another coronation feast in Westminster Hall, that of Richard III, was held on July 6, 1483. The chronicler's account is particularly interesting for the mention of the King's champion and other medieval details:

"About iiii of the clock the King and Queen entered the hall, and the King sat in the middle, and the Queen on the left hand of the table, and on every side of her stood a countess holding a cloth of pleasaunce[25] when she list to drink. And on the right hand of the King sat the Bishop of Canterbury: the ladies sat all on one side in the middle of the hall; and at the table against them sat the chancellor and all the lords. At the table next the cupboard sat the Mayor of London. And at the table behind the lords sat the barons of the ports: and at the other boards sat noble and worshipful personages. When all persons were set, the Duke of Norfolk, Earl Marshall, the Earl of Surrey, constable for that day, the Lord Stanley, Lord Steward, Sir William Hopton treasurer, and Sir Thomas Percy comptroller, came in and served the King solemnly with one dish of gold and another of silver; and the Queen all in gilt vessel, and the bishop all in silver. At the second course came into the hall Sir Robert Democke the King's champion, making a proclamation, that whosoever would say that King Richard was not lawful King he would fight with him at the utterance,[26] and threw down his gauntlet, and then all the hall cried 'King Richard!' and so he did in three parts of the hall; and then one brought him a cup of wine covered and when he had drunk, he cast out the drink, and departed with the cup. . . . After that the heralds cried a largess thrice in the hall, and so went up to their stage. At the end of dinner the Mayor of London served the King and Queen with sweet wine, and had each of them a cup of gold with a cover of gold. And by that time that all was done, it was dark night. And so the King returned to his chamber, and every man to his lodging."[27]

King Henry VII, the supplanter of Richard III, was averse to display involving expense that could be avoided, and hence we have little to record concerning banquets during his reign of nearly a quarter of a century. His reign carries us over into the beginning of the sixteenth century, but not to the end of medievalism. Notwithstanding the stirring of men's souls at the discovery of hitherto unknown lands across the seas and the still more profound awakening that came with the advent of the New Learning, the current of daily life still flowed on in the old channels. In so far as banquets were concerned, the setting of the feast became more brilliant and luxurious, but the food was prepared in much the same fashion as in the fifteenth century, and the standards of deportment remained substantially unchanged.

The accession of Henry VIII brought to the throne a brilliant young prince who, in the flush of his early manhood, aroused the highest expectations. Wealthy through the accumulations of his cautious and penurious father, he spared no expense in the magnificent entertainments which he devised, and he set a standard to which his subjects, when entertaining their royal master, endeavoured as far as possible to conform. Abundant illustration of the lavishness of the feasts of that time appears in the descriptions here presented. Henry's coronation feast was typical of the banquets throughout his reign. As we read in the contemporary chronicle: After the ceremony of the coronation had been finished, "the lords spiritual and temporal did to him homage and returned to Westminster hall, with the Queen's grace, every one under their canopies, where by the Lord Marshal and his tipped staves was made room, and every lord and other noble men, according to their tenures, before claimed and viewed. . . . At the bringing of the first course the trumpets blew up and in came the Duke of Buckingham, mounted upon a great courser, richly trapped and embroidered, and the lord Steward, in likewise on an horse, trapped in cloth of gold, riding before the service, which was sumptuous with many subtleties, strange devices with several posies[28] and many dainty dishes. At the King's feet under[29] the table, were certain gentlemen; and in likewise with the Queen, who there continued, during that long and royal feast. What should I speak or write of the sumptuous, fine, and delicate meats prepared for this high and honourable coronation, provided for as well in the parties beyond the sea, as in many and sundry places within this realm, where God so abundantly hath sent such plenty and foyson. . . .[30]

"The second course being served, the King's Champion, fully armed and wearing a great plume of ostrich feathers, rode through the hall and challenged the company to dispute the right of King Henry to the crown, afterward receiving a golden cup, with its cover, from which he drank to the health of the King and departed.

"The King of Arms and the heralds then made proclamations in various parts of the Hall, more wine was served, hands were washed, and all went

NOTABLE FEASTS

to their chambers."[31] I need not detail the jousts and tournaments that followed, but nothing more lavish appears in the romances.

In the second year of Henry's reign, "Against the XII day or the day of the Epiphany, at night, before the banquet in the hall at Richmond, was a pageant devised like a mountain glistering by night, as though it had been all of gold and set with stones, on the top of which mountain was a tree of gold, the branches and boughs friezed[32] with gold, spreading on every side over the mountain, with roses and pomegranates, the which mountain was with vises brought up towards the King, and out of the same came a lady, apparelled in cloth of gold, and the children of honour called the Henchmen, which were freshly disguised, and danced a morris[33] before the King. And that done, reentred the mountain, and then it was drawn back, and then was the wassail or banquet brought in, and so brake up Christmas."

On October 8, 1519, a great banquet was given in the palace at Greenwich, where the Master of the Rolls "made an eloquent proposition in praise of the matrimony to be had betwixt the Dauphin[34] and the lady Marie. All that day were the strangers feasted and at night they were brought into the hall," where "a pageant very sumptuous and of notable device" was shown. "After this pastime ended, the King and the ambassadors were served at a banquet with two hundred and sixty dishes, and after that a voidee[35] of spices with sixty spice plates of silver and gilt, as great as men with ease might bear. This night the cupboard in the hall was of twelve stages all of plate of gold, and no gilt plate. When that every man had been plenteously served, the tables were taken up, and the King with the Queen and all the strangers departed to their lodgings."[36]

As we have elsewhere noted, great banquets were by no means restricted to royal circles, though the presence of royalty necessarily imposed an entertainment worthy of a royal guest. Throughout the reign of Henry VIII no subject rivalled the luxury maintained in the household of Henry's favourite, Cardinal Wolsey, who lived amid splendour scarcely less than that of the King himself.

Not unnaturally, as we are told by Wolsey's biographer, "When it pleased the King's majesty, for his recreation, to repair unto the Cardinal's house, as he did divers times in the year, there wanted no preparations, or goodly furniture, with viands of the finest sort that might be provided for money or friendship, such pleasures were then devised for the King's comfort and consolation as might be invented or by man's wit imagined. The banquets were set forth, with masks and mummeries, in so gorgeous a sort, and costly manner, that it was a heaven to behold. There wanted no dames or damsels, meet or apt to dance with the maskers, or to garnish the place for the time, with other goodly disports. There was all kind of music and harmony set forth, with excellent voices both of men and children. I have seen the King suddenly come in thither in a mask, with a dozen of other maskers, all in garments

12. NEF OR SALT-CELLAR   KING, QUEEN, AND FOUR GUESTS
THE CARVER AT WORK

13. FEAST WITH KING AND QUEEN AT TABLE

like shepherds, made of fine cloth of gold and fine crimson satin paned,[37] and caps of the same, with visors of good proportion of visnomy; their hairs, and beards, either of fine gold wire or else of silver, and some being of black silk; having sixteen torch bearers, besides their drums, and other persons attending upon them, with visors, and clothed all in satin, of the same colours." On one such occasion, by prearrangement, short cannon were discharged as a salute, and the strangers then conducted to the banquet, accompanied by twenty new torches, along with many drums and fifes. After saluting all the ladies, they at length opened a cup full of gold to the value of two hundred crowns, and after some play, they poured all the crowns again into the cup. Then the Cardinal by a cast of dice won them all, "whereat great joy was made". Wolsey already suspected that the King was present and at last said, "Methinks the gentleman with the black beard should be he." The King laughed and "plucked down his visor", then retired to change his apparel. In his absence the tables were "spread again with new and sweet perfumed cloths", and "then the King took his seat under the cloth of estate, commanding no man to remove, but sit still as they did before. Then came in a new banquet before the King's majesty, and to all the rest through the tables, wherein, I suppose, were served two hundred dishes or above, of wondrous costly meats and devices, subtilly devised. Thus passed they forth the whole night with banqueting, dancing, and other triumphant devices to the great comfort of the King, and pleasant regard of the nobility there assembled." [38]

These earlier banquets, however, were quite eclipsed by Cardinal Wolsey's great feast given to the French embassy in October, 1527, on the conclusion of peace with France.

"This great embassy, long looked for, was now come over (with a great retinue), which were in number above fourscore persons, of the most noblest and worthiest gentlemen in all the court of France, who were right honourably received from place to place after their arrival, and so conveyed through London unto the Bishop's palace in Paul's Churchyard, where they were lodged. To whom divers noblemen resorted and gave them divers goodly presents; and in especial the Mayor and city of London, as wine, sugar, wax, capons, wild fowl, beefs, muttons, and other necessaries in great abundance, for the expenses of their house. Then the next Sunday after their resort to London, they repaired to the Court at Greenwich, and there, by the King's majesty [were] most highly received and entertained. They had a special commission to create and stall the King's highness in the Royal order of France; for which purpose they brought with them a collar of fine gold of the order, with a Michael[39] hanging thereat, and robes to the same appurtenant, the which was wondrous costly and comely, of purple velvet, richly embroidered; I saw the King in all this apparel and habit, passing through the chamber of presence unto his closet; and afterward in the same habit at mass beneath in the chapel. And to gratify the French King with like honour, [he] sent incontinent[40] unto [him] the like order of England by a nobleman [the Earl of Wiltshire], purposely for that intent, to create him one of the same order of England, accompanied with Garter the Herald, with all robes, garter, and other habiliments to the same belonging; as costly in every degree as the other was of the French King's, the which was done before the return of the great embassy."

Then ensued a solemn mass in St. Paul's, after which the treaty of peace and amity was read before the assembled multitude. From the cathedral "the King rode home to the Cardinal's house at Westminster, to dinner, with whom dined all the Frenchmen, passing all day after in consultation in weighty matters touching the conclusion of this peace and amity". The King then returned to Greenwich, making plans for the guests to hunt in the parks at Richmond and at Hampton Court, where, moreover, they were to be banqueted by Cardinal Wolsey.

"His pleasure once known, to accomplish his commandment they sent forth all the caterers, purveyors, and other persons to prepare of the finest viands that they could get, other [41] for money or friendship among my lord's friends. Also they sent for all the expertest cooks, besides my lord's, that they could get in all England, where they might be gotten to serve to garnish this feast.

"The purveyors brought and sent in such plenty of costly provision, as ye would wonder at the same.

The cooks wrought both night and day in divers subtleties and many crafty devices; where lacked neither gold, silver, ne[42] any other costly thing meet for the purpose.

"The yeomen and grooms of the wardrobes were busied in hanging of the chambers with costly hangings, and furnishing the same with beds of silk, and other furniture apt for the same in every degree. Then my Lord Cardinal sent me, being gentlemen usher, with two of my fellows to Hampton Court, to foresee all things touching our rooms, to be nobily garnished accordingly. Our pains were not small or light, but traveling daily from chamber to chamber. Then the carpenters, the joiners, the masons, the painters, and all other artificers necessary to glorify the house and feast were set at work. There was carriage and recarriage of plate, stuff [and] other rich implements; so that there was nothing lacking or to be imagined or devised for the purpose. There were also fourteen score beds provided and furnished with all manner of furniture to them belonging, too long particularly here to rehearse. But to all wise men it sufficeth to imagine, that knoweth what belongeth to the furniture of such triumphant feast or banquet.

"The day was come that to the Frenchmen was assigned, and they ready assembled at Hampton Court, something before the hour of their appointment. Wherefore the officers caused them to ride to Hanworth, a place and park of the King's, within two or three miles, there to hunt and spend the time until night. At which time they returned again to Hampton Court, and every of them conveyed to his chamber severally, having in them great fires and wine ready to refresh them, remaining there until their supper was ready, and the chambers where they should sup were ordered in due form. The first waiting-chamber was hanged with fine arras, and so was all the rest, one better than another, furnished with tall yeomen. There was set tables round about the chamber, banquet-wise, all covered with fine cloths of diaper. A cupboard of plate, parcel gilt, having also in the same chamber, to give the more light, four plates of silver, set with lights upon them, a great fire in the chimney.

"The next chamber, being the chamber of presence, [was] hanged with very rich arras, wherein was a gorgeous and a precious cloth of estate hanged up, replenished with many goodly gentlemen ready to serve. The boards were set as the other boards were in the other chamber before, save that the high table was set and removed beneath the cloth of estate, towards the midst of the chamber, covered with fine linen cloths of damask work, sweetly perfumed. There was a cupboard made, for the time, in length, of the breadth of the nether end of the same chamber, six desks high, full of gilt plate, very sumptuous, and of the newest fashions; and upon the nethermost desk garnished all with plate of clean gold, having two great candlesticks of silver and gilt, most curiously wrought, the workmanship whereof, with the silver, cost three hundred marks, and lights of wax as big as torches burning upon the same. This cupboard was barred in round about that no man might come nigh it; for there was none of the same plate occupied or stirred during this feast, for there was sufficient besides. The plates that hung on the walls to give light in the chamber were of silver and gilt, with lights burning in them, a great fire in the chimney, and all other things necessary for the furniture of so noble a feast.

"Now was all things in a readiness and supper time at hand. My lord's officers caused the trumpets to blow to warn to supper, and the said officers went right discreetly in due order and conducted these noble personage from their chambers unto the chamber of presence where they should sup. And they, being there, caused them to sit down; their service was brought up in such order and abundance both costly and full of subtleties, with such a pleasant noise of divers instruments of music, that the Frenchmen, as it seemed, were rapt into a heavenly paradise.

"Ye must understand that my lord was not there, ne yet come, but they being merry and pleasant with their fare, devising and wondering upon the subtleties. Before the second course, my Lord Cardinal came in among them, booted and spurred, all suddenly, and bade them *proface*[43]; at whose coming they would have risen and given place with much joy. Whom my lord commanded to sit still, and keep their rooms; and straitways, being not shifted of his riding apparel called for a chair, and sat himself down in the midst of the table, laughing and being as merry as ever I saw him in all my life. Anon came up the second course with so many dishes, subtleties, and curious devices, which were above a hundred in number, of so goodly proportion and costly, that I suppose the Frenchmen never saw the like. The wonder was no less than it was worthy in deed. There were castles and images in the same; Paul's church and steeple, in proportion for the quantity as well counterfeited as the painter should have painted it upon a cloth or wall. There were beasts, birds, fowls of divers kinds, and personages, most lively made and counterfeit in dishes; some fighting as it were with swords, some with guns and crossbows, some vaulting and leaping; some dancing with ladies, some in complete harness, jousting with spears, and with many more devices than I am able with my wit [to] describe. Among all, one I noted: there was a chess board subtilely made of spiced plate, with men to the same; and for the good proportion, because that Frenchmen be very expert in that play, my lord gave the same to a gentleman of France, commanding that a case should be made for the same in all haste, to preserve it from perishing in the conveyance thereof into his country. Then my lord took a bowl of gold, which was esteemed of the value of five hundred marks, filled with hippocras, whereof there was plenty, putting off his cap, said, 'I drink to the King my sovereign lord and master, and to the King your master', and therewith drank a good draught. And when he had done, he desired the Grand Master to pledge him, cup and all, the which cup he gave him; and so caused the other lords and gentlemen in other cups to pledge these two royal princes.

"Then went cups merrily about, that many of the Frenchmen were fain to be led to their beds. Then went my lord, leaving them sitting still, into his privy chamber to shift him; and making there a very short supper, or rather a small repast, returned again among them into the chamber of presence, using them so nobly, with so loving and familiar countenance and entertainment, that they could not commend him too much.

"And whilst they were in communication and other pastimes, all their liveries were served to their chambers. Every chamber had a bason and a ewer of silver, some gilt, and some parcel gilt; and some two great pots of silver, in like manner, and one pot at the least with wine and beer, a bowl or goblet, and a silver pot to drink beer in; a silver candlestick or two, with both white lights and yellow lights [of] three sizes of wax; and a staff torch; a fine manchet,[44] and a cheat loaf [45] of bread. Thus was every chamber furnished throughout the house, and yet the two cupboards in the two banqueting chambers not once touched." [46]

Gorgeous as this feast was, King Henry would not be outdone, and "gave a special commandment to all his officers to devise a far [more] sumptuous banquet for the strangers, otherwise than they had at Hampton Court." When the ambassadors returned from Windsor, whither they had gone from Hampton Court, "they were invited to the court at Greenwich" where the banquet was made ready.

"But", says Cavendish in his quaint phrasing, "to describe the dishes, the subtleties, the many strange devices and order in the same, I do both lack wit in my gross old head, and cunning in my bowels to declare the wonderful and curious imaginations in the same invented and devised. Yet this shall ye understand: that although it was at Hampton Court marvellous sumptuous, yet did this banquet far exceed the same, as fine gold doth silver in weight and value; and for my party I must needs confess (which saw them both), that I never saw the like, or read in any story or chronicle of such a feast. In the midst of this banquet, there was tourneying at the barriers (even in the chamber), with lusty gentlemen in gorgeous complete harness, on foot; then there was the like on horseback; and after all this there was the most goodliest disguising or interlude, made in Latin or French, whose apparel was of such exceeding riches, that it passeth my capacity to expound."

Following the banquet was a masquerade ball. "Thus was this night occupied and consumed from five of the clock until two or three after midnight; at which time it was convenient for all estates to draw to their rest." [47]

In 1533, the twenty-fourth year of Henry VIII's reign, the King went to France to discuss with Francis I the proposed separation from Catherine of Aragon, and at Calais sumptuously entertained Francis and his train.

"The King of England brought the French King to his lodging to the Staple Inn, where his chamber was hanged with so rich verdure[48] as hath not been seen, the ground of it was gold and damask and all over the tufts and flowers were of satin, silk, and silver, so curiously wrought that they seemed to grow, every chamber was richer than the other: the second chamber all of tissue with a cloth of estate of needle work set with great roses of large pearl. The third was hanged with velvet, upon velvet pirled,[49] green and crimson, and embroidered over with branches of flowers of gold bullion, and garnished with arms and beasts of the same gold, set with pearl and stone. If the French King made good cheer to the King of England and his train at Bulleyne,[50] I assure you he and his train were requited at Caleis,[51] for the plenty of wild fowl, venison, fish, and all other things which were there it was marvel to see, for the King's officers of England had made preparation in every place, so that the Frenchmen were served with such multitude of diverse fishes, this Friday and Saturday, that the masters of the French King's household much wondered at the provision. In like wise on the Sunday they had all manner of flesh, fowl, spice, venison, both of fallow deer and red deer, and as for wine they lacked none, so that well was the English man that might well entertain the French man.

"The Sunday at night the French King supped with the King of England in a chamber hanged with tissue, raised with silver, paned[52] with cloth of silver, raised with gold, and the seams of the same were covered with broad wreaths of goldsmith's work, full of stone and pearl. In this chamber was a cupboard of vii stages high, all of plate of gold and no gilt plate, beside that there hung in the said chamber x branches of silver and gilt x, and branches all white silver, every branch hanging by a long chain of the same suit[53] bearing v lights of wax. To tell the riches of the cloths of estates, the basins and other vessels which was there occupied, I assure you my wit is insufficient, for there was nothing occupied that night but all of gold. The French King was served iii courses, and his meat dressed after the French fashion, and the King of England had like courses after the English fashion, the first course of every king was xl dishes, the second lx, the third lxx, which were costly and pleasant." Masks and dancing followed the banquet.[54]

Hall describes in detail the coronation of Anne Boleyn in June, 1533, and the feast in Westminster Hall that followed:

"When all thing was ready, the Queen under her canopy came to the hall and washed and sat down in the midst of the table under the cloth of estate. . . . When all these things were thus ordered came in the Duke of Suffolk and the Lord William Haward on horseback and the sergeants of arms before them, and after them the sewer,[55] and then the Knights of the Bath bringing in the first course, which was xxviii dishes, besides subtleties and ships made of wax, marvellous gorgeous to behold, all which time of service the trumpets standing in the window at the nether end of the hall played melodiously. . . . As touching the fare, there could be devised no more costlier dishes nor subtleties. The Mayor of London was served with xxxiii dishes at two courses, and so were all his brethren, and such as sat at his table. The Queen had at her second course xxiii dishes, and thirty at the third course: and between the two last courses the Kings of arms cried largess in three parts of the hall."[56]

After the dinner, wafers and hippocras were served, followed by spice and comfits.

By way of comparison we may place along with the accounts of notable English feasts a few descriptions of feasts on the Continent portrayed by contemporary chroniclers. We observe at once that there is no essential difference,[57] though the continental feasts are perhaps on the whole more elaborate, and particularly notable for the excessive use of symbolic features.

As in the case of the English feasts, we may best arrange the accounts in chronological order.

In 1397 the "King of Almayne" at the invitation of the King of France came to Rheims. "And the French King made the King of Almayne[58] and his company a great dinner. At one table there sate, first, the Patriarch of Jerusalem, then the King of Almayne, and the French King, and the King of Navarre. There sate no more at that table. At the other tables sate the lords and prelates of Almayne: no lord of France sate that day, but served. To the King's board the meat was brought by the dukes of Berry and of Bourbon, the Earl of Saint Pol and by other great lords of France. The Duke of Orleans set every man down. Vessel of gold and silver ran plenteously through the palace, as though it had been but of wood or earth: it was a sumptuous dinner. And, as I was informed, the French King gave to his cousin the King of Almayne all the vessel and plate of gold and silver that was served that day in the palace at the dresser or elsewhere, and all other hangings and habiliments in the hall and chamber whereunto the King retrayed,[59] after dinner, and spice and wine taken. This gift was praised and valued to two hundred thousand florins; and moreover there was given to the other Almayns great gifts and goodly presents of vessel and plate of gold and silver, whereof the strangers that were there had great marvel of the state and puissance and great riches of the realm of France." [60]

The great feast given by Philip the Good at Lille in 1453 was a gorgeous affair. On the chief table was a well-built ship with sails spread. On the ship stood an armed knight with the arms of Cleves and before it swam a silver swan drawing the ship with a silver chain. At one end of the ship was a richly built castle, at the foot of which a falcon swam in a great river. The hall in which the feast was held was hung with tapestry depicting the labours of Hercules. Knights in damask and squires in silk served the banquet.

There were three tables in the hall, one large, one small, and one of medium size. Among the numerous ornaments was a church with a cross, chimes, and four singers. There was also a cargo ship at anchor laden with merchandise and provided with a crew. There was besides a beautiful fountain standing as it were in a little meadow surrounded with cliffs of sapphire and other rare stones. The second table had a great variety of marvels, among which was a huge pasty in which were twenty living musicians who played different instruments, each in their turn; a castle in the fashion of that of Lusignan, with Melusine in the form of a serpent; a windmill; a great wine cask lying in a vineyard and yielding two sorts of wine, one sweet, one bitter, and so on. In an uninhabited desert a lifelike tiger fought with a great serpent; a wild man rode upon a camel; a man with a pole was beating a bush full of little birds, and near by sat a gentleman and a lady who ate the birds that were struck down. Next to this pair was a fool riding a bear; then a lake surrounded by cities and castles, and on the lake a ship that sailed hither and thither. The third table showed a forest in India, with rare beasts that moved about. On the same table was a lion fettered to a tree in the midst of a meadow, and a man in front of the lion striking a dog. Lastly, an itinerant merchant went through a village bearing on his back a pack full of various wares.

The narrator describes many other notable details, but as for food he contents himself with saying that each platter was heaped with eight and forty sorts of food, and that the dishes containing the roasts were in the form of wagons adorned with blue and gold.[61]

Along with the actual banqueting at any of the

great continental feasts, particularly those that continued for several days, there were various entertainments, and, wherever possible, a tournament, with dancing in the evening, at which the ladies were the principal attraction.[62]

Superb as was the banquet at Lille, the festivities attending the marriage of Princess Margaret, sister of Edward IV of England, to Charles, Duke of Burgundy, in June 1468, appear to have been on a grander scale.[63]

On Saturday, June 18, 1468, the princess left London for Margate, and on Friday next after the nativity of John the Baptist she "was shipped" at Margate, arriving next day at Sluys in Flanders. She was there received in great state with lighted torches and with pinnacles "subtillie devised in the towne and in the castell", and with many bonfires in the streets. A multitude of pageants were presented, with inscriptions to ensure that the meaning should not be missed. In Sluys she remained several days and there was visited one night by the Duke of Burgundy. "My lady met him at the hall door, and he kissed her in the open sight of all the people of both nations. After this he kissed all the English ladies and gentlewomen, but no others. . . . On Sunday the Duke came in the morning betwixt V and VI of the clock, and the pair were wedded by the Bishop of Salisbury and the Bishop of Tournay in the presence of the old Duchess of Burgundy, lords, knights, and esquires, ladies and gentlemen that came with my lady of England." Then my lady was set in a litter richly apparelled with crimson cloth of gold, her surcoat and her mantle white cloth of gold furred with ermine, and she herself richly crowned. Before her rode kings at arms, heralds, lords and knights, lords and ladies, to the sound of trumpets. Before her entry into the town of Bruges the master of the Florentines met her and gave her four coursers trapped with white damask, bordered with blue, and honoured her with fifty burning torches. "And they that bore the torches were clothed in crimson velvet, and those that were servants were clothed in crimson cloth." There was much minstrelsy, casting of flowers, and rejoicing of the people.

The estates of Bruges presented her with wine and wax, in honour and sovereignty, and besought her to be good and gracious lady to the town. At the city gate, which was richly covered with tapestry, she was received with minstrelsy and casting of flowers, and with processions lighted with cressets. Then came nine elaborate pageants, biblical and mythological. Finally, she arrived at the great hall, sixty-five paces long and thirty-two paces wide, hung with cloth of gold and the Duke's colours, purple and black, richly fringed. Great candlesticks lighted the hall and the roof, which was covered with cloth, pale blue and white.

Most prominent in the hall was a great cupboard, nine stages high, displaying cups, flagons, and pots. "On every corner" of the cupboard were "unicorns'[64] horns, the points garnished, and other three in other places, 'accomplishing'[65] the cupboard". Then came the banquet: the princess, after water was offered for her hands, sat in the place of honour, "and at the one side of the table was fifty-two ladies and gentlewomen and, at the other, lords and knights of both the nations, then the cupboard standing on the right side of the hall. And after dinner the Duke addressed him to the jousts and after the jousts to the banquet. And at his entering into the hall, the high table and the table on the left hand was equally accomplished[66] with great silver chargers, full of delicate meats, every mess covered with dishes equally. And on the Tuesday the Duke dined in his great chamber, and after dinner went to the jousts in this habit ensuing.[67] His gown was richly adorned with diamonds and pearls, and the trappings of his horse were decked with gold and pearls. And after the jousts, at his entry into the hall, [were] upon the high table seven chargers with meat, every charger covered with a tent, and upon every tent two banners, and upon the said table sixteen dishes, every dish pavilioned, on every pavilion a pennon of arms. And when the Duke was set, the tents and pavilions were taken from the messes, among the common people, whoso would. The number of the tents and pavilions [was] forty-six. And in the midward of the hall, where the cupboard stood, there was a curiously wrought castle [with] a warden, the which, with high voice, called up his meine[68] to make watch about time of the midst of the banquet, and blew a horn, and at the four windows of the castle appeared four great bears: then the warden bade his trumpet blow fast to recomfort this my fortress. And then each of the said bears had a trumpet with a banner of the Duke's arms, and held it with his forefeet subtilly, and blew each one of them stoutly well; and after that he had so done, he called his minstrels to make melody, and at the same windows where the bears were appeared goats with long pipes, and piped, and after a great prologue of himself in speaking called again upon [his] people to watch his castle, and at every window there appeared wolves, and after that appeared asses at the same windows. The fifth time he called one [of] his people to search his place, that no prejudice to his place in any wise might approach, and at every window and door issued apes and searched the place, and in the basse[69] court they found a chapman asleep with ware— many small things, as brooches, purses, laces, and glasses—the which the apes distributed to the abundance of the people, and at the waking of the chapman so distressed, he made a heavy countenance. And on the Thursday next, the Duke kept his estate in a gown richly beseen[70] of goldsmith's work, and in his chamber, sitting at two tables, sixty barons and baronets, and on his head a black hat, one that had a balas[71] in a pani[72] . . . called the Balas of Flanders, a marvellous rich jewel. And at four of the clock he came into the mart to the jousts, and after the jousts, to the chamber, and soon after to the great hall. The Duke and the Duchess, with all the lords and ladies, the hall at that time accomplished[73] with the candlesticks afore rehearsed, sixty tortettes,[74] and all the foresaid tables set with divers meats: first, a great platter set with divers meats after the fashion of the country, and every mess an elephant bearing his castle, with a subtlety, a swan roasted and silvered, marvellously standing in [a] targe; a peacock in like form, every peacock having a mantle of arms of the brother of the fleece of gold and the livery of the fleece, and an unicorn bearing trussing coffers full of comfits; an hart charged with a basket filled with oranges, and many dishes of delicates, marvellous to me: and so from mess to mess the high table aforesaid, equally through the hall; at every other mess a tortes abroach,[75] the chandeliers of silver. And [at] the said banquet [were] four histories of Hercules, countenancing,[76] and no speech. The history of the Duke's great chamber was the marriage of the daughter of King Cloit [Clovis] of France and the King of Burgundy, and what issue that they had, right rich arras; and after that, other chambers hanged [with] arras, silk, and tapestry, thirty-two chambers. And on the Sunday, the eighth day of the feast, at banquets four stories of Hercules. The first was how he chastised the thieves with his own hands; the second was how he slew the boar; the third, how he chastised the wild men of the wilderness; the fourth, how he set pillars in the sea. The banquet on Monday, at night, the Duke and Duchess, with estates of Lords and Ladies, came into the hall, the table accomplished[77] as ensueth: thirty targes, on every targe a tree of gold, with green leaves and blossoms of divers fruit, and some with divers fruits ripe, as oranges, apples, pears, roses, white and red, pomegranates, hawthorns blown, and divers other things marvellously wrought. The targe before rehearsed [was] wattled with gold within the wattling about the said tree, and every [one] of them filled with meats, divers great abundance, the which signified thirty abbeys under the Duke's obedience, and upon every tree a pennon of the Duke's arms, and the names of the abbeys. Between every tree a baken meat covered with a vine bearing grapes; tovttes a broach, every tortettes standing on a chandelier of silver; to every tree through the hall divers subtleties, drawing to the number of sixty; as men and women, some two men bearing a bar between them loaden with subtleties, and some[78] bearing a basket load, in like wise. Some like wives, as they came to the market ward, with a basket on her head and another in her hand; and some as a labourer bearing a great basket on his back with both his hands; and some as maidens spinning; and some as gentlewomen bearing a gentleman's hat in both hands; some as gentlewomen bearing fans [baskets], lood [loaded] in like form; some as gentlewomen, in the Dutch manner afore her in their kerchief of their head[s] [a] subtlety, and such divers other, more than I can write of. . . . And upon the high table, afore the estate, was made a goodly tower with four turrets, curiously wrought, and over the midst of the said tower there was a great glass standing upon a chest of gold, the glass accompassed[79] with battling[80] of gold and pinnacles; and on the roof an image of a man bearing a pennon of the Duke's arms of

Burgundy; and before the gates of the said tower an arbour walled and craftily made with flowers and herbs, and in the midst of the arbour a fountain made VIII square, and over each other square a banner of the Duke's arms, and on the roof a little image of a prophet holding up his hand, and out of his forefinger running a mighty stream of water of Damask.[81]

"To write of the jousts that daily was during the foresaid IX days in the market place of Bruges is over long a thing to be written in this abbreviat"; and we may well follow the example of the chronicler.[82]

CHAPTER VIII

FOOD AND HEALTH

I

WHEN we put aside the idealized conceptions of the Middle Ages and consider actual conditions we find that on the average life was far shorter than in our own time,[1] in part, it may be, owing to early marriages with the consequent weak offspring,[2] in part to unwholesome sanitary conditions and to ignorance of the laws of transmission of disease,[3] and in part to immoderate eating,[4] particularly of food prepared according to the prescriptions of the fashionable cookery books. The Church included gluttony among the Seven Deadly Sins, but the definition of gluttony appears to have been somewhat elastic, for even the Church had no special revelation as to how much was to be eaten or what food was to be shunned, beyond the general principle that rich and dainty foods were unsuited to those who had chosen a life of self-denial.[5] The practical rule appears to have been that one might eat and drink what one pleased, and to any amount —except, of course, on days of abstinence and during Lent—provided no immediate ill result ensued.

The festal diet described in the foregoing chapters doubtless strongly appealed to medieval appetites, or it would not for generations have remained popular. Quite possibly many persons, accustomed from childhood to the strange compositions prepared for banquets, accepted them as part of the order of nature. And, moreover, it is to be remembered that men and women outside the cloister lived a vigorous animal life, passed much time in the open air, and easily developed habits of over-eating.

But it is not to be supposed that human constitutions in the Middle Ages were so unlike our own that men and women could with impunity go on for years devouring vast quantities of indigestible food without suffering serious consequences. Obviously, however, we cannot attribute every early death in the period we are discussing to immoderate indulgence in unwholesome food. There were innumerable unsuspected channels in the Middle Ages by which plague and fever and loathsome skin diseases could claim their victims among rich and poor. No one realized the dangers lurking in the feet of the common housefly, in dust, in over-kept food, in stale fish, and often even in clear water. The helplessness of our ancestors in the presence of diseases now almost entirely extirpated in civilized communities by means of intelligent sanitation is indeed one of the most striking differences between medieval times and our own.

II

Of late years much attention has been given to foods and their relation to health. Exhaustive analyses have been made to determine the exact number of calories in various articles of diet and the effect of each upon the working power of the individual. The growth of commerce and of rapid transportation has enormously increased the number of foods available from all parts of the earth, and the ingenuity of manufacturers has devised a vast number of "breakfast foods" and special preparations of ordinary food that were altogether unknown even a half century ago. We have, too, an endless number of modern books that prescribe a diet adapted to practically every emergency.

To some extent this was the case throughout the Middle Ages, and although medieval medicine never emerged from empiricism closely akin to quackery, there was no lack of dogmatic remedies for various ills and particularly of advice on what we may call personal hygiene. Typical suggestions on diet appear in the *Secret of Secrets*,[6] of which the following are fair examples: "Have placed upon the table the dishes among which you may choose what will best suit you. Let all the food be of good quality. Eat first the meats most 'soluble', that is, digestible; then those that are 'coarse'. The first open the way for the second as far as the bowels. Whoever drinks water while eating or immediately after, extinguishes in himself the natural heat and troubles the digestion by corrupting the foods that have been taken. In any case, if it is necessary, drink little, and cold; and if the water is mixed with wine it is less to be feared." [7]

Among the short popular treatises on the preservation of health that were addressed to the laity none was more notable than the little work credited to the famous medical school of Salerno. The widely used *Regimen Sanitatis Salerni*, designed to preserve health and ward off the ailments of old age, enjoyed popularity from the middle of the eleventh century to the sixteenth, and presented brief aphorisms concerning what food to avoid and what to accept. As was the case with many medieval productions, the original treatise was in the course of time freely interpolated with additional material, but for our purpose this is a matter of indifference. The order of treatment is somewhat confused, but a few of the most characteristic suggestions may be taken for what they are worth.[8] Some of them are, indeed, very singular:

"Avoid peaches, apples, pears, cheese, venison, salt meat, goat's flesh, and hare. Flesh of ducks and geese is salt; fried meats are injurious." vii.

"To be recommended are fresh eggs, rich broth, red wine, wheat, milk [new cheese], marrow, testicles, brains, ripe figs, grapes." viii, ix.

> No acid taste should lurk in wholesome beer,
> Brewed from sound grain, it should be old, and cleare.
> xvii, xviii, xlvi.

> Nor fresh nor old be bread, but spongy, light,
> Tasteful, well baked, freed from all blight,
> ... shun the crust lest some dark flux should smite.
> xxiv.

> Pork is inferior to lamb unless taken with much wine.
> xxv.

> Entrails of swine alone are fit for food,
> All other beasts' [entrails] should wholly be eschewed.
> xxv. Additional MS.

"New wine is diuretic. It congests the spleen and the liver and causes stone." xxvi, xlv.

"Water drinking at meals chills the stomach; wine is preferable. But if very thirsty, drink from a cool *fountain*. Rain water is best." xxvii.

"Waters that flow towards the East are wholesome, but not those flowing South"! xxvii. Additional MS.

"Flesh of sucking calves, when sound, is very nourishing." xxviii.

"Eating eels hurts the voice. Cheese eaten with eels requires much drink." xxxi.

"Bean skins cause constipation, dry the phlegm, injure the stomach and eyes." xxxiii. Additional. Paris ed. 1861.

"Prunes cool the body and move the bowels." xlvi.

"Figs breed lice and stir up lust." xliii. Additional A.V.

"Turnips cause flatulence and spoil the teeth, stimulate the kidneys, and when ill cooked cause indigestion." xlvii.

"Heart and tripe are hard to digest." xlviii.

"Anise seed 'comforts' the stomach and improves vision." l. "Excess of salt injures sight and impedes reproduction, besides causing scabies, itching, or cramps." lii.

"The daily diet should not be changed, except when necessary." lvi.

"Sage soothes the nerves and quiets trembling hands; drives away fever." lx.

"Onions rubbed on the scalp restore fallen hair."

FOOD AND HEALTH

lxii. Additional A.V. says that "they cure dog bites if triturated with honey and vinegar".

"Mustard removes poison." lxiii.

"Violets cure headache, catarrh, falling fits, and drunkenness." lxiv.

"Nettles aid slumber, check nausea; mingled with honey they are a remedy for colic. When stewed they cure an old cough." lxv.

"Honey mixed with pounded chervil cures cancer"! lxvii.

"Saffron restores weak limbs and regulates the liver." lxxvii.

"Pepper white or black aids digestion, cures coughs, checks fever." lxxv.

In the sixteenth century the somewhat crude suggestions of the *Regimen Sanitatis Salerni* largely yielded place, in England at least, to Sir Thomas Elyot's *Castel of Helth* (1534) and to Andrew Boorde's *Dyetary* [9] (1542).

Elyot's whole system was based upon the famous doctrine of the "four humours", which itself left much to be desired. As expounded by Skeat [10]: "Diseases were supposed to be caused by an undue excess of some one quality; and the mixture of prevalent qualities in a man's body determined his complexion or temperament. Thus the *sanguine* man was thought to be hot and moist; the *phlegmatic*, cold and moist; the *choleric*, hot and dry; the *melancholy*, cold and dry. The whole system rested on the teaching of Galen, and was fundamentally wrong, as it is assumed that the elements or 'simple bodies' were four, namely, earth, air, fire, and water. Of these, earth was said to be cold and dry; water, cold and moist; air, hot and moist; and fire, hot and dry. They thus correspond to the four complexions, viz. melancholy, phlegmatic, sanguine, and choleric. Each principal part of the body, as the brain, heart, liver, stomach, etc., could be 'distempered', and such distemperature could be either 'simple' or 'compound'. Thus a simple distemperature of the brain might be an 'excess of heat'; a compound one, an excess of heat and moisture."

In Sir Thomas Elyot's own words: "By the increase or diminution of any of them in quantity or quality, over or under their natural assignment, inequal temperature cometh into the body, which sickness followeth more or less according to the lapse or decay of the temperatures of the said humours" (p. 8).

Sir Thomas is thoroughly steeped in the science of his time, and although many of his suggestions display excellent sense he cannot escape some pitfalls:

"The causes whereby the air is corrupted be specially four: Influences of sundry stars, stagnant waters, carrion, over-crowding" (p. 22).

Almonds.—"Five or six of them eaten afore meat keep a man from being drunk; they be hot and moist in the first degree" (p. 22b).

Lettuce.—"Among all herbs none hath so good juice as lettuce: for some men do suppose that it maketh abundance of blood, albeit not very pure or perfect" (p. 23b).

Beans.—Of these Elyot speaks slightingly as causing flatulence and being indigestible, but he adds: "If onions be sodden with them, they be less noyful" (p. 25b).

Onions.—"They stir appetite to meat, and put away lothsomeness, and loose the belly, they quicken sight, and being eaten in great abundance with meat, they cause one to sleep soundly" (p. 26b).

Rosemary.—Among other virtues, "It helpeth the cough, taken with pepper and honey; it putteth away toothache, the root being chewed or the juice thereof put into the tooth; being burned, the fume thereof resisteth pestilence" (p. 27b).

Of cheese he says: "Cheese by the whole sentence of all ancient writers letteth [hinders] digestion and is enemy to the stomach. Also it engendereth ill humours and breedeth the stone" (p. 33).

On the other hand, he highly commends drinking water (pp. 33b–34). But "to drink between meals is not laudable, except very great thirst constraineth, for it interrupteth the office of the stomach in concoction [digestion] and causeth the meat to pass faster than it should do, and the drink being cold, it rebuketh natural heat that is working, and the meat remaining raw, it corrupteth digestion and maketh crudeness in the veins; wherefore he that is thrifty let him consider the occasion" (pp. 33–34).

"Honey, as well in meat as in drink, is of incomparable efficacy, for it not only cleanseth, altereth, and nourisheth, but also it long time preserveth that uncorrupted which is put into it" (p. 37b).

Sugar.—"It is now in daily experience that sugar is a thing very temperate and nourishing, and where there is choler in the stomach or that the stomach abhorreth the honey it may be used for honey in all things wherein honey is required to be" (p. 38b).

Meals.—"I suppose that in England young men until they come to the age of fifty years may well eat three meals in one day, as at breakfast, dinner and supper, so that between breakfast and dinner be the space of four hours at the least; between dinner and supper vi. hours; and the breakfast less than the dinner, and the dinner moderate; that is to say, less than satiety or fulness of belly, and the drink thereunto measurable according to the dryness or moistness of the meat" (p. 43).

Eight years after Sir Thomas Elyot's *Castel of Helth* appeared Andrew Boorde's *Dyetary*.[11] This contains many excellent precepts and illustrates the good sense and the humour of the author, but it does not escape some of the errors and whimsies that beset all the early treatises on medicine and hygiene.[12] Boorde certainly does not lack racy phraseology when commenting upon food that is not to his taste. But although some of his strictures are obviously due to personal dislike, his judgment in many instances coincides with that of modern dieticians.

Like most men of his time, Boorde had a suspicion of drinking water, not altogether ill founded, considering the normal medieval indifference to proper sanitation. "Water", says he, "is not wholesome, sole by itself, for an Englishman, considering the contrary usage, which is not concurrent with nature: water is cold, slow, and slack of digestion." Rain water is best. "Next to it is running water, the which doth swiftly run from East into the West upon stones or pebbles." River or brook water, according to him, is third in excellence.[13] We note that Boorde reverses the direction prescribed for running water in the *Regimen Sanitatis Salerni*. Fortunately, both were equally right!

"Pottage", he says, "is not so much used in all Christendom as it is used in England. Pottage is made of the liquor in the which flesh is sodden in, with putting to chopped herbs, and oatmeal and salt" (p. 262).

He names oatmeal gruel and frumenty, and says that pease pottage is better than bean pottage. He also recommends almond milk and rice pottage.

"Fish and flesh", he remarks, "ought not to be eaten together at one meal" (p. 269).

He finds that the best fowl is the pheasant, and the partridge soonest digested. Among edible fowl he enumerates cranes, herons, bustards, but he adds the warning: "All manner of wild fowl, the which liveth by the water, they be of discommendable nourishment." Of peacocks he says: "Young peachicken of half a year of age be praised: old peacocks be hard of digestion" (pp. 269–70).

"The brawn of a wild boar is much more better than brawn of a tame boar: if a man eat neither of them both, it shall never do him harm"! (p. 274).

"All the inwards of beasts and of fowls, as the

heart, the liver, the lungs, and tripes, and trillibubs [inwards] with all the entrails is hard of digestion, and doth increase gross humours" (p. 276).

"Sanguine men be hot and moist of complexion wherefore they must be circumspect in eating of their meat, considering that the purer the complexion is the sooner it may be corrupted and the blood maybe the sooner infected . . . ; they must refrain from eating of old flesh and eschew the usage of eating of the brains of beasts and from eating the udders of kine" (p. 287).

"Choler is hot and dry; wherefore choleric men must abstain from eating hot spices, and refrain from drinking of wine and eating of choleric meat" (p. 288).

Like Sir Thomas Elyot, Andrew Boorde paid deference to the doctrine of the four humours, and hence: "The xxiiij Chapter sheweth a diet for 'Fleumatycke' men. 'Fleumaticke' men be cold and moist, wherefore they must abstain from meats the which is cold" (p. 288).

"Melancholy is cold and dry; wherefore melancholy men must refrain from fried meat and meat the which is over-salt"[14] (p. 289).

I shall not attempt to estimate the comparative merits of the *Castel of Helth* and of Boorde's *Dyetary*, but merely note that Sir Thomas Elyot died at the age of fifty-six and Andrew Boorde at fifty-nine.

NOTES

PREFACE

(1) Although for the sake of brevity I have used the term medieval, I have not aimed to cover the long, indefinite period embraced in the loose term Middle Ages, but in the main have dealt with the feasting of the fourteenth and fifteenth centuries and the beginning of the sixteenth, while also taking some account of features of earlier English diet. Moreover, in order to confine the discussion within reasonable limits I have found it necessary to fix attention mainly upon conditions in England, though not forgetting the indebtedness of the English cookery books to French sources.

It may, perhaps, be superfluous to note that in discussing the feast I have occasionally for convenience used the term banquet as equivalent to feast. It was not until the sixteenth century that it was occasionally used to indicate "a course of sweetmeats, fruit, and wine . . . a dessert".

CHAPTER I

(1) In Wynkyn de Worde's *Boke of Kervynge*, *Babees Book*, pp. 274-282, are enumerated the foods that are suitable for the feasts from Easter to Christmas.

(2) The well-known passage in which Bishop Latimer recounts the changes he had noted in his own lifetime sufficiently illustrates the transformation that was taking place.

(3) Certainly, the bed of the princess described in the *Squyr of Lowe Degre* (ed. Mead), pp. 831-852, can hardly be regarded as typical of ordinary furniture, even in families of the nobility. At all events, the bedroom of Henry VIII, lavish as he was in expenditure, displayed no such luxury as that depicted in this romance.

(4) Despite municipal ordinances, offal and other unsavory heaps accumulated in the London streets. See Riley, *Memorials of London*, pp. 339-340. The first information we have concerning Shakespeare's father is that he was fined for allowing such a public nuisance to remain in front of his house in Stratford.

(5) As a curious fact, I note incidentally that in some parts of England "windows, doors, lattices, and locks were regarded as tenants' fixtures to be removed" when the tenant departed. See A. Abram, *English Life and Manners in the Later Middle Ages*, p. 178.

(6) The sort of supplies for illuminating purposes provided for a great house may be seen in the *Northumberland Household Book*: Candles, p. 2; Wicks, pp. 2, 13; Wax, p. 2; Wax in torches, p. 3; Wax in quarions*, p. 3; Wax in tapers, p. 3; Candles, p. 2; Rosin (for torches), p. 13; Parish candles, p. 14.

(7) Some notable feasts of the fifteenth century on the Continent were illuminated with torches. In the household of Philip the Bold, Duke of Burgundy, six servants were appointed to hold flambeaux in their hands throughout the feast. And at the great feast given by the Comte de Foix described by Froissart there were no less than twelve such torch-bearers. In France, at all events, this practice to some extent continued, for the sake of making more display, even after candelabra came into fashion.

See Le Grand d'Aussy, *La Vie Privée des François d'Autrefois*, ed. de Roquefort, III, 170–171.

(8) See *Household Book*, fagots, pp. 3, 21; sea coal, p. 20; charcoal, p. 21.

(9) Sumptuous furred mantles were part of the equipment of a great house, and were handed down from one generation to another, so that we may perhaps imagine the state of these garments when they had arrived at the age of maturity.

CHAPTER II

(1) Ed. Percy, pp. 102–108.

(2) A typical entry is that relating to the number of swans provided yearly: "*Item*, a Warraunte to be servide oute Yerelie at Michalmes for twentie *Swannis* for th' Expencis of my Lordis House; As to saye for Cristynmas daie V— Sainte Stephins daie two—Sainte John daie two—Childremas

---

* Quarions were "square lumps of wax with a wick in the centre", *Our English Home*, p. 91.

daie ij—Sainte Thomas daie ij—Newyere daie iij—and for the xijth daie of Cristynmas iiij Swannes", p. 206.

(3) Long feasts are a feature of medieval romances. See *The Squyr of Lowe Degre*, l. 1114, for a feast lasting forty days. For other feasts of the same length, see *Havelok*, l. 2,344, (and Skeat's note), l. 2,950; *Libeaus Desconus*, ll. 1,048, 2,221. Cf. also Kölbing's note to *Amis and Amiloun*, l. 100; my note in *Selections from* Malory's *Morte Darthur*, p. 255; and Kaluza's note to *Libeaus Desconus*, l. 1,048. It is hardly necessary to remark that feasts protracted through several days included a great variety of entertainments and were not merely devoted to gormandizing, though that feature was by no means neglected.

(4) Warner, *Antiquitates Culinariae*, pp. 93-94.

(5) However moderate this sum may now appear, we have only to consider the changed value of money in the last four centuries to realize that it then represented a considerable fortune, probably more than $50,000, or some £10,000.

(6) See details in Warner's *Antiquitates Culinariae*, pp. 107-124.

(7) There were supplied: 8 oxen, 24 calves, 24 sheep, 20 lambs, 30 pigs, 12 pheasants, 108 capons, 240 chickens, 120 rabbits, 800 eggs, butter, iij*s*. VI*d*., 140 pair of pigeons, 32 gallons of milk, bread, iij. *li*., ix*s*., 20 barrels of "dobelle bere", 16 barrels of "syngelle bere", hogsheads of wine worth iij. *li*., xiii*s*. iiij*d*., besides XIII*s*. ii*d*. worth at "gentylmennes logenges".

The account includes also 10 loads of wood, 12s. 8d., 8 bushels of flour, 6s. 8d., salt, 3s. 6d., ale, 24s., hiring napery and washing, 6s. 8d., pepper, 14d., cloves and maces, 2s. 8d., saffron, honey, and "sawndres", 4s., "reysans of corauns", i.e. dried currants, 18d., powder of "sinamon, gynger and suger", 5s., candles, 2s. 6d., "erbes", 8d., mustard, 6d., "makenge of rakkes of tre to roste one", i.e. wooden racks for roasting, xij*d*., 12 labourers to help the cooks in the kitchen, 4s., 6 lads more to help, 18d., 4 washers of vessels, 12d., 12 dozen white cups, 10s., 64 great earthen pots, 3s. 4d., 12 ells linen cloth, 5s. 4d., hiring of pewter vessels and for loss, 19s. 4d., hire of xx doz. stone pots, 8s., 4 of the chief cooks' rewards, 13s. 4d., 2 porters for loading and unloading wine, 8d., expenses of "my masters horses at theyr ynnes", 44s. 6d.

228   THE ENGLISH MEDIEVAL FEAST

Expenses of Sir John Howard, 1462-1469, ed. Botfield, pp. 398-400.

(8) The expense for robes and other adornments and for the dinner itself made a total of £61 8s. 8d., or more than 6,000 dollars in money of to-day. The supplies included 3 hogsheads of wine, one white, one red, one claret, 2 oxen, 2 brawns, 2 (for 6) swans, 9 cranes, 16 heronsews, 10 bitterns, 60 couple of conies, as much wild fowl, 16 capons of grease (i.e. fat capons), 30 other capons, 10 pigs, 6 calves, 1 other calf, 7 lambs, 6 withers (wethers), 8 quarters of barley malt, 3 quarters of wheat, 4 dozen of chickens, besides butter, eggs, verjuice, and vinegar. See Samuel Pegge, *The Forme of Cury*, pp. 165-170.

Another Neville wedding feast on Jan. 14, 1526, cost £27 8s. Idem, pp. 171-174.

(9) I copy Stow's quaint spelling: "24 great beefes, 1 carcasse of an Oxe, 100 fat muttons, 51 great veals, 34 porks, 91 pigs, 10 dozen 'capons of grece' (i.e. fat), 9 dozen capons of Kent, 7 dozen cocks of 'grose', 19 dozen capons course, 14 dozen & 8 cockes, course, pullets the best, 2d. ob. (farthing), other pullets, 2d., 37 dozen pigeons, 14 dozen swans, 340 dozen larks at 5d. the dozen." *Survey of London*, ed. Kingsford, II, 36.

(10) See the Introduction by Raines, pp. VIII, XIII.

(11) "Already in the time of Henry III sugar, cummin, almonds, brazil, quicksilver, ginger, cetewal,* lake, liquorice, small spices, [such as cloves, mace, cubebs, and nutmegs] vermilion, glass, figs, raisins, shumac, sulphur, ivory, cinnamon, gingerbread, rice, turpentine, cotton, whalebone, frankincense, pyome [peony?], anise, dates, chestnuts, orpimemt, olive oil, etc., are noted as imports at the port of London." H. T. Riley, *Liber Albus*, p. 202.

(12) For interesting details of early English foreign trade, see Mrs. Green's *Town Life in the Fifteenth Century*, I, 77, 83, 84, 89, and especially Georg Schanz, *Englische Handelspolitik*, 2 vols., Leipzig, 1881.

(13) The official charged with purchasing supplies for the household of the Earl of Northumberland is required to be

---

* A stimulant having an aromatic, warm, bitter taste.

NOTES

if possible "at all fairs to buy supplies for the entire year—wine, wax, beeves, multons [i.e. sheep], wheat and malt. If he cannot go he is to appoint a substitute". *Northumberland Household Book*, p. 407.

(14) Cf. the comments of Le Grand d'Aussy on the housekeeping of Charles IX and Henry III as compared with that of Francis I, Henry II, and Francis II in *Histoire de la Vie Privée des François d'Autrefois*, ed. de Roquefort, III, 281–2.

(15) Much material for determining the cost of food and other household material is brought together in Bishop Fleetwood's "*Chronicon Preciosum* or Account of English Money, the Price of Corn and other Commodities, For the last 600 Years". London, 1707, pp. 181–186.

Even allowing for the difference in the purchasing power of money in the last six hundred years, many of the prices appear astonishingly low.

(16) H. T. Riley, *Memorials of London and London Life*, p. 426.

(17) *Liber Albus*, ed. Riley, p. 401. These and the preceding prices cited by Riley, it must be remembered, should be multiplied by at least fifteen or twenty before they can be compared with prices in our own day.

We may note also the caution suggested by Denton, *England in the Fifteenth Century*, pp. 94 ff., "Owing to the ravages of war and pestilence, prices fluctuated widely, so that too much dependence should not be put upon the prices recorded at any particular time as indicating the average for a number of years."

(18) Riley, *Liber Albus*, p. 624.
(19) Riley, *Memorials of London*, etc., p. 666.
(20) The caution is given that "no payhennes [are] to be bought". *Northumberland Household Book*, p. 191.
(21) See Riley, *Memorials*, pp. 37, 180, 323.
(22) Riley, p. 121.
(23) Idem, p. 423.
(24) "Of the finest wheaten flour."
(25) Paindemain and manchet.
(26) "Made of unbolted meal."
(27) Brown bread.
(28) Common white bread. See Riley, pp. 644–645.
(29) Idem, p. 121.
(30) Riley, p. 432.

CHAPTER III

(1) Some of the details here given are found in H. J. Feasey's *Monasticon*, p. 193.
(2) *Two Fifteenth Century Cookery Books*, p. 22, lxxxix.
(3) Idem, p. 28, Nos. 118, 119, 121.
(4) Idem, p. 31.
(5) Idem, p. 25. Cf. the similar receipt, Idem, p. 87.
(6) Idem, p. 98.
(7) Idem, p. 54. Compare the similar receipt, p. 76.
(8) "All ovens were of brick, some of them of immense size, and in kitchens of importance a double fireplace was usual to accommodate all the meats to be roasted." Percy Macquaid, in *Shakespeare's England*, II, 138-139.
(9) A. Franklin, *La Cuisine*, pp. 43, 44.
(10) At all events, there is no mention of it in the Oxford English Dictionary before 1599, when it appears in Ben Jonson's *Cynthia's Revels*, II, 1.
(11) All from Harleian MS. 279. Harleian MS. 4016 yields also more than can be quoted. Both in Austin, *Two Fifteenth Century Cookery Books*.
(12) See *Two Fifteenth Century Cookery Books*, p. 85. A more elaborate receipt appears on p. 21.
(13) Idem, p. 50, No. xvi.
(14) A notable exception is furmenty. To prepare this favourite dish, wheat is to be picked clean, hulled, winnowed, and washed; then boiled until it bursts, beaten up with milk, mixed with yolks of eggs, heated but not burned, coloured with saffron, seasoned with sugar and salt, and served.*
(15) Le Grand d'Aussy, *La Vie Privée des François d'Autrefois*, ed. de Roquefort, II, 19, 182.
(16) Le Grand d'Aussy, op. cit. II, 22. Cf. the derogatory remarks of de Roquefort on the swan, II, 24, note.
(17) A. Franklin, *La Cuisine*, p. 70.

---

* *A Noble Boke off Cookry*, ed Napier, p. 100. More complicated types of furmenty are found in *Two Fifteenth Century Cookery Books*. See Index.

NOTES

(18) *Oeuvres* (1607), p. 1,065, quoted by A. Franklin, op. cit., p. 19. Cf. *Le Ménagier de Paris*, II, 200, note 2.

(19) Various other receipts are found in the *Two Fifteenth Century Cookery Books*, pp. 17, 42, 105, and Index, s.v. "porpeys".

(20) Cf. S. Pegge, *The Forme of Cury*, pp. 176, 180, 184.

(21) *Two Fifteenth Century Cookery Books*, ed. Austin, p. 13, No. xl.

(22) Idem, p. 43.

(23) Cited by C. V. Langlois, *La Vie en France au Moyen Age de la Fin du XIIe au Milieu du XIVe Siècle d'après les Romans Mondains*, pp. 269–70. Illustrated ed. 1924.

(24) *La Cuisine*, p. 214.

(25) *Tableau de Paris*, IV, 123.

(26) In the entire range of medieval cookery books that we have enumerated the number of simple receipts is altogether negligible.

(27) *Two Fifteenth Century Cookery Books*, pp. 72 and 6 (the latter quoted also in the text, Chap. III, sec. xii, p. 81).

(28) Idem, p. 24.

(29) This powder, according to Cotgrave, was "compounded of Ginger, Cinnamon, and Nutmegs; in use among Cookes". As illustrating how persistent some of the old types of cookery are in out-of-the-way parts of the world, I may note that I myself had a poached egg served with a sprinkle of sugar in the island of Crete, but I found it uneatable.

(30) *Two Fifteenth Century Cookery Books*, p. 20.

(31) Idem, p. 113.

(32) Idem, p. 97.

(33) I.e. in thin long strips.

(34) Not in the Glossary or the Oxford Dictionary.

(35) *Two Fifteenth Century Cookery Books*, p. 15.

(36) Le Grand d'Aussy, *La Vie Privée des François d'Autrefois*, ed. de Roquefort, II, 254.

(37) Idem, op. cit., III, 340.

(38) Idem, op. cit., III, 256.

Worth quoting also is Alfred Franklin's comment upon the so-called *mets*, which persisted both in France and in England: "Dans une immense marmite on entassait des chapons, des perdrix, des canards, des dindonneaux, des cailles, des pigeons, qu'on laissait cuire pendant dix ou douze heures, mêlés à une foule de substances aromatiques, muscade, gingembre, poivre, thym, etc." *La Cuisine*, pp. 127-128. See also his remarks on p. 46 ff.

Though the roast meats on the same dish made a "mess", the various sauces were served separately, each for its appropriate meat.

(39) In the *Ménagier de Paris*, II, 155, specific directions are given for making a piece of beef taste like venison of the stag or like bear's flesh; or even (II, 200) how to make sturgeon imitate veal. In general, the highest aim of the medieval cook seems to have been to transform food of one sort into something quite different.

(40) *Two Fifteenth Century Cookery Books*, ed. Austin, p. 24, (C^{iii}).

(41) Idem, p. 72.

(42) Idem, p. 76.

(43) Idem, p. 49 (xij).

(44) Idem, p. 76.

(45) Idem, p. 7.

(46) Idem, p. 9 (xx).

(47) The reader may easily test these directions.

(48) For numerous other vague receipts see Idem, pp. 11, 12, 15, 16, 33, 35, 36, 37, etc.

(49) Idem, p. 22.

(50) Idem, Amidons are made of "wheat flour, steeped strained, and dried in the sun".

(51) Idem, p. 25.

(52) Cut in slices.

(53) *Two Fifteenth Century Books*, p. 35.

(54) They were legally entitled to a certain proportion of the meal, but since they measured as well as ground, they had frequent occasion to take advantage of the unsuspicious.

(55) Oxford English Dictionary, s.v.

(56) Cf. The *Northumberland Household Book*, p. xi. In England barley bread was commonly given to horses in the eighteenth century. See Le Grand d'Aussy, *La Vie Privée des François d'Autrefois*, ed. de Roquefort, I, 129.

(57) *The Bread of Our Forefathers* (Clarendon Press), pp. 132-133.

(58) Commenting upon the same topic, A. Redford, in the *Economic Journal*, September 1928, p. 458, remarks: "Even

NOTES

in the Middle Ages the bread corn of these privileged classes [colleges, cathedral chapters, great nobles] was admittedly wheat; and it is therefore natural to find wheat predominating in the cultivation of the demesnes. Not only nobles and monks but also merchants and well-to-do craftsmen in the great towns were already, by the middle of the thirteenth century, beginning to demand wheaten bread."

(59) Variously spelled, paynemain, paynemaynne, etc.
(60) Austin, *Two Fifteenth Century Cookery Books*, Glossary.
(61) Idem, Glossary.
(62) *A Noble Boke off Cookry*, p. 46.
(63) That is, originally, "keeper and cutter up of bread".
(64) *Babees Book*, p. 266.
(65) See *Northumberland Household Book*, pp. xv, 73, 75, 78.
(66) *Dyetary*, p. 261.
(67) Bile.
(68) Gloomy.
(69) In the *Northumberland Household Book*, p. 353, the chippings of trencher bread are directed to be kept for feeding the hounds.
(70) Modern English translation in the *Babees Book*, Part II, p. 37.
(71) Idem, Part I, 6/141.
(72) William Harrison, *Description of England*, Book III, Chap. I (1577), in *Elizabethan England*, ed. Withington, p. 96 f.
(73) A. Franklin, *La Cuisine*, p. 87, note 4. Marrow from long bones is fat and easy to get.
(74) Dickenmann, *Das Nahrungswesen in England*, *Anglia*, 27: 457.
(75) See S. Pegge's remark in *The Forme of Cury*, Introduction, p. xxii.
(76) See Glossary, "boter" and "butter".
(77) *Anglia*, 27, 470.
(78) Doubtless olive oil, which, of course, had to be imported. The frequently mentioned "grece" or "white grece" is the same as our lard.
(79) Napier, *A Noble Boke off Cookry*, p. 114.
(80) "Bruet of Almony", *The Forme of Cury*, (Warner), 47.
(81) Rabbits more than a year old.
(82) *The Forme of Cury* (Warner), 14.
(83) Idem, No. 131.

(84) Idem, No. 134.

(85) For the share of German merchant vessels in the spice trade, see Heyd, *Histoire du Commerce du Levant au Moyen Age*, I, 87-88; 726-727 (1886).

(86) "Spices were known in France", says Le Grand d'Aussy, "long before the Crusades, but they were not common until commerce with the Levant became active. Even then the expense of bringing them from India via Alexandria, or Smyrna, or Kaffa (Feodosia) made them enormously dear", *La Vie Privée des François d'Autrefois*, ed. de Roquefort, II, 174. He adds: "As long as the spices of the East arrived only via the Mediterranean they were brought by the Italians. But when the Portuguese by doubling the Cape of Good Hope to go to the Indies had found a route easier and safer, though longer, they got control of the commerce with those rich countries. In due time they were driven out by the Dutch, who appropriated their trade." II, 176.

(87) The kitchen of Jeanne d'Evreux, widow of King Charles le Bel, contained: 3 bales of almonds, 6 pounds of pepper, 13½ pounds of cinnamon, 23½ pounds of ginger, 5 pounds of grains of paradise (cardamon), 3½ pounds of cloves, 1½ pounds of saffron, ¼ pound of long pepper, 1 quarteron and ½ of massis (mastic?) ½ quarteron of cinnamon powder, 46 pounds of rice, 20 pounds of amidon (steeped, dried flour), 3 quarterons of aspic (the common name of lavender), 5 pounds of cummin, 20 pounds of sugar in four loaves. See Alfred Franklin, *La Cuisine*, pp. 45-46.

(88) The Expense Book was edited by Rev. John Webb (Camden Soc.), I, 115. See also Introduction, p. li.

(89) Pepper, p. 3; mace and cloves, pp. 3, 19; Ginger, p. 3; cinnamon, p. 19; anise, p. 19; saffron, pp. 3, 19; blaynsch powder,* pp. 3, 19; tornesole (sunflower), pp. 3, 19; mustard, pp. 18, 63; spices, p. 19; nutmegs, p. 19; galingale (cypress root).

(90) *Two Fifteenth Century Cookery Books*, p. 8.

(91) Idem, p. 9.

(92) Idem, p. 10.

---

* Blank powder is a mixture of ginger, cinnamon, and nutmegs. See *Two Fifteenth Century Cookery Books*, ed. Austin, Glossary.

NOTES

(93) Idem, p. 10.
(94) Idem, p. 18.
(95) Idem, p. 26.
(96) Idem, p. 18 (No. lxi), p. 19 (No. lxvii) (No. lxix), p. 21 (No. lxxxiii).
(97) Idem, p. 20 (No. lxxvi), p. 21 (No. lxxx), p. 22 (No. lxxxix), p. 23 (Nos. lxxxiv-lxxxviii), etc.
(98) Idem, p. 27 (No. cxv).
(99) Idem, p. 29.
(100) Idem, p. 29.
(101) The elaborate ceremony with which the spiced wine was served is described in detail in Warner's *Antiquitates Culinariae*, p. xli, note. The modern reader is tempted to scoff at such solemn fooling. For further comments upon spices at feasts, see Le Grand d'Aussy, *La Vie Privée des François d'Autrefois*, ed. de Roquefort, II, 307–310.
(102) Heyd, *Histoire du Commerce*, II, 683 ff. The sugar most prized was that from Cyprus; then that of Rhodes, of Syria, of Kerek, of Egypt, II, 693. Highly prized in the seventeenth century was the sugar of Madeira. See Moffett, *Health's Improvement* (1655), p. 250.
(103) *Our English Home*, p. 86.
(104) Heyd, *Histoire du Commerce*, II, 692–693.
(105) *Paston Letters*, ed. Gairdner, II, 102.
(106) Idem, iv, 210. See also V, 119–120.
(107) See *Two Fifteenth Century Cookery Books*, pp. 26, 27, 28, 29, 30, 31, 41, 51, etc., etc.
(108) Idem, p. 28, No. 120. See also, *The Forme of Cury* (Warner), No. 45, p. 41.
(109) There was abundance of salt in Cheshire and elsewhere, to say nothing of the unlimited supply of sea-water.
(110) Considerable quantities of meat, we are told, were also preserved by being covered with pigs' lard. See George Roberts, *Social History of the Southern Counties*, p. 334.
(111) "The verjuice of the English grape was boiled in an abundance of honey and spice and, being intended for immediate use, was seldom left to undergo the process of fermentation." *Our English Home*, p. 82.
(112) Le Grand d'Aussy, *La Vie Privée des François d'Autrefois*, ed. de Roquefort, II, 154–157.
(113) *Le Ménagier de Paris*, II, 248.

(114) See *Two Fifteenth Century Cookery Books*, p. 6. This receipt quite eclipses the one already presented in section vi.
(115) Idem, p. 72.
(116) Idem, p. 13, No. 36.
(117) Idem, p. 19.
(118) *Anglia*, 27, 458.
(119) *Two Fifteenth Century Cookery Books*, p. 40.
(120) Of bakemeats no less than thirty-eight varieties are enumerated in the *Two Fifteenth Century Cookery Books*, see pp. 47–56.
(121) *Dyetary*, p. 277.
(122) Le Grand d'Aussy, *La Vie Privée des François d'Autrefois*, ed. de Roquefort, II, 273.
(123) Op. cit., II, 277.
(124) *Two Fifteenth Century Cookery Books*, p. 53.
(125) Idem, p. 73.
(126) Idem, p. 38, No. 20.
(127) See *Fretoure* in *Two Fifteenth Century Cookery Books*, Index.
(128) Pages 34–46.
(129) Indigestible.
(130) Notwithstanding the vast consumption of meats variously minced and spiced, there appears to have been little or no use of sausage, at least under that name. The first mention of sausage (as an English word) in the Oxford English Dictionary is under the year 1553. Puddings, however, which appear to be substantially the same as sausages, are mentioned in the *Land of Cockayne* (1305), l. 59, and are common throughout the medieval period.
(131) A kind of heron.
(132) *Two Fifteenth Century Cookery Books*, pp. 57–58.
(133) Idem, p. 58.
(134) Idem, p. 62.
(135) Idem, p. 63. In the *Northumberland Household Book*, p. 183, we find the following entry: "It is thought good that sea gulls be hadde for my Lords owne Meas And none other. So they be good ande in Season and at id. a pece or id. ob. at the moiste."
(136) Idem, p. 67. See also *Our English Home*, p. 64.
(137) A favourite phrase in the *Forme of Cury* is "smyte hem to gobbets".

NOTES 237

(138) For roasting swans, cranes, pheasants, partridges, herons, bitterns, curlews, aigrettes, quails, plovers, woodcocks, etc., see Austin, *Two Fifteenth Century Cookery Books*, pp. 78–80.

(139) *Two Fifteenth Century Cookery Books*, p. 79. See also Chap. VI, sec. iii.

(140) For the use of peacocks, swans, and cranes on the tables of the German nobility, see A. Schultz, *Das höfische Leben zur Zeit der Minnesinger*, I, 284 ff.

(141) *Two Fifteenth Century Cookery Books*, p. 41.

(142) Two quarts.

(143) Skewer.

(144) Idem, p. 73.

(145) Idem, p. 9.

(146) Idem, p. 9 (xix).

(147) Idem, p. 40 (xxviii).

(148) *A Noble Boke off Cookry*, ed. Mrs. Napier, p. 36.

(149) *Dyetary*, p. 270.

(150) Details in *Two Fifteenth Century Cookery Books*, pp. 58, 59.

(151) Idem, pp. 59, 60.

(152) Idem, pp. 61–62.

(153) II, 101–103.

(154) Idem, Glossary.

(155) Le Grand d'Aussy, *La Vie Privée des François d'Autrefois*, ed. de Roquefort, II, 139–145.

(156) This commendation appears in Topsell's *Four-footed Beasts*, ed. Rowland, 1658, p. 36.

(157) In the Markets of Paris in 1393 one could similarly choose from a long list. See A. Franklin, *La Cuisine*, p. 18 f.

(158) *Two Fifteenth Century Cookery Books*, p. 106.

(159) Idem, p. 102.

(160) Idem, p. 103.

(161) See A. Franklin, *La Cuisine*, p. 19 and note.

(162) *Our English Home*, p. 69.

(163) *Two Fifteenth Century Cookery Books*, p. 42. See also *The Forme of Cury* (Warner), Nos. 69, 108, 116.

(164) *Two Fifteenth Century Cookery Books*, p. 52.

(165) La Rousse, *Dictionnaire Universel*, s.v. "sauce".

(166) Le Grand d'Aussy, *La Vie Privée des François d'Autrefois*, ed. Roquefort, II, 250.

(167) Peculiarly repulsive to modern taste would be the

perfumes that French cooks, especially of the seventeenth century, commonly added to their sauces and ragouts, notably rose-water and musk. Sauces that were not "piquant" contained sugar. Idem, II, 244.

(168) *Canterbury Tales* (Skeat), A 351-2.
(169) *Two Fifteenth Century Cookery Books*, p. 108.
(170) Idem, p. 109.
(171) See *The Forme of Cury*, No. 30, p. 9, in Warner's *Antiquitates Culinariae*.
(172) The "soul" is the "spongy lining of a goose's frame".
(173) Mrs. Napier, *A Noble Boke off Cookry*, p. 48.
(174) Pp. 108–110. Another group of seven appears on p. 77.
(175) Quite likely the fresh, mildly sharp, sour taste of the sorrel was deemed sufficient without further additions.
(176) A. Franklin, *La Cuisine*, p. 93.
(177) Kymer was Dean of Salisbury and Chancellor of the University of Oxford. He was also a physician of reputation and wrote a Dietary.
(178) B. Botfield, *Manners and Household Expenses in England in the Thirteenth and Fifteenth Centuries*, pp. xlvi–xlvii.
(179) Of "herbs" Andrew Boorde makes mention of borage, bugloss, artichokes, "rocket", chicory, endive, white beets, purslane, thyme, parsley, lettuce, sorrel, pennyroyal, hyssop, rosemary, roses, fennel, anise, sage, mandragora, with their qualities, and adds, "There is no Herbe nor weede but God hath gyven vertue them to helpe man." *Dyetary*, pp. 280 ff. (E.E.T.S.)
(180) Cf. the *Ménagier de Paris*, II, Table alphabetique des matières, laitue. There is no indication as to how it was prepared. When onions and cucumbers were used for salad in France they were recommended to be soaked several hours in vinegar.
(181) Cotgrave calls "composte a pickled or winter sallet of hearbes, fruits or flowers, condited in vinegar, salt, sugar, or sweet wine".
(182) Young onions.
(183) Small onions.
(184) Le Grand d'Aussy, *La Vie Privée des François d'Autrefois*, ed. de Roquefort, II, 264-265.
(185) See *Victorian County History*—Essex.

NOTES

(186) *A Noble Boke off Cookry*, pp. 25–112.
(187) *Liber Cure Cocorum*, p. 49.
(188) *A Noble Boke Off Cookry*, p. 34.
(189) Idem, p. 36. On page 37 the author suggests, "To roast eggs in lent—colour half with saffron."
(190) *Two Fifteenth Century Cookery Books*, p. 35, No. 4.
(191) Idem, p. 38, No. 20.
(192) Idem, p. 38, No. 19.
(193) Idem, p. 39, No. 22.
(194) Idem, p. 40, No. 28.
(195) Idem, p. 29, No. 129.
(196) Idem, p. 34, No. 152.
(197) Idem, p. 29, No. 124.
(198) Idem, p. 78.
(199) Idem, p. 36, No. 8. Cf. also p. 37, No. 17.
(200) *A Noble Boke Off Cookry*, p. 38.
(201) Idem, p. 87.
(202) Idem, p. 98.
(203) *Liber Cure Cocorum*, p. 37. This is for "powme dorrys", i.e., rissoles endored.
(204) "Un Vyaunde furnez sanz nom de chare", *Two Fifteenth Century Cookery Books*, p. 49, No. xiii, the *simpler* of the two receipts for this dish.
(205) For various other coloured foods, see Mrs. Napier, *A Noble Boke off Cookry*, pp. 59, 103, 106; *Liber Cure Cocorum*, p. 23. On p. 10 one is directed to colour "Nombuls" with "Brende [toasted] bred or with blode"; *Two Fifteenth Century Cookery Books*, p. 36, etc. This last receipt deals with "Lete lardes". One far more elaborate appears in *The Forme of Cury*, No. 68.
(206) *Two Fifteenth Century Cookery Books*, p. 7.
(207) Idem, p. 96. Caudell of almondes.
(208) Idem, see Glossary, "Allemaundys".
(209) Gerard in his famous *Herbal* (1597), p. 1, 256, remarks, "The naturall place of the Almond is in the hot regions, yet we have them in our London gardens and orchards in good plentie."
(210) See table of contents, Book I, *Two Fifteenth Century Cookery Books*.
(211) The last three are also in Book II, along with duplicate receipts of those in Book I.

(212) See the "Kalender" of the *Boke*.
(213) *A Noble Boke off Cookry*, p. 76.
(214) *Two Fifteenth Century Cookery Books*, p. 7.
(215) I.e. the time required to walk a furlong.
(216) Ground or pounded meat.
(217) Idem, *Books*, p. 24.
(218) Idem, pp. 12, 37, 88.
(219) Idem, pp. 12, 87.
(220) Idem, p. 20.
(221) Idem, pp. 27, 51, 97.
(222) Idem, pp. 30, 113 (and *Ancient Cookery*, No. 2 (Warner) pp. 39, 42).
(223) Idem, p. 28.
(224) Idem, p. 29.
(225) Idem, p. 51.
(226) Idem, p. 12, No. 35.
(227) *Two Fifteenth Century Cookery Books*, p. 12, No. 34.
(228) The peel is "a flat, spade-shaped tool used by bakers to take dishes, etc., out of the oven".
(229) Idem, p. 50, No. xv.
(230) Idem, p. 75. Compare the similar receipt on page 53.
(231) Baker's flat shovel.
(232) *Two Fifteenth Century Cookery Books*, p. 51, No. xviii. A somewhat similar receipt appears on p. 73.
(233) Idem, p. 16, No. 54.
(234) Idem, p. 37, No. 16.
(235) Idem, p. 92.
(236) Idem, p. 93.
(237) Idem, p. 92.
(238) Idem, p. 93.
(239) Incidentally, we may note that in the course of time the fashion of perfuming food, particularly in France, became popular. English cooks, as a rule, were less extreme in thus "improving" the flavour or odour of the festal diet than the French, but they went farther than modern taste can follow them. Musk was freely used in perfuming desserts, to say nothing of gloves and other wearing apparel. Into various English receipts in the fifteenth century and later enter roses, violets, primroses, and flowers of hawthorne, whether for the perfume or the flavour we are not informed. See *Two Fifteenth Century Cookery Books*, Glossary—Hawthorn,

NOTES

Primrose, Roseye, Vyolet; Warner's *Antiquitates Culinariae, A Noble Boke off Cookry*, etc. As for France, Alfred Franklin remarks, "The rage for perfumes which infected the court from the sixteenth century up to the middle of the reign of Louis XIV did not even respect the ragouts, the pastry, the liqueurs, and so forth. There were mingled iris, rose-water, marjoram; and the cook had always to keep under his hand musk and ambergris. Grilled tongue of pork was perfumed. Little patés and cakes were made with musk. Confitures, pralines, and marchpane were also saturated with musk." See *La Cuisine*, pp. 128, 129. See also Le Grand d'Aussy, op. cit. II, 244.

(240) The first mention of breakfast in the Oxford English Dictionary is under the year 1463, but with no indication of what it consisted. The old romances afford some help. For example, in the Didot *Perceval*, ed. Hucher, p. 478, the breakfast, after mass is heard, consists of bread and wine. To this day, the traveller through Central and Southern France may often see people dipping bread or light rusk into wine as their sole allowance for the early breakfast, which is literally a break-fast.

(241) *Orders and Rules of the House of the Princess Cecile*, Mother of Edward IV, in *Ordinances and Regulations of the Royal Household*, p. 39. The hours prescribed for meals in her household are not without interest. Upon "eating days" dinner is to be served by eleven of the clock for carvers, sewers, and officers; upon fasting days by twelve of the clock, and a later dinner for carvers and waiters. Supper for carvers and officers comes at four o'clock: for my lady and household at five o'clock.

(242) For all details, see *Northumberland Household Book*, ed. Percy, pp. 75, 76, 78, 79. For food in Lent, see pp. 80–87.

(243) *Household Book*, pp. 88–95.

(244) The picture that Chaucer presents of the poor widow who lived mostly on white and b ack (milk and brown bread), broiled bacon, and sometimes an egg or two (*Nonnes Preestes Tale*, B. ll. 4,022 ff.), and the suggestive allusions in *Piers Plowman* to the beggarly diet of the labouring classes, sufficiently indicate that the type of food described in the medieval cookery books was designed for those to whom economy was not a necessity.

(245) Ordinances made at Eltham in *Ordinances for the Royal Expenses*, p. 164.
(246) *Two Fifteenth Century Cookery Books*, p. 11, No. xxix.
(247) Idem, p. 104.
(248) Although in the English fifteenth-century cookery books simple receipts are rare, there are in the considerably earlier *Ménagier de Paris* (1393) a good number that would be acceptable in our time. Possibly it is significant that the *Ménagier* was written by an elderly husband for a young wife.
(249) See *Household Book*, p. 165, middle.
(250) See pp. 57 f. 60, 115 ff. (indicating prices to be paid for food, etc.), 173–176.
(251) Idem, p. 206.
(252) Idem, p. 205.
(253) Idem, p. 214.
(254) See Idem, pp. 280 ff. for the scattered items.
(255) For *succade*, "sweetmeats of candied fruits or vegetable products".
(256) Quince marmalades.
(257) "A kind of pie or tart", especially a baked meat pie.
(258) *Description of England*, Book III, Chap. I (1577), ed. Withington, pp. 91–93, 98.

CHAPTER IV

(1) The condemnation of drunkenness repeatedly expressed by Chaucer, himself the son of a vintner, is particularly interesting.

(2) As a manufacturing industry, the distillation of brandy in France began in the fourteenth century. But it appears to have been regarded rather as a medicine than as a beverage; and at all events it seems to have played no part in English feasts. See *Encyclopedia Britannica*, 13th edition, xxv, 694–695.

(3) The Anglo-Saxon hall was commonly called a mead hall, clearly indicating its primary purpose. It is suggestive, too, that in Anglo-Saxon poetry a feast is regularly called a *bēorscipe*, the food apparently being regarded as a negligible item, since it is never mentioned.

(4) A. Boorde, *Dyetary of Helth*, p. 257.
(5) Weinhold, *Die Deutschen Frauen im Mittelalter*, II, 15.

NOTES

(6) "Bride-ale was so called from the bride selling ale on the wedding day and friends contributing what they liked in payment of it." Richard Valpy French, *Nineteen Centuries of Drink*, p. 123.

(7) "In 1309 London is said to have contained 354 taverns and 1,334 breweries."—Charles Pendrell, *London Life in the Fourteenth Century*, p. 105. He adds: The population of London "according to the statistics in connection with the poll tax of 1380, numbered 20,397 persons over the age of fifteen; and so providing there had been no material variation in the intervening years, we have the astonishing result of one drink shop to every twelve inhabitants".

(8) *Our English Home*, p. 88.

(9) *Encyclopedia Britannica*, 11th ed., s.v. *Ale*. See also Heyn, *Migration of Plants and Animals*, translated by Stallybrass, pp. 358, 359.

(10) Godesgood is an old term for barm or yeast.

(11) *Dyetary of Helth*, p. 256.

(12) Idem, p. 256. Boorde mentions also "cyder", "meade", "metheglyn", "whay", "poset ale", pp. 256-257.

(13) R. V. French, *Nineteen Centuries of Drink*, p. 133.

(14) Le Grand d'Aussy, *La Vie Privée des François d'Autrefois*, ed. de Roquefort, II, 400. See also his entire fourth chapter on "Medieval Wines". He adds in a note that Champier, who wrote about a hundred and fifty years after Froissart, observes that in his time England consumed scarcely any other wines or grains than those of France and that when the commerce was checked by war she suffered famine. On French wines imported into England, see also R. V. French, *Nineteen Centuries of Drink*, pp. 66, 67.

(15) *Our English Home*, p. 81.

(16) R. V. French, op. cit., p. 109. Cf. also Charles Pendrell, *London Life in the Fourteenth Century*, p. 106.

(17) *Boke of Kervynge* (*Babees Book*), p. 267.

(18) See the long list in *Colyn Blowbol's Testament* (?1475-1500 A.D.), printed in Halliwell's *Nugae Poeticae*, 1844, and *Hazlitt's Popular Poetry*, I, 106, II, 324-341; *The Squyr of Lowe Degre*, ed. Mead, ll. 753-762; Furnivall's note to Andrew Boorde's Works, E.E.T.S. Extra Series, X, p. 327.

(19) *Babees Book*, pp. 202-203.

(20) R. V. French, op. cit., p. 121.

(21) For the allowance of ale, see the *Household Book*, p. 2; beer, p. 2; hops, pp. 2, 11; malt, p. 4.
(22) *The Losely MSS.*, ed. Alfred John Kempe, 1835, p. 11.
(23) R. V. French, op. cit., p. 130.
(24) Idem, p. 131–132.
(25) Sunflower seeds?
(26) For these receipts, see Pegge, *The Forme of Cury*, p. 161.
(27) See Henderson, *History of Modern Wines*, pp. 283–284.
(28) Le Grand d'Aussy, *La Vie Privée des François d'Autrefois*, ed. Roquefort, III, 65–68.
(29) Page 5, iiij. back.
(30) Hindreth.
(31) Embers.

CHAPTER V

(1) In the Household Statutes of Bishop Grossetest, c. 1450–60, the ninth provision is that all the household are to dine together in the hall. See *Babees Book*, E.E.T.S., p. 329.
(2) Sixty-five by forty-three feet. See illustration in H. W. C. Davis's *Mediaeval England*, pp. 55–57.
(3) This is one hundred and six feet long, forty feet wide, and sixty feet high. The massive ceiling is of oak, with the beams exposed, and the windows are filled with stained glass. It is pictured in colour in Charles Knight's *Old England*, II, 14.
(4) Among the more notable halls in England may be cited the hall of the Middle Temple and the Guil hall in London; Crosby Hall, of the fifteenth century, formerly in the City of London, now removed to Chelsea, stone by stone, and rebuilt; St. Mary's Hall at Coventry; the great hall at Knole Park, Sevenoaks, Kent, with its carved musicians' gallery, its ceiling, panelling, and oak screen; and the famous hall of Penshurst Castle, with its central brazier and its louvre in the roof.
(5) J. A. Gotch in H. W. C. Davis's *Mediaeval England*, p. 61.
(6) *Our English Home*, p. 22.
(7) In the course of time the great fireplace in the chimney at one of the long sides of the hall was substituted for the brazier in the centre, but in severe weather even this left something to be desired.

NOTES

(8) *Our English Home*, p. 145.

(9) In J. H. Parker's *Domestic Architecture in England from Edward I to Richard II*, p. 40, is an illustration of the dais with the high table and tapestry, taken from Brit. Mus. Add. MS. 12228, fol. 126. There are six guests—a king and queen with two men and two women. The diners sit only on the *inner* side of the table.

(10) See the reproduction in Warner's *Antiquitates Culinariae*, p. xxii f. Most likely, what is here pictured is the chief table, which, of course, would be placed upon the dais.

(11) This is quoted in Jortin's *Life of Erasmus*, I, 69 (1801), and in the *Babees Book*, p. lxvi.

(12) In some great houses a permanent table, known as a "table dormant", was maintained. Such a table, richly supplied, Chaucer credits to his Franklin.

(13) The term *banquet* is from "A. F. *banquet*, dim. of *banc* bench—cf. *table*, board, in sense of meals". *Oxford English Dictionary*, s.v.

(14) *Merlin, or the Early History of King Arthur*, edited by H. B. Wheatley, E.E.T.S., 1869, pp. 614–615.

(15) Great.
(16) Held.
(17) Baronage.
(18) Pavilions.
(19) Such.
(20) Becoming.
(21) Offering.
(22) Bare.
(23) Honour.
(24) Leapt.
(25) Each.
(26) Them.
(27) Heads.
(28) Dais.
(29) In a row.

CHAPTER VI

(1) The description is taken from Bartholomew Anglicus, *De Proprietatibus Rerum* and printed in G. C. Coulton's *Social Life in Britain from the Conquest to the Reformation*, pp. 374–375.

The quaint English translation is that of Trevisa (ed. 1536), f. 81a, Liber VI, Chap. 23-24. To the average reader the passage presents small difficulty, but I have ventured to modernize the antiquated spelling and substitute an occasional modern word for an old one.

(2) Appropriate.
(3) Made ready.
(4) Divided.
(5) For *when?*
(6) Scraps.
(7) *Atte mere.* As a rule, *mere* means boundary, and a reasonable interpretation here seems to be *threshold.*
(8) Do honour to.
(9) Suitable.
(10) *Text,* siker.
(11) *Text,* kynde.
(12) Are not accustomed.
(13) Tapers.
(14) Especially.
(15) Duration, continuance.
(16) Toward.
(17) Invited.
(18) Agreeable.
(19) Most of the silks brought into Europe in the Middle Ages came from Alexandria, Tripoli, Damascus, Antioch, Syria, Cyprus, Asia Minor, Greece, but Spain, Sicily, and some parts of Italy produced a good deal. See Heyd, *Geschichte des Levantehandels im Mittelalter* II, 670-696.
(20) Note, for example, the various descriptions of feasts and public celebrations in the chronicles of Edward Hall.
(21) See the *Babees Book,* 129/187, 268/23. Note the care with which the cloth must be removed from the table. Ibid., 343/399.
(22) See Le Grand d'Aussy, *La Vie Privée des François d'Autrefois,* ed. de Roquefort, III, 285-289.
(23) Idem, II, 246.
(24) *Our English Home,* p. 40.
(25) Description of England in Holinshed's *Chronicles* (1575), Book III, Chap. I.
(26) See the detailed description, with coloured illustration, of *The Royal Gold Cup in the British Museum,* London,

1924. "The cover, bowl, and standard, all of solid gold, are magnificently decorated with enamelled subjects in the manner of the fourteenth century, to which period the costumes represented belong", p. 1. The cup dates from the end of the fourteenth or the beginning of the fifteenth century and is of French workmanship.

(27) In France and pretty certainly also in England, middle-class households contented themselves with a salt-cellar consisting of a piece of bread hollowed out in the centre. A. Franklin, *La Cuisine*, p. 57, note 6.

(28) An English lady told me recently of a dinner that she attended at a country house in Yorkshire where a peacock in his plumage adorned the table.

(29) See Le Grand d'Aussy, *La Vie Privée des François d'Autrefois*, ed. Roquefort, I, 362-367, and De la Curne de Sainte-Palaye, *Memoires sur l'Ancienne Chevalerie*, I, 184, 187, 244, 246, III, 394, English translation, 1784.

(30) Le Grand d'Aussy, *La Vie Privée des François d'Autrefois*, ed. Roquefort I, 318-319.

(31) See *Household Book*, pp. 253-258, for their duties and wages. See also the list of servants working in the kitchen, larder, scullery, bakehouse, brewhouse, wardrobe, armoury, and mill, pp. 325-328.

(32) *Household Book*, pp. 408-410.

(33) The vast household of Warwick the Kingmaker (1428-71), with its great array of servants and men at arms, has become proverbial.

(34) George Cavendish, *Life of Cardinal Wolsey*, ed. Singer, pp. 34-35.

(35) Idem, p. 37. The estimates of the size of Wolsey's household differ widely. In Wordsworth's edition of Cavendish it is 180; in Singer's (1825), 500; in the edition of 1641, 800.

(36) This included: Marshall of the hall, 1; Ushers of the hall, 2; Usher of the chamber, 1; Sewers of the hall, 6; Herbergers, 2; Master cooks, 3; Queen's butler, 1; Total 16. *Ordinances and Regulations of the Royal Household*, p. 4.

(37) See the *Babees Book*, E.E.T.S., pp. 299-321.

(38) Much of Wynkyn de Worde's *Boke of Kervynge*, e.g. p. 272 f., follows rather closely the wording of Russell's *Boke of Nurture*, p. 140, ll. 377 ff., with intermittent omissions. Cf. Russell's recipe for Ypocras with W. de Worde's, p. 267.

See also Furnivall's comments on this same matter, *Babees Book*, p. CXI.

(39) See the *Babees Book* (E.E.T.S.), p. 265.

(40) Idem., p. 271.

(41) The *Babees Book*, E.E.T.S., p. 276.

(42) Le Grand d'Aussy, *La Vie Privée des François d'Autrefois*, ed. de Roquefort, III, 346.

(43) Cf. *Our English Home*, pp. 61, 62.

(44) "Forks for special purposes [i.e. to assist the carver] had been known in England since the middle of the fifteenth century; a bequest of 1463 includes 'a silver forke for grene gyngour', and one of 1554 mentions a 'spone with a forke in the end'." Percy Macquoid *Shakespeare's England*, II, 133, note.

(45) *Canterbury Tales*, Prologue, ll. 127 ff.

(46) Le Grand d'Aussy remarks in 1783 that apparently up to the epoch when forks began to be employed "On se servoit du couteau pour porter à la bouche les morceaux coupés; ainsi que font encore les Anglois, qui ont pour cela des couteaux dont la lame est arrondie et très large par le bout." *La Vie Privée des François d'Autrefois*, ed. de Roquefort, III, 179.

(47) Cited in *Oxford English Dictionary*, s.v.

(48) *La Vie Privée des François d'Autrefois*, ed. de Roquefort, III, 167. For evidence of the early use of serviettes and napkins in England, see the *Oxford English Dictionary*, s.v.

(49) *Old English Cookery*, in *Quarterly Review* (1894), clxxviii, 86.

(50) An illustration of a gentleman and a lady washing before dinner, taken from Thomas Wright's *History of Domestic Manners and Customs*, p. 156, is among the wood-cuts prefacing Furnivall's *Babees Book*, E.E.T.S., 1868. For various details, see also Le Grand d'Aussy, *La Vie Privée des François d'Autrefois*, ed. de Roquefort, III, 310, 312; *Ménagier de Paris*, II, 247; *Our English Home*, p. 53; *Archaeologia*, X, 252; and innumerable passages in medieval romances.

(51) Edited by Dr. Furnivall in 1869 for the E.E.T.S., Extra Series, VIII.

(52) See Russell's *Boke of Nurture*, ll. 1,195 ff. The tasting was thought to be unnecessary for any under the rank of earl.

(53) A. Franklin, *Les Repas*, p. 21.

(54) A. Franklin, *La Cuisine*, p. 22.

NOTES

(55) *Babees Book*, II, 35-53.
(56) Austin, *Two Fifteenth Century Cookery Books*, pp. 57-58.
(57) Although most feasts were more notable for their abundance than for the delicacy of the dishes, they had already in the ninth year of the reign of Edward II become so luxurious that by proclamation the King decreed that his subjects "should have only two courses of flesh meat served up to their tables, each course consisting of only two kinds of flesh meat", and "on fish days only two courses of fish, each course of two kinds, with an intermeat, if they saw fit". *Introduction to Ordinances and Regulations of the Royal Household*, pp. VIII, IX. Needless to remark, the feasts of Edward II's successors were unhampered by the royal proclamation.
(58) Warner, *Antiquitates Culinariae*, p. 98.
(59) *Ménagier de Paris*, II, 91.
(60) Idem, II, 92.
(61) Idem, II, 93, see the entire list, pp. 91-103.
(62) See *Two Fifteenth Century Cookery Books*, pp. 59-62.
(63) See A. Franklin, *Les Repas*, p. 60.
(64) For the entertainment of guests during and after the feast, see section VII.
(65) Until recently America lagged far behind England.
(66) *Babees Book*, p. 303, ll. 134-135.
(67) In the old sense of the word, *mess* signifies the portion provided for one or more persons, and has none of the disagreeable modern implications.
(68) The temptation must have been almost irresistible, and there is abundant evidence that the knife was often used when a spoon would have better served the purpose.
(69) A typical group of these little treatises in Latin, French, Italian, and English are conveniently brought together in Furnivall's *Babees Book*, E.E.T.S., 1868.
(70) *Boke of Nurture*, ll. 189-192.
(71) Ll. 217-220.
(72) Ill-smelling breath, ll. 229-230.
(73) Ll. 237-238.
(74) *Boke of Nurture*, ll. 241-242.
(75) Ll. 249-252.
(76) Ll. 261-263.
(77) Ll. 281-284.
(78) Ll. 289-292.

(79) Ll. 308-312.

(80) Erasmus says: "It is a great piece of incivility, when you have your fingers dirty and greasy, to carry them to your mouth to lick them, or to wipe them on your jacket: it will be more decent to do it on the tablecloth or napkin." See his *De Civilitate Morum Puerilium*, Basel, 1530.

(81) Ll. 333-336.

(82) Even in France the usages of polite society appear strangely primitive to well-bred people of our time: "Up to the middle of the sixteenth century", in France at least, "there was often only a single drinking-glass for the entire table. Hence before drinking, a man well brought up had to wipe his mouth on his serviette or on the table-cloth. If one dined with a wealthy host and there was a glass for [eve y] two guests, one was advised to empty it completely every time that one drank so as to leave nothing for his companion." A. Franklin, *Les Repas*, p. 104.

(83) Quoted by Warton, *History of English Poetry*, ed. Hazlitt, III, 200.

(84) See the menu in *Two Fifteenth Century Cookery Books*, pp. 57, 58.

(85) See the account in Le Grand d'Aussy, op. cit.

(86) In the old use of the word a *cake* is merely a term for a flat or thin loaf of bread.

(87) *Two Fifteenth Century Cookery Books*, p. 39, No. 24. I have slightly modernized the phraseology.

(88) It is interesting to note that the famous English plum cake is not mentioned before 1635.

(89) A. Franklin, *Les Repas*, p. 63.

(90) Le Grand d'Aussy, *La Vie Privée des François d'Autrefois*, ed. de Roquefort, III, 323.

(91) Idem, III, 334.

(92) Idem, III, 337.

(93) Hence even in the sixteenth century, "Champier advises thus to be eaten early in the meal the fruits that are naturally watery, refres ing, and likely to decay readily, such as cherries, mulberries, strawberries, plums, peaches, apricots, etc. He allows for dessert none but astringent fruits, such as medlars, apples, quinces, and pears, besides pistache, filberts, and almonds." Le Grand d'Aussy, op. cit. III, 332-333.

(94) *Encyclopedia Britannica*, 11th ed, s.v. "lemon".

(95) In *The Forme of Cury*, dating from the reign of Richard II, a good number of fruits are named as forming part of the ingredients in various receipts. The list here given is not exhaustive and is made up from Warner's reprint in his *Antiquitates Culinariae*, pp. 1–35. The figures indicate the numbers of the receipts: Apples, 79, 156, 182; cherries, 58; dates, 167; figs, 167, 182; grapes, 30 (used for stuffing geese) and 34 (for stuffing chickens); mulberries, 99, 132; pears, 30, 132, 158, 182; pomegranates, 27, 84; prunes "damsyns", 156, 158, 167; quinces, 30; raisins, 130, 154, 167, 182; raisins (currants), 154, 156.

(96) See pp. 3–19.

(97) He gives warning, p. 285, that "Mylons doth engender evyl humours".

(98) The interesting information is given in Champier's *Rosa Gallica*, Book III, pars. iv, Chap. 16, that figs breed lice! "Si quis vero ficum frequentem comestionem pediculi in corpore eius generantur."

(99) Honey was often substituted for sugar in preserving fruit.

(100) A. Franklin, *La Cuisine*, p. 90, quotes a singular passage from Lemery, *Traité des Aliments* (1705), p. 57: "Les dactes ne sont guère en usage ici que pour médicine. On les estime propre pour fortifier l'enfant dans le ventre de sa mère."

(101) *Antiquitates Culinariae*, pp. 91–92.

(102) Le Grand d'Aussy, *La Vie Privée des François d'Autrefois*, ed. de Roquefort, II, 317.

(103) The dragées were notably popular in the sixteenth century and later. For a detailed account of their manufacture and use, see Larousse, *Grand Dictionnaire Universel*, s.v.

(104) In the menus of the feasts cited in *Two Fifteenth Century Cookery Books*, ed. Austin, pp. 56–63, the "sotelties" are regularly cited along with the food, as part of the banquet. See also pp. X, XIV. The same is true of the descriptions of medieval feasts in the old *Chronicles* and elsewhere. See S. Pegge, *Forme of Cury*, Glossary; Napier, *A Noble Boke off Cookry*, p. 133.

(105) See the complete menu in Mrs. Napier's edition of *A Noble Boke off Cookry*, pp. 4–6.

(106) Ensueth.
(107) *Fleur de lis.*
(108) Ostrich.
(109) Fabyan's *Chronicle*, ed. H. Ellis, pp. 599–601.
(110) See Warner's *Antiquitates Culinariae*, pp. 107–124.
(111) Substantially the same as folding.
(112) Anyone interested in the elaborate foolery involved in removing the surnappe will find the whole described in full in Warner's *Antiquitates Culinariae*, p. 105.
(113) *Void* is for *voidee*, a supplementary collection of wine, spices, comfits, etc., served at the close of the feast.
(114) Pastry puffs.
(115) Warner, op. cit., pp. 114–115.
(116) Cf. Floire et Blanceflor, ll. 2,872 ff.
(117) A similar tale is related in Larousse's *Encyclopedie* (s.v. Nain) of a dwarf at the wedding feast of a duke of Wurtemberg.
(118) By no means was the fondness for amusement limited to the aristocracy: "The townspeople all took their part not only in the serious and responsible duties of town life, but apparently in an incessant round of gaieties as well. All the commons shared in supporting the minstrels and players of the borough. Mrs. Alice Green, *Town Life in the Fifteenth Century*, I, 145.
(119) See the illustrations prefixed to the *Babees Book*, ed. Furnivall, E.E.T.S., 1868.
(120) For these instruments, see Cutts, *Scenes and Characters of the Middle Ages*, 3rd ed., 1911, p. 109. He says, in part, "The most common are the harp, fiddle, cittern or lute, hand-organ, the shalm or psaltery, the pipe and tabour, pipes of various sizes played like clarionets but called flutes, the double pipe, hand bells, trumpets and horns, bagpipes, tambourine, tabret, drum and cymbals." See also his comments, pp. 267–308. Illustrations of most of these instruments are given by Cutts.
(121) In the enthusiastic words of Rosières, *Histoire de la Société Française au Moyen Age*, p. 482, "Des ménétiers accompagnent les barons aux chevauchées; à toutes les fêtes royales, à toutes les cérémonies des châteaux, à toutes les solennités religieuses, aux grands festins, aux pas d'armes, aux tournois, aus cavalcades, aux chasses, des symphonies retentissent.

Bien des barons savent jouer de la harpe, les clercs les moins lettrés composent des hymnes et écrivent des traites sur l'harmonie, les riches bourgeois eux-mêmes se plaisent souvent à réunir dans leur maison des instruments de toutes sortes. Et les ménétriers de Par s sont si nombreux qu'ils occupent a eux seuls toute une rue, si riches qu'ils possedent un hôpital et une église, si puissant que, des 1407, leur roi commande aux ménétriers de la France entière."

(122) For two long lists of minstrels of the early fourteenth century (1306) comprising a total of 176, see *Manners and Expenses of England in the Thirteenth and Fifteenth Centuries*, pp. 140–145, Roxburghe Club, 1841. It is notable that most of the names are French.

(123) In the household of King Edward III the list of musicians is given as follows:

Trompettes	5	Clarions	2
Citolers	1	Nakerers	1
Pipers	5	Fidelers	1
Taberett	1	Waytes	3

Ordinances and Regulations of the Royal Household, Introduction, p. 4.

(124) In the *Northumberland Household Book*, ed. Percy, p. 2, mention is made of "A Tabarett, a Luyte, and a Rebecc". See also pp. 339, 343–344.

(125) See a long note in Warton's *History of English Poetry*, ed. Hazlitt, II, 98.

(126) Brand, *Popular Antiquities of Great Britain*, ed. Hazlitt, I, 259.

(127) See the *Northumberland Household Book*, ed. Percy, pp. 331–339. The highest sum directed to be paid is six shill'ngs and eightpence.

(128) Le Grand d'Aussy, *La Vie Privée des François d'Autrefois*, ed. de Roquefort, III, 366.

(129) Idem, III, 369.

(130) For jesters, see Warton, *History of English Poetry*, Index.

(131) See illustration, p. 5, in the *Babees Book*.
(132) Shoes of Cordovan leather.
(133) Adorned with gold.
(134) Impaired.

(135) Eyes.
(136) Spaniel.
(137) Refrain.
(138) *Romance of Merlin*, pp. 614–615, ed. by H. B. Wheatley, E.E.T.S., 1869. This scene is obviously one of pure romance, and it belongs to the thirteenth century. But in many essentials it faithfu ly depicts the type of entertainment common to English feasts in the fourteenth and fifteenth centuries.
(139) *Chronicle*, VI, 346.
(140) Error for *rochettes*.
(141) Piacenza in Italy.
(142) Thin.
(143) Negroes.
(144) Hall's *Chronicle*, pp. 513–14.

CHAPTER VII

(1) A table of ivory.
(2) Cloths with towels spread before the lord of the feast.
(3) See *Sir Degrevant* (ed. Halliwell, *Thornton Romances*), ll. 1,377–1,424. I have ventured to paraphrase the lines, since they require too much glossarial addition for the average reader.
(4) Persons of high rank.
(5) Holinshed, *Chronicle* (1586), p. 254.
(6) *Chronicle* (ed. Ker), l. 65.
(7) *Mediaeval London*, I, 69.
(8) Adorned.
(9) Froissart, *Chronicle* (ed. Ker).
(10) Endowed.
(11) Froissart, *Chronicle* (ed. Ker), I, 232–233.
(12) Laundresses.
(13) Costly.
(14) Since.
(15) Appliqué work cut out.
(16) Embroidery.
(17) Ever.
(18) Hardyng's *Chronicle* (ed. Ellis), pp. 346–347.
(19) See the long account in Froissart's *Chronicle* (ed. Ker), V, 419–425.

NOTES

(20) Stow's *Survey of London* (ed. Kingsford), II, 116.
(21) Had the place of honour upon the dais.
(22) Fabyan's *Chronicle* (ed. Ellis), p. 581.
(23) See the whole account in Fabyan's *Chronicle*, p. 585 f. For some further details, see Austin, *Two Fifteenth Century Cookery Books*, p. XIV.
(24) Place of honour.
(25) A fine kind of lawn or gauze made at Placentia in Italy.
(26) To the last extremity.
(27) Grafton's *Continuation of Hardyng's Chronicle*, p. 517.
(28) Mottoes.
(29) That is, at the foot of the table.
(30) Abundance.
(31) Hall's *Chronicle* (ed. Ellis, 1809), pp. 509 ff.
(32) Adorned.
(33) A morris dance.
(34) Hall's *Chronicle*, p. 510.
(35) A dish or course eaten just before leaving the table.
(36) Holinshed, *Chronicle* (1586), p. 849.
(37) Made up of coloured strips joined side by side.
(38) Cavendish, *Life of Cardinal Wolsey*, ed. Singer, pp. 49–55.
(39) Image of Saint Michael.
(40) Immediately.
(41) Either.
(42) Nor.
(43) About equivalent to the expression *Prosit!* used in Germany when drinking a health.
(44) The finest kind of wheat bread.
(45) Wheat bread of the second grade.
(46) George Cavendish, *Life of Cardinal Wolsey*, ed. Singer, I, 124–135.
(47) Cavendish, *Life of Cardinal Wolsey*, ed. Singer, pp. 135–138.
(48) Tapestry representing trees or flowers.
(49) Twisted.
(50) Boulogne.
(51) Calais.
(52) Striped.
(53) Material.

(54) Hall, *Chronicle*, p. 793.
(55) Server at table, often of high rank.
(56) Hall, *Chronicle*, p. 804.
(57) A. Schultz, *Deutsches Leben im XIV und XV Jahrhundert*, Chap. IV, pp. 398–534, observes that German feasts of the fourteenth and fifteenth centuries were substantially like those of France and England.
(58) Germany.
(59) Withdrew.
(60) Froissart, *Chronicle* (ed. Ker), XI, 304.
(61) The whole account, which is taken from the description in de la Marche's *Memoires*, Paris, 1857, is found in A. Schultz's *Deutsches Leben im XIV. und XV. Jahrhundert*, pp. 462–467.
(62) See Schultz, op. cit., pp. 474 ff.
(63) The very curious and prolix account of the wedding fills many pages of *Archaeologia*, 31 : 326 ff., but the essentials can be briefly presented. It need hardly be remarked that much of the English of the description, though vivid, is very ragged.
(64) The horn of the unicorn—or what was supposed to be the unicorn—was thought to be an infallible protection against poison.
(65) Furnishing or adorning.
(66) Furnished.
(67) As follows.
(68) Retinue.
(69) Lower.
(70) Adorned.
(71) Ruby.
(72) Word unfinished. Is *panicle* meant?
(73) Furnished.
(74) *Tortettes* appear to be large wax candles twisted. See also the form torttes.
(75) The candles put upon a broach.
(76) That is, with the stories presented in pictures or moulded figures.
(77) Adorned.
(78) Text, upon some.
(79) Encompassed.
(80) Battlements.

(81) "Rose water distilled from damask roses."

(82) Throughout the Middle Ages there were on the Continent an infinite number of other feasts in France, in Flanders, in Germany, in Italy, in Spain well deserving a place here, but we must stop somewhere. Incidentally, we may note in Holinshed's *Chronicle* (1586), p. 825, the account of Henry VIII's feast after the taking of Tournay in 1514, and on p. 1425 the description of the feast given to the Earl of Leicester on Christmas Eve, 1585, by "the states of the town of Middleboro" in Holland.

And as illustrating the persistence in England of the medieval type of banquet, with enormous quantities of meat and fish, we note the great feast at Knole in Kent, July 3 1636.

1. Rice pottage.
2. Barley broth.
3. Buttered pickrell.
4. Butter and burned eggs.
5. Boiled teats.
6. Roast tongues.
7. Bream.
8. Perches.
9. Chine of veal roast.
10. Hash of mutton with anchovies.
11. Great pike.
12. Fish chuits [*sic*] (chewets?).
13. Roast venison in blood.
14. Capons (2).
15. Wild ducks (3).
16. Salmon, whole hot.
17. Tenches, boiled.
18. Crabs.
19. Tench pie.
20. Venison pasty of a doe.
21. Swans (2).
22. Herons (3).
23. Cold lamb.
24. Custard.
25. Venison, boiled.
26. Potatoes, stewed.
27. Gr. Salad.
28. Redeeve [*sic*] pie hot.
29. Almond pudding.
30. Made dishes.
31. Boiled salad.
32. Pig, whole.
33. Rabbits.

1. Soup, 2 kinds.
2. Fish, 7 kinds and crabs.
3. Eggs.
4. Meat, 9 kinds.
5. Fowl, 4 kinds.
6. Salad, 2
7. Vegetable: potatoes, stewed.
8. Desserts, 1 or 2.

Another Menu

1. Jelly of tench. Jelly of hartshorn.
2. White gingerbread.
3. Puits (peewits).
4. Curlew.
5. Ruffes.
6. Fried perches.
7. Fried eels.
8. Skirret pie.
9. Larks (3 doz.).
10. Plovers (12).
11. Teals (12).
12. Fried pickrell.
13. Fried tench.
14. Salmon soused.
15. Soused eel.
16. Esconechia [sic]?
17. Sea gulls (6).
18. Ham of bacon.
19. Sturgeon.
20. Lark pie.
21. Lobster pie.
22. Crayfishes (3 doz.).
23. Dried tongues.
24. Anchovies.
25. Artichokes.
26. Peas.
27. Fool (gooseberry?).
28. Second porridge.
29. Reddeeve, pie [sic]?
30. Cherry tart.
31. Laid tart.
32. Carps, 2.
33. Polony sasag [sic].

1. Meat.
2. Fish and shell fish, eels, all kinds.
3. Fowl (birds), 6 kinds.
4. Ruffes (sea breams).

See V. Sackville-West, *Knole and the Sackvilles*, p. 94.

CHAPTER VIII

(1) "A very competent authority says 'that in the Middle Ages the deaths of a great part of the nobility, even when occasioned by natural causes, occurred under the age of forty'. Indeed, 'as large a number of persons now live to seventy as lived to forty in the year 1500'." Quoted from Amyot, in *Archaeologia*, XXII, 241, by Denton, *England in the Fifteenth Century*, p. 211.

(2) See the chapter by G. C. Coulton on "Husbands at the Church Door" in *Chaucer and his England*, pp. 202–216.

(3) To an astonishing extent the streets were used as stercoraceous depositaries by all classes of citizens. Filthy dis-

charges from upper windows were normal in large, as well as in small, towns.

(4) As we might expect, the penalty for excesses at the table followed swiftly and drew the attention of satirists. One of the most notable attacks is *La Condamnacion du Banquet* (Paris, 1507), by Nicole de la Chesnaye, physician to Louis XII. The plot is somewhat too complicated to present here, but the piece points out the diseases that are the natural sequence of excess—apoplexy, paralysis, epilepsy, pleurisy, colic, quinsy, dropsy, jaundice, gravel, gout. Modern medical science rejects from this list epilepsy, dropsy, pleurisy, quinsy— except indirectly—but the author was in harmony with the teaching of his time. The piece was edited by P. L. Jacob, *Recueil de Farces, Sotiès, et Moralités du Quinzième Siècle*, Paris, 1859.

(5) Few medieval banquets, however, can have exhibited more extravagant profusion of indigestibles than the feast at the enthronization of Archbishop Neville in the sixth year of the reign of Edward IV, and that of Archbishop Warham in 1504.

(6) *Secretum Secretorum*, attributed throughout the Middle Ages to Aristotle.

(7) Quoted by C. V. Langlois in *La Connaissance de la Nature et du Monde*, p. 94.

(8) The phrasing is for the most part that of Ordonaux, Philadelphia, 1870.

(9) With the later dietaries may be compared the English *Diatorie* about 1430 and the Latin version about 1460, printed in Furnivall's *Babees Book*, pp. 54–59.

(10) Chaucer, V, 40–41.

(11) Reprinted by the Early English Text Society, Extra Series X, pp. 223–303.

(12) A typical example is afforded by Thomas Muffett (1553–1604), one of the leading physicians of the sixteenth century. In *Health's Improvement*, p. 77 (ed. of 1655), he highly commends the flesh of the hedgehog as a preservative against various ills.

(13) *Dyetary*, pp. 252–253.

(14) As a result of the constant eating of salted meat, especially in winter, and the enormous consumption of highly spiced food, the system of most men became disordered or,

according to the physic of the time, the blood became "heated" and bleeding was thought to be necessary. The practice of frequent blood-letting continued well into the middle of the nineteenth century and even later. In medieval times, monks, we are told, "were bled four, five, or six times a year, according to the rules of the order". See Feasey, *Monasticism—What is it?* p. 244.

BIBLIOGRAPHICAL NOTE

THE following list of books, revised and brought up to date for this 1967 reprint, comprises those that have furnished the most important data for the history of the Medieval Feast in England. Ordinary books of reference and the general histories of the period have not been included.

Abram, A. English Life and Manners in the Later Middle Ages. London, 1913.
Ainsworth-Davis, J. R. Cooking through the Centuries. London, 1931.
Anglia. Vol. 27. Halle, 1885.
Antiquaries, Society of. Ordinances and Regulations for the Government of the Royal Household. London, 1790.
Aresty, Esther B. The Delectable Past. London, 1965.
d'Aussy, Le Grand. Histoire de la Vie Privée des François d'Autrefois depuis l'Origine de la Nation jusqu'à nos Jours (1783). Ed. J. B. B. de Roquefort. 3 vols. Paris, 1815.
Austin, Thomas. Two Fifteenth-century Cookery Books. Harleian MS. 279 . . . and Harl. MS. 4016. London, 1888. Early English Text Society, Original Series, No. 91.
Avila, Ludovicus Lobera d'. Ein Nutzlich Regiment der Gesundheit, 1531.
The Babees Book. Containing Stans Puer ad Mensam, The Bokes of Nurture of Hugh Rhodes and John Russell, Wynkyn de Worde's Boke of Kervynge, The Boke of Curtasye, etc., etc. Ed. F. I. Furnivall. In two parts. E.E.T.S. No. 32. London, 1868.
Bataille des Vices. Ed. Barbazan. Paris, 1808.
Bitting, Katherine G. Gastronomic Bibliography. San Francisco, 1939.
Boorde, Andrew. A Compendious Regiment, or a Dyetary of Helth (1542). Ed. F. J. Furnivall. E.E.T.S., 1870.
Boorde, Andrew. The Wisdom of Andrew Boorde; edited by H. Edmund Poole. Leicester, 1936.
Brand, John. Popular Antiquities of Great Britain. Ed. W. C. Hazlitt. 3 vols. London, 1870.
Browne, Matthew (William Brighty Rands). Chaucer's England. 2 vols. London, 1869.

Carter, Charles. The Complete Practical Cook or, A New System of the Whole Art and Mystery of Cookery. London, 1730.
Cavendish, George. Life of Cardinal Wolsey. Ed. S. W. Singer. 2 vols. Chiswick, 1825.
Caxton, William. Book of Curtesye. In Babees Book. E.E.T.S. London, 1868.
Chadwick, W. Social Life in the Days of Piers the Plowman. London, 1922.
Champier, Symphorien. Rosa Gallica. Paris, 1514.
Chesnaye, Nicole de la. Condamnacion du Banquet. Ed. Paris, 1857.
Coulton, G. C. Social Life in Britain from the Norman Conquest to the Reformation. London, 1918.
Coulton, G. C. Chaucer and his England. London, 1927.
Craig, Elizabeth. Court Favourites: recipes from royal kitchens. London, 1953.
Curtis-Bennett, Noel. The Food of the People. London, 1949.
Cutts, Edward L. Scenes and Characters of the Middle Ages. 3rd Ed. London, 1911.
Davis, H. W. C. Medieval England. Oxford, 1924.
Dickenmann, J. J. Das Nahrungswesen in England vom 12 bis 15 Jahrhundert. Anglia, XXVII, 453–515. Bibliography, pp. 513–515.
Drummond, J. C. and Wilbraham, Anne. The Englishman's Food: a history of five centuries of English diet. London, 1939.
Eccleston, James. An Introduction to English Antiquities. London, 1847.
Elyot, Sir Thomas. The Castel of Helth. London, 1539. (Original ed. London, 1534, lost.)
Emmison, F. G. Tudor Food and Pastimes. London, 1964.
Erasmus. De Civilitate Morum Puerilium. Translated R. Whitington. (Latin and English texts.) London, 1554.
Feasey, H. J. Monasticism—What is it? London, 1898.
A Fifteenth Century Courtesy Book. Ed. R. W. Chambers. E.E.T.S. London, 1914.
Fleetwood, William. Chronicon Preciosum. London, 1707.
The Forme of Cury. (Ed.) Rev. Samuel Pegge. London, 1780.
Franklin, Alfred. La Vie Privée d'Autrefois. Vol. 3. La Cuisine. Vol. 6. Les Repas. La Civilité de la Table. Paris, 1893.

The French Pastery Cooke. (Translated from Le Patissier Français, 1655.) London, 1656.
French, Richard Valpy. Nineteen Centuries of Drink in England. London, 1884.
Froissart, Jean. Chronicles. Tudor translations. Ed. Ker and Henley. London, 1901.
Froissart, Jean. Chronicles. Translated by Lord Berners. 7 vols. Oxford, 1927-8.
Furnivall, F. J. Early English Meals and Manners. London, 1868. Early English Text Society, Original Series, No. 32.
Furnivall, F. J. See Babees Book.
Gerarde, J. The Herball. London, 1597.
Gesner, Conrad. Sanitatis tuendae praecepta . . . contra luxum conviviorum, etc. Tiguri (1556).
Glasse, Hannah. The Art of Cookery Made Plain and Easy. London, 1747.
Gottschschalk, Alred. Histoire de l'alimentation et de la gastronomie depuis la préhistoire jusqu' à nos jours. 2 tom. Paris, 1948.
Hackwood, Frederick W. Good Cheer: the romance of food and feasting. London, 1911.
Hall, Edward. Chronicle. Ed. H. Ellis. London, 1809.
Hartley, Dorothy. Food in England. London, 1954.
Hazlitt, William Carew. Bibliographical Collections and Notes on Early English Literature. London, 1876.
Henderson, Alexander. History of Ancient and Modern Wines. London. 1824.
Heyd, Histoire du Commerce du Levant au Moyen Âge. Leipzig-Dessau. 2 vols. 1885-6.
Hintze, K. Geographie und Geschichte der Ernährung. Leipzig, 1934. (Pp. 75-92, Europa: Mittelalter.)
Household Roll of Eleanor, Countess of Leicester, 1215. London, 1841.
Huon de Bordeaux. Ed. S. Lee. E.E.T.S., 40, 41, 43, 50. London, 1882 ff.
Knight, Charles. Old England. London. 2 vols. Illus. 1845.
Langlois, Ch. V. La Société Française au XIIIe Siècle d'apres Dix Romans d'Aventure. Paris, 1904.
Langlois, Ch. V. La Vie en France au Moyen Âge, 12me à 14me Siècle. Paris, 1924.
Leland, John. Collectanea. Ed. T. Hernius, 1715. 6 vols. 1770.

THE ENGLISH MEDIEVAL FEAST

Liber Albus: The White Book of the City of London (1419). Ed. H. T. Riley. Public Record Series. London. 2 vols. 1859–62.

Liber Cure Cocorum (1420). Ed. R. Morris. Transactions, Philological Society. Berlin, 1862.

Losely MSS. Illustrative of English History, Biography, and Manners, from the reign of Henry VIII to that of James I. London, 1835.

Le Ménagier de Paris (*circa* 1393). Publié de la Société des Bibliophiles François. 2 vols. Paris, 1846.

Merlin, The Romance of, Edited by Henry B. Wheatley, E.E.T.S. 4 vols. London, 1899.

Moufet, Thomas. Health's Improvement, etc. London, 1655.

Napier, Mrs. Alexander. A Noble Boke off Cookry. London, 1882.

Newman, L. F. Some Notes on Food and Diatetics in the 16th and 17th Centuries. *In* Journal of the Royal Anthropological Institute of Great Britain and Ireland, vol. 76, pt. 1, 1936, pp. 39–49.

Nichols, John. Illustrations of the Manners and Expences of Ancient Times in England. London, 1797.

Ordinances for the Royal Household. Ed. J. P. Collier. London, 1790.

Our English Home. Oxford, 1861.

Paston Letters. Ed. James Gairdner. London. 6. vols. 1904.

Le Patissier Français. Amsterdam, 1658.

Paynell, Thomas. Regimen Sanitatis. (English translation.) London, 1528.

Peacham, Henry. The Compleat Gentleman. London, 1627.

Pegge, Samuel. Illustrations of the Manners and Expences of Antient Times. London, 1797.

Pendrell, Charles. London Life in the 14th Century. London, 1925.

Percy, Thomas. Household Book of the Earl of Northumberland in 1512. London, 1770.

The Perfect English Cooke. London, 1656.

Power, Eileen. The Goodman of Paris. London, 1928. A translation of Le Ménagier de Paris.

Quarterly Review. London, 1894.

Queen Elizabeth's Achademy. Ed. F. J. Furnivall. E.E.T.S. London, 1869.

Riley, Henry Thomas. Liber Albus: The White Book of the City of London. (Compiled 1419.) London, 1862.
Riley, Henry Thomas. Memorials of London Life in the 13th, 14th and 15th Centuries (1276–1419). London, 1868.
Reliquiae Antiquae. Ed. T. Wright and J. O. Halliwell. London. 2 vols. 1845.
Ritson, Joseph. Ancient English Metrical Romances. Ed. by E. Goldsmid. Edinburgh, 1884–5.
Roberts, George. The Social History of the People of the Southern Counties of England in Past Centuries. London, 1856.
Rosières, R. Histoire de la Société Française au Moyen Age, 987–1483. 2 vols. Paris, 1884.
Sacchi, Bartholomaeus de Platina. Platynae de honesta voluptate et valitudine: vel de obsoniis, et arte Coquinaria libri decem, 1498.
Salzmann, L. F. English Industries of the Middle Ages. London, 1924.
Schultz, Alwin. Das höfische Leben zur Zeit der Minnesinger. With 372 illustrations. 2 vols. Leipzig, 1889.
Schultz, A. Deutsches Leben im XIV und XV Jahrhundert. Wien, 1892.
Serjeantson, M. S. Vocabulary of Cookery in the 15th Century. *In* Essays and Studies, vol. 23 (1937), pp. 25–37.
Shakespeare's England. Oxford University Press. 2 vols. Oxford, 1916.
Stark, Lewis M. The Whitney Cookery Collection. New York Public Library, 1946. (A bibliography of cookery books from the 15th to the 20th century.)
Stow, John. Survey of London. Ed. C. L. Kingsford. 3 vols. Oxford, 1908 f.
Strutt, Joseph. Horda Angel-Cynnan or, A Compleat View of the Manners, Customs, Arms, Habits, etc., of the Inhabitants of England. 3 vols. London, 1775–6.
Tirel, G. (Taillever.) Le Viandier de Guillaume Tirel. . . . 1326–1395. Two Parts. Paris, 1892.
Traill, H. D. and Mann, J. Social England. Vols. 1–4. London, 1901–4.
Turner, Thomas Hudson. Manners and Household Expenses of England in the 13th and 15th Centuries. Illustrated by Original Records. Roxburghe Club. London, 1841.

Two Fifteenth Century Cookery Books. Harleian MSS. 279 (ab. 1430), and Harl. MS. 4016 (ab. 1450), etc. Edited by Thomas Austin. E.E.T.S., London, 1888.

Vicaire, Georges. Bibliographie Gastronomique. Avec une préface de P. Ginisty. Paris, 1898.

Vollmer, F. Studien zu dem römischen Kochbuche von Apicius. Sitzungsberichte der Bayerischen Academie. No. 6. 1920.

Warner, Richard. Antiquitates Culinariae: Tracts on Culinary Affairs of the Old English. London, 1791.

Way, Arthur S. Food Hygiene of the Middle Ages. *In* The London Quarterly Review, vol. 153, January and April, 1930, pp. 40–52.

Way, Arthur S. The Science of Dining (Mensa Philosophica a medieval treatise on the hygiene of the table and the laws of health). London, 1936.

Webb, Rev. John. A Roll of the Household Expenses of Richard de Swinfield. Camden Society. 2 vols. London, 1854.

Webb, Margaret J. Early English Recipes selected from the Harleian MS. 279 of about 1430 A.D. Cambridge, 1937.

White, Florence. Good Things in England: a practical cookery book for everyday use containing traditional and regional recipes ... between 1399 and 1932. London, 1932.

Whitmore, Mary E. Medieval English Domestic Life and Amusements in the Works of Chaucer: a dissertation. Catholic University of America. Washington, D.C., 1937.

Wilson, John D. Life in Shakespeare's England: a book of Elizabeth prose. Cambridge, 1913.

Wright, Thomas. A History of Domestic Manners and Sentiments in England during the Middle Ages. London, 1862. (Reproduced in 1871 as Homes of Other Days.)

INDEX AND GLOSSARY[1]

Africa, trade with, 36
Ale, home brewed, 35; freely used, 124 ff.
Alexander, King, feast given to, 181
Allegory in Middle Ages, 144, 165 ff.
Almonds, lavish use of, 105–108
Ames, *sb.*, for *amice*, "A hood, or cape with a hood, lined with fur of the marten or grey squirrel", 178
Anne Boleyn, coronation feast of, 203 f.
Apples, stewed, 59

Bakemeats, 84 f.
Banquet, occasions for a, 16; great, at Knole, 257
Barclay, Alexander, description of table manners, 159
Bawdrike, *sb.*, baldric, belt, 173
Beef, stewed, 58
Beer, 122, 125, 127
Birds (small), 90
Blancmange, 52
Blood for colouring food, 104
Bokeled, *adj.*, buckled, 174
Boorde, Andrew, 68, 84, 91, 124; his *Dyetary*, 222–224
Bread, 66–69
Breakfasts, 115, 116, 241
Brewing, 124
Broth, 71, 72
Butter, 70

Cakes, 161 f.
Capon, stuffed, 88; stewed, 89; two capons made of one, 91
Carter, Charles, his *Complete Practical Cook* (1730), 119 f.
Carver, duties and methods of, 148–150
Castel of Helth (1534), 219 ff.
Castle, evolution of medieval, 140
Cavendish, George, 146
Chandeler, Bishop John, 160
Chaucer, Franklin, 128; Squire, 149; Prioress, 150
Cheat loaf, *sb.*, "Wheaten bread of the second quality, made of flour more coarsely sifted than that for Manchet, the finest quality", 116
Cheyne, *sb.*, chain, 174
Christ Church College, 129
Church, festivals of, and feasts, 16
Cider, 123
Claret, 127
Coffin, a pastry crust, 84, 85, 96, etc.
Cokyntryce, 91
Colouring food, 102–105, 121, 144
Condé, Prince of, 88
Cookery books, 49–51
Cookery, revolution in art of, 118 ff.

[1] The index to the Notes is not intended to be exhaustive, since the references in the text are in most cases sufficient. Most of the unusual terms employed in the old texts have been explained where found, but for the convenience of readers unfamiliar with the English of four or five centuries ago a brief glossary is incorporated in the Index.

Cooks, medieval, their methods, 44–46, 96; importance, 47; Wolsey's, 146
Courses of a feast, 153 ff.
Courtesy at table, 156–159
Crane, carving a, 148
Crusades, influence of the, 24, 140
Custard, 52

Dancers at feasts, 173, 174
Degrevant, Sir, feast in romance of, 180–181
Derby, Earl of, his servants, flocks, herds, weekly supply of food, 35
Desserts, 112, 159–165; order of, 160 f.
Devonshire, Earl of, wedding feast of, 87
Diaper, *sb.*, cloth ornamented with units of design evenly spaced, 197
Diseases in Middle Ages, 215
Doket, *sb.*, ducat, 178
Doucetys, sweetmeats, 160
Dragées, 165, 251
Drinks, lacking in Middle Ages, 48; beer and wines in Middle Ages, 242–244

Edward III, officials in household of, 147
Egg, poached, 59, 231
Egypt, trade with, 36
Elyot, Sir Thomas, his *Castel of Helth* (1534), 219–222
England, order of feasts in, 155
English trade in fifteenth century, 36
Entertainments, 171 ff., 181, 182
d'Eutrapel, Contes, 61
Ewrie, 151

Fairs, medieval, 37
Fats in medieval cookery, 69 f.
Feast, essentials of a thirteenth-century, 137 f.; courses at a, 153 ff.
Feast, of Archbishop Neville, 33; of five days, 34; of Archbishop Warham, 34; of Sir John Howard, 34; of Gaston, Count de Foix, 160; of Henry V, 166; of Henry VI, 166 ff.; in Romance of Sir Degrevant, 180; of King Alexander and Queen Margaret, 181; of Edward III, 181–183; of Henry Picard, *c.* 1348, 182; of Richard II, 184–186; of Henry V, 186–187; of Richard III, 187 f.; of Henry VIII, 176 ff., 189 f., 191 f., 201 f.; of Cardinal Wolsey, 192 f., 194–200; coronation feast of Anne Boleyn, 202 f.; of King of France at Rheims (1397), 204 f.; of Philip the Good at Lille (1453), 205 f.; at marriage of Margaret, sister of Edward IV, to Charles, Duke of Burgundy, 207–213
Feasting, fondness of Middle Ages for, 16
Feasts, cost of, 227–229
Feasts, long, 227
Feasts, mainly given by the aristocracy and royalty, 17
Festivals of Church, relation of feasts to, 16
Fish, 33; feasts all of, 92; list of, eaten in Middle Ages, 93 f.; when served, 154–155
Flemming, Bishop, 160
Floor of hall, covering for, 132–133

INDEX AND GLOSSARY 269

Flour delices, *sb.*, fleurs de lys, 178
Foix, Gaston, Count de, his great feast, 160 f.
Food, enormous quantities consumed at feasts, 33, 34; native supplies of, 33, 35; cost of, in fourteenth and fifteenth centuries, 38–40; see also 227–228; penalties for falsifying, 40; chopping and macerating, 44; mixtures for, 44; types of, lacking in Middle Ages, 48; types of, no longer eaten, 54–56; monotony of medieval, 57; disguised, 61, 62; heaps of, 62; perfumed, 240
Food and health, 214–224; suitable for the feasts from Easter to Christmas, 225
Fool, Court, 173
Fork, the ordinary table, 45; brought by Thomas Coryat, 149
France, order of a feast in, 155
French influence upon English cookery, 50–51
Froissart, 61, 175, 181, 182
Fruit, 109–114; receipts for preparing, 75, 110–114; raw, dried, preserved, 162 f.; caution in eating, 217 f.; see also 250, 251
Furmenty, 230
Furniture in Middle Ages, 225

Galantine, *sb.*, meat, boned, tied up, and served cold, 78
Garbage in streets, 225
Gingerbread, 65
Gotland, 36
Greece, wines from, 36

Hall, English medieval, 129ff.; plan of, 130; the, in festal array, 139 f.
Hampton Court, 129, 140
Hands, washing, 151 f.
Hanseatic League, 36
Harrison, William, 69, 120–122
Heating, see Lighting and Heating
Henry II, 125
Henry III, 124
Henry IV, 87, 160, 165
Henry V, feasts of, 166, 186–187
Henry VI, coronation feast of, 166 ff.
Henry VII, 189
Henry VIII, 116, 125, 129, 175; great feast of, 176 ff., 189 f., 191 f., 201 f.; coronation feast of Anne Boleyn, 202 f.
Herbs, 238
Heron, carving a, 149
Hippocras, 127, 170
Howard Household Book, 101
Humours, Four, doctrine of the, 219 f.

India, trade with, 36

Joinville, 149

King's champion on horseback in feasting hall, 188
Kitchens, medieval, 42–44
Kymer, Gilbert, 100

Lamprey, baked, 95
Lased, *adj.*, laced, 177
Latimer, Bishop, social changes in his lifetime, 225
Leched meats (sliced), 86
Leicester, Roll of Countess of, 100

Lighting and heating in the Middle Ages, 26–31; illumination at feasts, 133, 226; lighting of Northumberland Castle, 226
Lille, feast at, in 1453, 205 f.
Losely MSS., 73
Louis IX, 149

Malmsey, 126–127
Mammenye bastarde, 65
Manners at table, 156–159; in time of Elizabeth, 158
Mansel, John, his feast for King Alexander of Scotland, 181
Mantles, furred, 30, 226
Marche, Olivier de la, 155
Marshal of Hall, 147
Maw, *sb.*, stomach, 85
Mead, 123
Meals, hours for, 222, 241
Meas, mese, *sb.*, mess, portion, 115, 173
Meat in medieval cookery, 78–86; salted, 80; pork, 79; boiled, 81; beef, stewed, 81, 82; hares, 82, 83; venison 83, 85; hedgehogs, 85; fried meats, 85; poultry, 87–92
Mediterranean trade, 36
Ménagier de Paris, 92, 154; see also Notes to Chap. III and VI
Merlin as a minstrel, 173 f.
Merlin, Romance of, feast described in, 135–136
Metheglin, 123
Mets, 231
Middle Ages, character of, 15 ff., 20 ff.; transitions from 1050 to 1550, 17 f.; persistence of medieval features, 18; difficulty of understanding, 19; everyday life in, 21; discomforts of, 22 ff.; misconceptions of, 22 f.; lack of comfort in, 25 ff.; filth in, 25; lighting and heating in, 26–31; not a time of plain living, 58; spices in, 73–77; allegory in, 144; conventional usages in, 144; multiplicity of servants in, 145; persistence of usages of, 189; disease in, 214 f.; medical theory in, 216 f.
Minstrels, 171 f., 252–253
Modus Cenandi, 153
Money, changed values of, 227
Moreskoes, *sb.*, Moors, 177
Mortar, for macerating food, 44–45
Music at feasts, 171–174, 252–253

Napkins, 150
Nef, 142
Neville, Archbishop, food supplied at installation of, 33, 154
Northumberland Household Book, 32, 73, 115; economy indicated in, 117–118; servants, 145; fruits, 163
Nuts, in England, 106; imported, 164; see also Almonds

Oakham Castle, 129
Other half-pound, one and a half pounds, 65

Panter, 151
Paris, pies of, 84
Partridge, 90
Paynell, Thomas, 79
Peacock, roasting, 88; stuffed, 143; vow of, 143
Pepperers of Soper Lane, 40
Perfuming food, 240 f.
Pheasants, 88

INDEX AND GLOSSARY

Philip the Good, his feast at Lille (1453), 205 f.
Pies containing live birds, 170; a dwarf, 170
Plain living, 114 ff., 249
Plate of gold and silver, 141 ff.
Poison, tasting for, 153
Pomegranaltes, *sb.*, pomegranates, 178
Pork, see Meat
Porpoise, 93–95
Pottle, *sb.*, two quarts, 65
Poultry, 32, 33, 38, 39, 87–92
Powdered, *ppl. adj.*, spangled, 176
Precedence, order of, 152 f.
Primrose, 65

Receipts, misleading names of medieval, 52; vagueness, 63 ff.
Regimen Sanitatis, 79, 128, 217; directions concerning diet, 217–219
Revolution in art of cookery, 118 ff.
Rheims, feast at, in 1397, 204 f.
Rhodes, Hugh, *Boke of Nurture, or Schoole of Good Manners*, 158
Richard II, 87, 129, 176, 184–186
Rissoles of fruit, 60
Robes, fur-lined, 30
Romances and feasts, 23
Russell, John, *Boke of Nurture*, 86, 93
Russia, trade with, 36

Saffron, 102–104, etc.
Salads, 101 f.
Salewed, saluted, 174
Sauces, 96–99
Saunders, *sb.* (*Sanders*), an old name for sandal wood, used as a red dye, 103, 104, etc.
Seal, 94
  eats at feasts, 133

Servants, multiplicity in Middle Ages, 145; in household of Cardinal Wolsey, 146 f.; duties of, in Middle Ages, 147 f.; see also 247
Sewer, an upper servant, a table waiter, 147, 151
Sewte, *sb.*, suit, 178
Shives, *sb.*, thin pieces, 67
Simple food, 114–116
Sixteenth century, food in the late, 120 ff.; wine and beer, 121–122
Skeat, Wm. W., 219
Sop, 128, 150; see also Wine sop
Soups, 70–72
Spices in medieval cookery, 72–77; in modern cookery, 76; spice plates, 76; in stewed beef, 81, etc., etc.; see also pp. 228, 234–235
Spring, medieval enthusiasm for, 30
Stafford, John, Bishop of Wells, 87
Steelyard, in London, 36
Sturmye, 75
Subtleties, 160, 165 ff.
Sugar, 77–78
Swans, 33, 226
Swinfield, Richard de, 73, 100

Tables for feasts, 133, 141; decorations of, 141 ff.
Tapestry, medieval, 131 f.
Tasting food, 151, 153
Tiers, *sb.* (for *tires*), headdresses, 178
Trade, foreign, 36
Trenchers, 67, 68, 142 f.
Tryon's *Way to Health*, 161

Vegetables, 100
Verjuice, 80, 235
Visby, 36

Voyded lowe, *ppl. adj.*, cut low, 177
Vynettes, vignettes, *sb.*, 178

Wafers, 161
Warham, Archbishop, food at enthronization of, 34; feast of, 168–170
Warner, 169
Washing before and after meals, 151–152
Water perfumed for washing hands, 152
Whale, 93, 94
Wheaten bread, 233
Wine sop, 128; see also Sop
Wine, 34, 36, in late sixteenth century, 121 f.; native and imported, 125–126; cost of, 126; character of medieval, 127; spiced, 165
Wolsey, Cardinal, 129, 146; his servants, 146 f.; his feasts, 192 f., 194–200
Worde, Wynkyn de, 68, 148, 150

For Product Safety Concerns and Information please contact our EU
representative GPSR@taylorandfrancis.com
Taylor & Francis Verlag GmbH, Kaufingerstraße 24, 80331 München, Germany

www.ingramcontent.com/pod-product-compliance
Lightning Source LLC
Chambersburg PA
CBHW071809300426
44116CB00009B/1255